FROM VIS   LITY IN COMMUNITY CARE

CHANGING DIRECTION AT THE LOCAL LEVEL

From Vision to Reality in Community Care

Changing Direction at the Local Level

Chris Gostick, Bleddyn Davies, Robyn Lawson
and Charlotte Salter

PSSRU
at the University of Kent at Canterbury,
the London School of Economics
and the University of Manchester

First published in Great Britain in 1997

Arena
Ashgate Publishing Ltd
Gower House
Croft Road
Aldershot
Hants GU11 3HR
England

Ashgate Publishing Company
Old Post Road
Brookfield
Vermont
U.S.A.

British Library Cataloguing in Publication Data
From vision to reality in community care: changing
   direction at the local level. - (PSSRU)
   1. Community health services - Great Britain
   2. Deinstitutionalization - Great Britain
   I. Gostick, Chris
   362.1'2'0941

ISBN 1 85742 409 3 (pbk)
     1 85742 408 5 (hbk)

Typeset by Jane Dennett at the PSSRU, University of Kent at Canterbury
Printed and bound in Great Britain by Hartnolls Limited, Bodmin, Cornwall

Contents

Boxes

Preface

This book describes the first stages of the local development of the community care policy reforms articulated in the 1989 *Caring for People* White Paper and the subsequent 1990 NHS and Community Care Act, with a particular emphasis on the needs and services for elderly people. It discusses the period between the mid-1980s, when the policy initially began to crystallise, and the beginning of 1993, when the reforms were formally implemented. The study is based partly on analysis of the wide range of documentary material now available on the development and implementation of community care during this period, and partly on interviews and material collected from each of five authorities by Robyn Lawson, Charlotte Salter and Bleddyn Davies. The interviews all took place between 1990 and 1992. We already knew something of the history of these five authorities. Four of them were among the ten on which a larger 'production of welfare' study had been based in the mid-1980s (Davies et al., 1990), and we had a long history of working in the fifth authority, although the collections there had in earlier work been more narrowly focused. This five-authority study itself has already been the basis of various papers,[1] but the aims of this book are different.

First, it is an attempt to map the initial responses of authorities at the beginning of what we expected to be a long journey of community care reform. We were at that time quoting with approval the views of the Australian Commonwealth Auditor General, who argued that the reform of long-term care there would take 'perhaps 15 to 25 years' (Auditor General, 1988). In *Resources, Needs and Outcomes* (Davies et al., 1990) and associated papers the state of play in the late 1980s had been systematically described, but great changes had been made since data for that collection were compiled in the mid-1980s in response to the stimulus from central government given by the 1989 *Caring for People* White Paper and the NHS and community care legislation that immediately followed. The various monitoring and other studies by the Department of Health, Social Services Inspectorate and the National Health viii

Service Executive were to do much to fill that gap more fully, and with much greater resources once their operations started. But these activities were not yet running, indeed had scarcely been conceived, at the time of our research. To pursue that goal we sought closer contact with authorities than was characteristic of most other investigations of the early stages of the reforms. For instance, we interviewed many officials rather than a few; and read much rather than little produced by the authorities, because we suspected that without this we would gain less understanding of what really was happening and why. For instance, we should be less able to sort rationalisation and partial or biased vision from a broad and valid view.

The material is of value for a second reason. There is nothing like the violent bombardment of matter to reveal the fundamentals of micro-physics. For the violent bombardment of matter in this case read the community care reforms and its accompanying events and crises; and for the fundamental physics of microcosms read the nature of social services as organisations. It is particularly important to understand the nature of social services organisations for the timing, the content and the handling of central government's community care policy reforms. Organisations retain cultural continuities even at a time of rapid change, so that insights into them will retain practical significance for long periods. More important, local authorities have always differed greatly one from another.[2] It would be too easy for distant policy-makers to assume that the headline-catching pressures from the central government — at one level similar bombardments on each social services department microcosm — would have the same effects. No one who has had much contact with local authorities would think that for one moment. So it is valuable to describe the differences in the behaviour of microcosms similarly bombarded with matter.

There was a third aim. The study of ten authorities from 1984 had mapped the basic production of welfare parameters of that period. It had yielded insights both into the proximate causal processes which led them to differ, and into the reasons why the proximate causes had come to differ between areas. That is, the study had used the usual range of production of welfare modelling techniques to answer the main production of welfare questions: who gets how much of what, with what effect, and at what costs to whom; and had supported these with descriptions of how and why these differed between authorities. It was anticipated that another such study would be necessary and be undertaken during the mid-1990s in order to tune policy and implementation, the community care *Policy Guidance* (Department of Health, 1990b), having clearly indicated that the evaluation of the impact of the changes would be an important task for centrally commissioned research. A before/after study design would be possible were the investigation to be conducted in the same areas. To lose contact with the authorities for more than a decade would undermine our capacity in the mid-1990s to understand why the production of welfare parameters of community care would be so different in the 1990s.

Of these three objectives, the first was the immediate aim of the research collection. However, it is the second which is the most important aim of this book. The PSSRU is now in the middle of the field stage of the project describing and explaining the production of welfare parameters in the ten authorities during the mid-1990s. Great changes are still in process in the policy world, and soon there will be evidence which will throw new light on the issues discussed here. Therefore, we use the evidence of the project and draw on other material and our experience to formulate some issues and messages rather than attempt to provide an authoritative review.

ACKNOWLEDGEMENTS

In retrospect it is always difficult to disentangle the division of labour among all of those most actively involved in the work, but Robyn Lawson and Charlotte Salter did most of the field interviews and the initial drafting of the chapters in Part Two. Bleddyn Davies supervised the project, did some field interviews, participated in some of the drafting of the Part Two chapters and contributed sections for the remaining chapters. Chris Gostick joined the project after the fieldwork had been completed, but as Director of Social Services for the City of Westminster during the early period of the reforms, and later as Community Care Development Manager for North West Thames Regional Health Authority, brought the insight and knowledge of an insider to our emerging view of the local implementation of community care in a way that academics can seldom achieve. He breathed new life into the work, undertaking the greater part of the editing of the manuscript, and producing drafts of most of the first and last sections of the book after team work-ins on the various topics.

We are particularly grateful to the wide range of individuals at all levels within our sample authorities for answering our endless questions so fully and helpfully, and for the stream of documents made so freely available to us by those authorities. Administrative and secretarial support at the PSSRU was provided by Anita Whitley and Audrey Walker, and at North Thames by Gill Entwistle. Their efficiency at coping with the flow of paper has been little short of remarkable. We also thank Jane Dennett and Nick Brawn of the PSSRU publications and dissemination office for the preparation of camera-ready copy for the publishers. Special thanks are due to the officials in the Research and Development Directorate at the Department of Health who supported this work as part of the Monitoring Social Care for Elderly People Project. Finally, we remain grateful to those many friends and colleagues throughout the health and social care services on whom we have endlessly tested our emerging ideas over the past three years. Needless to say, we alone remain responsible for the interpretation and presentation of the resulting material.

This work was undertaken by the PSSRU which receives support from the Department of Health. The views expressed in this publication are those of the authors and not necessarily those of the Department of Health.

NOTES

1 For example: Salter (1992); Lawson (1993); Davies (1993, 1994).
2 'Any County Borough with over 75 years of history behind it can make out a good claim to be regarded as *sui generis*' (Pear, 1966).

1 Introduction

From Vision to Reality is primarily an essay, but also a description of policy processes and structures. Our objective has been to use our comparison of the initial stages of the local development of community care with the emerging policy vision at the centre as a basis for ideas about how to reform community care with still greater success.

By *vision* we mean the fundamental logic and content of policy at the highest level of generality, as it exists when the synthesis is at its clearest and purest. It is about ends and means at their most abstract; about what might potentially be achieved, and by what means, where the means include strategic features of structures and commitments. It is the assumptive basis of policy derived from that highest common factor intellectual framework shared by the small in-group of officials who have influenced, and to a high degree understood and become committed to, the key elements of the most general policy statements. This group forms the priesthood of the policy paradigm first synthesised in the Griffiths Report *Community Care: Agenda for Action* (1988) and the White Paper *Caring for People*: Community Care in the Next Decade and Beyond (Secretaries of State, 1989b).

By reality, on the other hand, we mean those elements of the community care world which are adapted and used purposefully to achieve the policy ends: structures; policies and procedures; material and human resources; practices, values and commitments. This reality can only respond partially and inadequately to the vision. We are all conscious of the practical constraints on the degree to which reality can respond to the initiating visions. The community care priesthood always included some people in field agencies, notably in social services departments. Equally, there was also some constraining 'reality' in our sense at the centre. However, there is a strong sense in which more of the vision was radiated from the centre than from field agencies; while the areas in which the contests between vision and reality were most weighted in favour of the latter were inevitably mostly to be found in local agencies.

The main players in the contests form an *implementation community* whose members are expected to reconcile the influence of the paradigm with other factors. They are expected to interpret and take out of the national policy paradigm what can be used by local corporate policy cultures and values. They are expected to balance the logical requirements for the success of the paradigm with the demands of competing policy imperatives (avoiding bed-blocking, for example). They are expected to juggle the policy and task specifications of the new paradigm with long-standing professional or political values and images of the nature of that area of the welfare state (in interpreting attitudes to charging, in responding to targeting priorities). They are expected to balance the paradigm-generated demand to redefine occupational activities against the imperative to protect traditional professional values. They are expected to reinterpret the old tensions between bureaucratic and managerial priorities and those of the caring professions. They are expected actually to try to follow the lead, precepts and instructions of those who articulate the paradigm within the contexts of uneven human and financial resources, intense everyday pressures, and the continuous emergence of the unexpected.

At its most basic level, therefore, *From Vision to Reality* is about central-local relations, and field agency response to a major new central policy initiative. But it also has important lessons to impart about the process by which policy is elaborated and developed by central government officials; about the manner in which that essential policy vision becomes progressively reinterpreted in response to emerging events and constraints; and about the nature of local government itself.

There are two particular features of the study which enable these wider issues to be addressed.

The author of the Chinese proverb must have been in the public service. Few of us will have worked in an environment which has changed so much or so rapidly as health and social care during the past decade. The change has been fundamental in at least three ways: intellectual, structural and assumptive. It is easy to recognise more of the same but at a faster rate, but these changes have also been genuinely exciting and innovative, with Damascene visions and upended logics; the creation of new forces and structures; the emergence of new processes; and the transformation of some traditional health and social care activities almost beyond recognition.

Some of these changes have elements in common with changes in other countries,[1] but few countries have changed so much or so quickly. Outside the UK, the best-publicised major contemporary policy proposal is probably the Clinton health plan. Yet its long-term care element is modest (although expensive), amounting to little more than a benefit to finance the home care of the most disabled — and whether it will ever be enacted still remains uncertain at the time of writing. We also have much to learn in the UK of the potential dangers of service specialisation and fragmentation arising from a largely unregulated mixed health and social care economy such as the United States (Davies, 1986b, for example).

The German and Austrian governments have also enacted legislation for new social insurance benefits, but the pace of change has been much slower, and has not involved the reconstruction of major parts of the logic of an already complex long-term care system. Their state-financed, brokered and planned provision of home and community social services have been and remain primitive by British standards. The Netherlands have a more elaborate system with a greater welfare state commitment, but the radical changes proposed by the Dekker report (1987) have not been enacted, and instead change has been initiated from below. While the Dutch economy of ideas is as open as its trade in commodities, there remain powerful barriers to change in the political structures, and perhaps in their consensus ideology. Elsewhere in Europe, the Danes have been building on their systems of the 1970s and before, rather than radically changing the logics to conform to the new ideologies of the late 1980s.

Perhaps only in Australia has the scale of the reforms been as extensive as in the UK, although it is possible to overstate the magnitude of these changes because the division of responsibility between the Commonwealth and the States, with provision in a mixed supply economy, forces the changes to take highly visible forms mandated by central policy-makers. Perhaps more significantly, the changes in Australia represent a much clearer reflection of the learning processes of the community care world, rather than the translation of foreign concepts from other areas of public policy into social care activities (Auditor General, 1988).

Experiences of the UK policy transformation in community care over the past few years have been extremely varied, often depending on the type of agency and the position of the observer within it. The experience has also differed between those individuals playing the same roles in similar agencies. This diversity of experience perhaps tells us something significant about the nature of the changes themselves. Despite this variety, common patterns can still begin to be traced (see Taylor-Gooby and Lawson, 1993, for example). Our task has been to begin to sketch them a little more clearly. We are acutely conscious that our evidence is limited, and that the speed of change makes the emerging patterns as kaleidoscopic as the opinions and perspectives of those involved.

Almost all social policy analysis is at least by implication evaluatory, and from this perspective the UK reforms of community care have two distinctive features to predispose the academic towards pessimism about their outcomes. First, hardly anything about the reforms reflects trends at the grassroots, or even in most field authorities. The initial policy analysis was from above and from outside, from the very fringes of the policy community. The Financial

Management Initiative was particularly influential, and led directly to the establishment of the Audit Commission and the creation of the new Social Services Inspectorate. Other significant influences have been almost entirely from among policy analysts in academe. In most respects this early policy logic was synthesised by Sir Roy Griffiths, and subsequently adapted (and in important ways fundamentally changed) by a small group of officials at the Department of Health. Once adopted as formal policy, the implications of the fundamental logic began to be developed and programmed into a sequence of actions that were still directed from the top, although the number of participants grew enormously. The subsequent process of dissemination and implementation has been almost exclusively dominated by the mechanisms established by central government. The central vision on which this policy logic was based differed markedly from that in the majority of field agencies at each stage of the policy process, but particularly at the beginning. So in every important respect, these reforms are an apotheosis of top-down policy initiative.

A further important feature adding to the complexity is that the field organisations in this case are not (formally at any rate) simply agents of the central policy-makers. They are constitutionally independent local authorities. The aspiration of many of them, and the aspirations for them of some of the most influential of theoreticians of government, has been to govern rather than to administer; to put the stamp of local values, as brokered by lively and imaginative political processes, on the priorities in policy development; to see the policy process in a corporate way, not as narrowly defined as by central government departments (Stewart, 1986). These aspirations were reflected in, and reinforced by, local government reform in the mid-1970s which created some of the largest multi-purpose authorities in any country. Almost immediately the 1974 oil crisis set in motion a separate chain of events leading to significant fiscal stress and profound political changes, which were eventually reflected in the redefinition of the central role of the state, just at the time these new local authorities were achieving maturity and competence.

The politics of local government have been transformed since 1974, although some movements had waxed and been largely extinguished before the period of the community care reforms. Few if any local authorities now remain the small or more amateur local policy agencies typical of the 1960s. Yet to be effective, local government must remain just that: local (even perhaps parochial) in its orientation, and extremely heterogeneous. Just over twenty years ago, a distinguished political scientist could write of local government:

> Each town is unique: it has its own environment, its own problems ... most of all, each town throws up its own unique individuals (Jones, 1969).

While the dramatic changes in central control during the last few years have tended to dominate debates about the role and responsibilities of local government (Stewart, 1986), changes in control alone do not spell the transformation of either political or policy cultures. And some of the authorities created in 1963 and 1974 were direct successors of, and dominated by, the traditions of their predecessors; while many others survived the 1974 reforms virtually unscathed.[2] However, the classic literature about top-down change of the 1970s and later makes gloomy reading, whether home-grown (Barrett and Fudge, 1981) or trans-Atlantic (Pressman and Wildawsky, 1973). It creates a presumption that top-down policy all too frequently results in fiasco, and rarely delivers what was intended within the parameters envisaged. Schools of analysts have vied in providing alternative explanations: the pressure to adapt to change at all levels in the local negotiation of policy (Straus et al., 1963) or practice (Smith, 1980); the particular imperative to pervert in order actually to survive, while still appearing to conform to the street-level bureaucrat (Lipsky, 1980). These examples from the classic theoretical streams of policy analysis are the core of both graduate and undergraduate courses.

The fundamental question, therefore, is whether the first stages of the community care reforms are laying the foundations for ultimate success. The odds against are all the greater because of the scale and ambition of the reforms.

The context also suggests a testable proposition, although at this stage more a mixed metaphor than a precise scientific hypothesis: the further from the epicentre at which the new policy stone was cast into the social welfare pond, the weaker the ripples, and the more distorted they are likely to be by waves caused by other events. We will use the data we have to explore this proposition, although the research was not undertaken for the purposes to which this essay is putting it. The small collection of evidence on which it is based was made for two other reasons.

One was to fill the gap between two major production of welfare studies which both asked the traditional descriptive production of welfare questions of community care of elderly people about 'Who gets how much of what resource at what cost, where, with what effect on whom?' The second study is a follow-up of the first, creating a classic 'before-after' design for the evaluation of changes in community care over the decade. However, the two studies are separated by a period of such unprecedented change and turbulence that at least some contemporary evidence for the period in between is required if a full understanding of local policy development is to be achieved.

The second reason was to evaluate how far the community care changes were likely to affect the critical targeting and production of welfare parameters identified in the earlier study (Davies et al., 1990). This too required a close description of what was being put into place at the local level.

As a result, the project was small, and uncomfortably and distractingly sandwiched between two major studies. The first was still being worked through during much of the life of this project, for instance in the completion of *Resources Needs and Outcomes*, the drafting of *Community Services and the*

Social Production of Welfare, while the second project was being prepared during its later stages.

Despite these difficulties, our general proposition has provided us with a usable framework for telling the story of the early years of community care reform in Britain, and the way in which the central policy vision was translated into action at a local level. We start with a detailed review of the policy implementation process undertaken by the Department of Health, derived from a close analysis of the rich vein of documentary sources now available. In Part Two we then use the research data generated from our small sample of authorities to outline the emerging local response. Finally, in a short closing chapter in Part Three, we begin to elaborate some tentative conclusions derived from this analysis.

NOTES

1   Dekker (1987); Davies (1986a, 1992); Baldock and Evers (1991); Baldock (1993);
    Challis et al. (1994).
2   For example, at least one authority has had as its social services chair the chair
    of the welfare committee of the authority whose ethos was taken by its successor.

PART ONE
THE POLICY VISION

2 The New Policy Framework

Over the past decade social policy in the United Kingdom has undergone a revolution. What would once have been unthinkable is now commonplace, and becoming more so each day, as the full implications of the new organisational arrangements begin to transform practice and service delivery. It has been difficult to see either the extent or the direction of the transformation. But now that the new policy direction has been clearly set, and with the essential clarity of hindsight, it is possible to see that the current community care reforms are an essential component of the fundamental policy revolution which took place in Britain during the 1980s, triggered by a conjunction of events and ideas originating and emerging in the mid-1970s. These powerful forces for change influenced all public policy, not just the developing critiques of health and social care services. But they emerged only gradually, and within the social welfare arena developed coherence and force relatively late in the 1980s.

The major event to trigger this transformation was the oil crisis of 1974. This profoundly affected all major economies, particularly in Western Europe and Japan. In Britain, it led directly to the collapse of the growth-focused economic policies which had been sustained with varying degrees of emphasis (or success) by all major political parties, whether in government or opposition, since the end of the Second World War. The oil crisis led in turn to currency devaluation, which focused attention specifically on the home economy, producing narrow domestic policies, with a marked emphasis on reducing the influence of government on the market. This was achieved by decreasing the role of the managed economy through an increasingly vigorous search for public expenditure reductions.

An important consequence of this change in emphasis was the breaking up of the long consensus over the role of the welfare state, and the broad co-operation between employers, unions and government which had been sustained over succeeding administrations. Rose (1975) and others have identified these developments as a response to the increasing requirement for national government policy objectives to grapple with international economic systems, and the increasing gap between policy ambitions and actual achievements, sometimes referred to as 'government overload'.

From the mid-1970s onwards, the increasingly recognised failure of centralised economic management (corporatism) was accompanied by a stream of policy analysis from 'new right' research centres, repackaging for broader public consumption the theoretical arguments of American public choice economists and others. These new centres, both of the left and the right, were themselves largely a creation of the breaking down of the old consensus, and the essential search for new policy alternatives. Such centres created increasing public awareness as well as media debate about social issues through the publication of regular bulletins, reports and briefings.

The increasingly obvious failure of policy to achieve effective outcomes created a major opportunity for the hardening 'new right' increasingly to identify and interpret the inflexibility and inefficiencies of government (both national and local) as inevitable tendencies of public bureaucracies. At the same time, competitive markets were increasingly interpreted as a preferable alternative, leading to pressures for the 'privatisation' of public utilities and enterprises, and the creation of autonomous agencies to perform traditional government activities. This approach also had the significant advantage of improving the government's cash-flow position, without requiring either major reductions in public spending commitments or any increase in taxation.

A supporting development was the re-emergence of so-called 'traditional values', especially the concept of family and kinship links as an essential social component, and the downgrading of the concept of community. Such themes were to provide an important component in the second and third Thatcher administrations (1984-1990) (Thatcher, 1993). In combination, these forces were eventually to lead to the restructuring of the NHS around the concept of an internal market, and the changing emphasis in the role of local government.

For local government the changes were most clearly signalled by the statutory requirement for compulsory competitive tendering (CCT) of many key services in the 1988 Local Government Act, and in the move away from a local property tax based on rateable values, to the successive introduction of individualised personal local taxation through the community charge or poll tax in April 1991, and its subsequent replacement by the hybrid council tax in 1993. The same period also saw a further increase in central government control over local authority activities through a progressively regressive operation of the revenue grant mechanism, whereby central government provided (and so controlled) an increasing proportion of local authority revenue expenditure from central taxation, and the introduction of increased powers to cap individual local authority total expenditure levels.

The overall responsibilities of local government were also gradually reduced, for example by the move to local management of schools (LMS), and the ability of individual schools to opt out of local authority control altogether. As a result, over the past decade local authorities have increasingly become little more than local agents for central government, rather than independent authorities in their own right.

This fundamental move from a centrally planned to a market economy was heralded in a variety of ways. Environment Secretary Michael Heseltine contrasted accountability through the ballot box in a public bureaucracy with accountability to consumers in a market, with the latter promoted as a better alternative as a principle of reform. Nicholas Ridley, a predecessor to Heseltine at the Department of Environment (a portfolio which includes responsibility for local government affairs), had earlier defined the concept of an *enabling authority* as that of regulator, sponsor and co-ordinator rather than provider; contracting with independent providers in a competitive market for the supply of services for those for whom it had responsibility.

The Secretary of State of the DHSS had earlier anticipated these arguments in his speech to the annual Social Services Conference at Buxton in September 1984 (Fowler, 1984). Our memory is that some of the movers and shakers among officials and others were reading far more of the history of the late 1980s and 1990s from that speech than the words themselves now convey. This change in emphasis reflected both the change of thinking among Departmental officials in the early 1980s, as well as the prevailing economic and social philosophy which emerged from the second Thatcher election victory in June 1983. It can hardly have been coincidence that Norman Fowler was a member of the ad hoc group of senior ministers known as the 'Family Policy Group' established by Margaret Thatcher as early as June 1982 with specific responsibility to develop this whole area of policy (Thatcher, 1993).

This change in Department of Health thinking was in response to challenges to the traditional agencies of the local welfare state from different quarters, with criticisms first heard during the 1960s. These had much in common with criticisms of the 'new right'; particularly charges of professional domination, bureaucratisation and unresponsiveness to user needs and wishes. By the late 1970s, academic critiques of inflexibility, and empirical evidence of poor targeting and outcomes, were becoming more common in a wide range of policy areas, including community care, both in terms of a general vagueness about both ends and means (Goldberg and Connelly, 1982), and to new approaches to targeting and innovation (Davies , 1981).

In health and personal social services policy-making, the initial effect of the turmoil of the late 1970s was to hamper progress in implementing old policies, without the development of new alternatives. One example of this was the short-lived flirtation with community social work signalled by the Barclay review in the early 1980s (Barclay, 1982).

Not all arguments that public authorities should play more ambitious enabling roles came from the 'new right'. Some commentators increasingly argued for flexibly purchasing local services as a development from, rather than a reaction against, the centralising reforms of the 1960s. This movement was nourished by the clear lessons beginning to emerge from overseas experience (Davies, 1986b, 1992), as well as from empirical research (Davies and Challis, 1986).

One early development by the Thatcher administration was the Financial Management Initiative (FMI), which led to the replacement of the Audit Office by a new Audit Commission for Local Government, whose initial focus was cost-effectiveness (White Paper, 1983). The Commission did much to introduce and popularise the new managerialist ideas to a local government system still conditioned by the centralised provider agenda of the early 1970s. The Audit Commission very quickly produced powerful critiques of the wide variations in the relative efficiencies of local authorities, as well as of the effectiveness of government community care policy (Audit Commission, 1985, 1986). There are foci for these criticisms. One is the existence of perverse incentives to enter residential care rather than remain at home. It was created by the free availability of social security payments for those people entering independent sector residential or nursing care homes without any requirement for an assessment of their need for such services. A second was the failure to shift the balance of care from hospitals and other residential institutions to community-based services. A third was the vagueness and apparent confusion of existing targeting policy for the provision of care services well adapted to the specific needs of priority users in cost-effective ways.

The Department of Health contributed to these emerging developments by the replacement of the Social Work Service (focused on professional effectiveness, particularly in child welfare) with a new Social Services Inspectorate (SSI), with a duty to promote efficiency as well as effectiveness. These new-style inspections undertaken by SSI in the latter 1980s were already being influenced by new academic arguments, particularly the failure to match resources to needs in community care, and the effects on the targeting of resources and impact on outcomes (see Social Services Inspectorate, 1987, for example).

Both the new SSI and the Audit Commission were influential because their writings were widely studied by managers and policy-makers at both central and local levels. Being inspectorates, both also worked to programmes which allowed them to follow up the impact of their earlier findings about individual agencies by further studies.

During this same period the concept of *new managerialism* also began to emerge, and interestingly was used to describe two sets of related phenomena. One was the adoption in government generally of many of the values, assumptions and techniques of private sector management, such as clear mission statements and objectives for managers, regularly reviewed against short-term time scales; 'cost' and 'profit' centres; performance monitoring; and financial incentives using process and outcome indicators rather than the more traditional input data (Davies and Ferlie, 1982; Pollitt, 1990). *Quality assurance* and *total quality management* also emerged as important themes, together with more extensive management training and the delegation of authority and responsibility with cash-limited budgets for achieving the goals within more effective accountability systems.

These approaches were all designed to encourage resourcefulness and responsiveness; adaptiveness about means with constancy about ends (Klein and O'Higgins, 1985), and spawned an increasing array of new management gurus, mainly emanating from North America, each with a seminal text or cook-book of ideas (for example, Peters and Waterman, 1982). Increasing numbers of young British social welfare managers exposed to these new ideas began to emerge and form networks during the late 1980s. In this sense, the new managerialism was a powerful influence in all government agencies.

The second way in which new managerialism was conceptualised related mainly to post-1974 reorganisation local authorities, with local government emerging as a 'political institution constituted for local choice' (Stewart, 1986). This approach added a political dimension to 'learning, choice, flexibility and responsiveness' in Stewart's vision of 'new managerialism'. Reflecting this second sense, local authorities were increasingly defined as 'public sector organisations, not market organisations', making their decisions 'subject to political control rather than market discipline' (ibid). For Stewart, this emerging response was a reaction to the break-up of consensus, and the spread of party conflict in local government, in the years following the 1974 reorganisation. In many ways this emerging politicisation of local government simply added to its problems by creating a yet stronger managerial response from the centre.

By the late 1980s the role and responsibilities of local government were increasingly coming into question as they moved away from being major service providers to commissioners and enablers as a result of compulsory competitive tendering, particularly the complex two-tier system that remained from 1974. In 1985 the Greater London Council (GLC) and the six metropolitan counties were abolished, and the following year the Inner London Education Authority (ILEA) was decentralised to its component authorities. But this was still not sufficient. In 1991 Environment Secretary Michael Heseltine established the Local Government Commission under the chairmanship of Sir John Banham (first Director of the Audit Commission) to review all county and district authorities in England, with a view to a movement away from the existing dual structure to a single system of unitary authorities similar to that already operating in London and the metropolitan districts (Department of Environment, 1991). The respective Secretaries of State for Scotland

and Wales subsequently outlined proposals for the establishment of similar new unitary authorities in their regions. Only in Northern Ireland does the future remain in any doubt, largely because of the existence of direct rule from Whitehall since 1984.

It was against this more general background of political transformation and the refocusing of economic and social policy that the more specific developments in health and social care policy, particularly for elderly people, that form the major focus of this monograph began to emerge in the mid-1980s. And it is against this background that the actual impacts and achievements of the new central government policy initiatives need to be measured and evaluated.

3 Evolution of the New Community Care Vision

The reforms of the United Kingdom health and social care services embodied in the 1990 NHS and Community Care Act are bringing about the most significant changes since the inception of the welfare state, and accelerating the transformation of both the National Health Service and of local authority social services departments. These reflect the changes (and fragmentation) in social values and the breakdown of the welfare consensus during the early 1980s.

The past decade has seen a sustained erosion of the independence and responsibilities of local authorities, and increased centralisation of power towards Whitehall. The only area of significant increase in local authority responsibilities has been in social services, where the introduction of community care has been accompanied by the phased transfer of significant new resources (£1,588 million over three years) from the Department of Social Security to local authorities, beginning in April 1993.

These changes, together with the implementation of the 1989 Children Act in November 1991, have led local authority social services departments into the most significant transformation since their creation in 1971 following the recommendations of the Seebohm Committee (Secretary of State, 1968). The impact of these changes is still far from clear, but the degree of change has been so rapid and significant that it is important to chart developments on both the way in which the policy has emerged, and the response to that policy shift within individual local authorities.

Although April 1993 was the critical date for full implementation of the 1990 NHS and Community Care Act, the process had started with the creation of the NHS internal market in April 1991 and the phased introduction of the local authority elements of community care over the following two years. This period of phased introduction culminated with the ending of Department of Social Security responsibility for public financing for the care of people entering non-local authority residential or nursing care on 31 March 1993, and the beginning of the phased transfer of ring-fenced financial resources to local authorities to take over these responsibilities.

CONFUSED CROSS-CURRENTS OF THE PRE-VISION WORLD

In retrospect, it seems that during the fifteen years preceding the Griffiths Report we were searching for a unifying vision. The assumptions of the years which immediately followed the Seebohm Report and the Royal Commission on Local Government could no longer hold in the difficult years for British society and economy following the oil crisis. There were many currents of thought. But some were barely elaborated; others were the projections forward of the ideas of the previous decade and took little account of the new currents and constraints. Nowhere were they brought together within a coherent framework.

While April 1993 may be seen as the formal start of community care, use of the term began much earlier, and has been traced back to at least the 1920s (Wistow et al., 1994). In its current form the concept was originally articulated by Richard Titmuss in the 1960s, but came to more general prominence in the early 1970s with proposals first outlined by Enoch Powell (1961) when Minister of Health, for the movement of long-stay hospital patients from the old Victorian asylums back into the community (DHSS, 1976, 1977). It is at this point that the general policy of broadly preferring community care to more institutional alternatives may be said to have its origins. Even then the term was the subject of confusion as to whether it was a *description* of the services or resources involved (for example, those services provided outside of institutions), or a *statement of objectives* (for example, to treat mentally ill patients as near as possible to their local communities). Those differences were explicitly recognised by a Government Review Group on community care (DHSS, 1981b).

The same period saw a deepening professional emphasis on care *by* the community rather than *in* the community (Webb and Wistow, 1987), or *by AND with* the community (Bayley, 1982), largely as a result of the more widespread acceptance of the Wolfensberger (1972) concept of *normalisation*, and the provision of more ordinary facilities and life-styles for sick or disabled people (Ovretveit, 1993). The growing popularity of community social work throughout the late 1970s and early 1980s (Barclay, 1982), coupled with a general demise of social case work and an increasing emphasis on a crisis intervention approach (Gostick and Scott, 1982; Challis and Ferlie, 1988), also characterised this period as social services attempted to regroup in response to the more constrained financial circumstances of local authorities and the demand for more evidence of social work effectiveness.

These developments were possibly the inevitable consequence of the post-Younghusband and post-Seebohm changes as they worked their way through to influence both the nature of the workers being employed and the underlying beliefs and values of the new departments in which they worked. The new social services departments were much less social work agencies than had originally been envisaged by the profession, and although the Seebohm ambitions for breadth were clear enough, there was certainly an assumption that the social work professionals would be the high priests of the new welfare temple. But social services authorities became interested in value for money and more effective management long before the creation of the Audit Commission, as is well illustrated by the studies of trends in the organisation of the new departments at both field and middle management levels (for example, Black et al., 1983), and the studies of patterns of innovation during the late 1970s and early 1980s (Ferlie, 1980; Ferlie et al., 1989).

The Barclay report (1982) provides an interesting example of the confusion over policy and practice that characterised the 1980s social services departments. Barclay was in fact three reports: the main report signed by fourteen of the eighteen members of the committee, together with two minority reports. One of these minority report took a more extreme view of the need for a community social work or 'patch' approach (Brown et al., 1982), which grew out of Professor Hadley's extensive work on neighbourhood and community activities (Hadley and McGrath, 1981). The second, by Professor Pinker (1982), argued for a sustained re-emphasis on the centrality of social casework to social services activities. All three approaches may usefully be contrasted with the alternative concept of *social maintenance* being developed and articulated in successive books by Professor Martin Davies (1981, 1985).

These various approaches reflect in part the emerging debate between generic and specialist social work on the one hand, and between professional elitism or non-directive egalitarianism on the other (Brewer and Lait, 1980; Glastonbury et al., 1980). It was during this period that the British Association of Social Workers (BASW) abolished formal entry qualifications for membership. In retrospect this can be seen as a sterile debate which deflected social services authorities away from the crucial issues of identifying clear intervention goals and evaluating outcomes, although good examples of both appear in the literature of the period (Goldberg and Warburton, 1979; Mattison and Sinclair, 1979). In this sense, Barclay was a major distraction from the central concern of establishing an effective balance of care, especially in relation to services for elderly people, between the various potential interventions (Shenfield, 1957).

In the early 1980s, Martin Knapp (1984) argued that the logic of matching mode of case to costs and benefits had been little applied by local authorities. A decade later, care managers not just assume that most persons would prefer to remain at home, they receive it almost as doctrine. However, researchers must admit that the logic linking people's circumstances and the supply and

prices of inputs to the targeting of modes of care remains in important ways
vague and unsupported by rigorous analysis of evidence.

It has been suggested (Isaacs et al., 1972) that the origins of the prevalent
modern concept of community care may be found in the increasing tendency
for home care workers such as home helps and district nurses, as well as
family, neighbours and other carers, to support and sustain elderly and
disabled people in the community, often at great personal cost and with little
or no recognition, long after they could more appropriately have been sustained in hospital or residential care. Similarly, Bayley (1982) has argued that
our contemporary concept of care tends to be very individualised, with one
person (usually a daughter) becoming identified as the carer, so freeing others
(including statutory agencies) from responsibility until some major breakdown occurs. Once this happens care then tends to become professionalised
and increasingly institutionalised. What needs to be stressed is the general
lack of any consistent empirical evidence as to the patterns of care most likely
to provide either an efficient or effective response, or an improved quality
of life, in response to individual personal needs. The assumption that community care is somehow superior to other forms of care is just that; and has
yet to be demonstrated.

It was against this generally confused background, and the sustained pressure to reduce public expenditure in local authorities throughout the 1980s,
that the new social policy vision began to emerge. But it became coherent
only gradually, and some distinctive strands in its development can be identified. One of the most significant was signalled by Social Services Secretary
Norman Fowler in his speech to the 1984 Social Services Conference at Buxton.
This gave an early glimpse of the change in conceptual framework within
which the new policy alternatives were to be developed, by emphasising the
emerging principles of new managerialism that needed to be applied, although at this stage endeavouring to make links with the broad social concepts
outlined in the Seebohm report (Secretary of State, 1968). This was taken as
a warning shot by many local authorities, emphasising the need for improved
management, efficiency and effectiveness.

A complementary strand also beginning to emerge more generally during
this period was the increasing emphasis in government and media rhetoric
on 'traditional family values', with its emphasis on informal care networks
sustained by practical activities rather than on the basis of professional intervention. It is now a matter of record that Norman Fowler was a prominent
member of the so-called 'Family Policy Group' established by Margaret Thatcher to develop this approach (Thatcher, 1993), which was eventually to
embrace the development of a complementary independent sector social care
market, and the targeting of state resources on those with greatest needs.

In the meantime, during the mid-1980s, while these policy initiatives were
still in an embryonic state, a very powerful additional strand began to emerge:
a strand that would eventually come to dominate the public agenda. This

was the result of minor changes to the income support system in 1979, which led to the ready availability of social security funding to support elderly and other disabled adults in independent sector residential (or nursing) care homes (Wistow et al., 1994). In time this fuelled the massive expansion of independent (mainly private) residential and nursing care homes which occurred throughout the 1980s. Income support payments for care in private and voluntary residential and nursing homes totalled £1,300 million in March 1991, and perhaps as much as £2,480 million by April 1993, compared to supplementary benefit payments of £10 million in 1979 (Henwood et al., 1991; Wistow et al., 1994). In response the number of residential home places grew by 57 per cent between 1980 and 1991, and there was an almost four-fold increase in the number of nursing home places. By 1988, the private sector had displaced local government as the largest provider in the residential care sector (Wistow et al., 1994).

It is unclear how far availability of social security support, subject only to a simple financial means test and with no cash limit, merely financed a latent preference for independent institutional care among elderly people and their families rather than encouraged it. Whatever the reason, the private residential and nursing care sector grew spectacularly throughout the 1980s, particularly in popular retirement areas on the south and east coast of England. As a result, many people who could probably have managed quite adequately in the community with a modest amount of support found the financial advantages and relative security of publicly financed residential care too attractive to refuse, and by March 1991 60 per cent of elderly people in private or voluntary residential care in England were financed by social security income support, compared to 14 per cent in 1979 and 36 per cent in the mid-1980s, while only 20 per cent were financed by local authorities (Wistow et al., 1994).

Despite the potential consequences of these emerging financial and political trends, DHSS officials still appeared more concerned with ensuring better collaboration between health and social services authorities than in evaluating the effectiveness of existing community care policy. A *Progress in Partnership* working group was established, which reported in 1985 (DHSS, 1985), with 44 detailed recommendations on how joint planning might be improved, but was precluded by its terms of reference from addressing the underlying themes of the effectiveness of existing policy, or the adequacy of resources (Wistow and Brooks, 1988).

By contrast, the House of Commons Social Services Committee was less inhibited, and in a critical report on community care (1985) brought the issue back to a prominent position on the policy agenda. This was reinforced the following year when the newly established Audit Commission in an early report (1986) raised serious concerns about the effectiveness of existing community care policy, and questioned just how far government policy objectives were being achieved. The Audit Commission report identified a problem of 'slow and uneven progress' due to 'fundamental underlying problems' reflecting 'policy contradictions' and 'perverse incentives', for which central government bore substantial responsibility. The conclusions were expressed in strong terms, warning that: 'if nothing changes the outlook is bleak' (para. 48), with 'a continued waste of resources' (p.5). The report called upon central government to initiate radical change by the establishment of a high-level review, and emphasised that 'the one option which is not tenable is to do nothing' (p.4).

The government was also beset by increasing problems over the financing and priorities of the NHS during this period. These issues grabbed the headlines when a number of operations were cancelled by the Birmingham Children's Hospital, causing a national outcry by the media. As a result the Prime Minister herself became involved, and established (and personally chaired) a high level internal review into the reform of the NHS (Thatcher, 1993). On the community care front, the government responded equally rapidly, and in December 1986 appointed Sir Roy Griffiths, the Prime Minister's personal adviser on health services matters, to lead an enquiry into community care. An earlier report by Sir Roy Griffiths into the organisation and management of the NHS (Griffiths, 1983) had led to the introduction of general management into the health services, which paved the way for the eventual development of the NHS internal market (Thatcher, 1993).

THE GRIFFITHS ARGUMENT

Sir Roy Griffiths responded promptly, and his recommendations were published in *Community Care: Agenda for Action* in February 1988. The report identified the theme of policy failure in unequivocal terms: 'In few areas can the gap between political rhetoric and policy on the one hand, or between policy and reality in the field on the other hand have been so great' (p.iv). The report did not review all the evidence again, but accepted that the essential facts were contained in the reports of the Social Services Committee and Audit Commission. In the meantime, information on the developing financial consequences of existing policies had been supplemented by two internal DHSS reviews on the use of supplementary benefit for residential care (Scott-Whyte, 1985; Firth, 1987).

Griffiths was admirably succinct and to the point, focusing on contradictions (or 'roadblocks') in the existing systems of care, and concentrating on recommendations for change, set out in an agenda for action. In particular the report did not dwell on the issue of resources, except to emphasise that policy and resources must be brought into better balance, and that the ready availability of social security support for residential care compared to a cash-limited priority system for community care was inevitably limiting the opportunity for the development of potentially more effective community-based alternatives. The report pointed out that the system for the distribution of local authority funding through the rate support grant mechanism made it extremely difficult for social services authorities to commit themselves confidently to collaboration with health authorities (ibid, p.v).

The report also emphasised that publicly provided care represented only a small part of the total social care provided to people in need, and recommended that the future role of the state should be to support and reinforce such informal care rather than to replace it, so echoing the underlying principles of *social maintenance* as outlined by Professor Martin Davies (1985). The report supported the need for individuals to be maintained in local communities rather than be cared for in long-stay hospitals or other institutions, with resources being targeted explicitly towards those in greatest need. Finally, the report highlighted the need for the appointment of *care managers* with responsibility to identify individual needs, devise packages of care, and co-ordinate the delivery of services (ibid, p.vii).

The report made no mention of individual care groups, and implied that a similar mechanism could usefully be applied to all major client groups. This was potentially very significant, for while the potential of the care management approach adopted by Griffiths had been clearly demonstrated for the care of elderly people (Davies and Challis, 1986), no such evidence was available for other client groups, and indeed recent evidence on the poor implementation of the similar Care Programme Approach (CPA) for mentally ill people, such as the report of the Christopher Clunis enquiry (Ritchie et al., 1994), suggested that alternative systems might need to be devised and tested for each of the major client groups. In the United States, for example, care management was available for a wide variety of groups, but set in teams with different organisational focus, different compositions, and with different balances of core care management and clinical or therapeutic tasks (Davies, 1986a). The main recommendations from *Agenda for Action* are summarised in Box 1.

The Griffiths report devised a mechanism whereby the existing haemorrhage of income support into independent residential and nursing care might be controlled, and diverted into a range of community alternatives that over time should lead to a better balance between individual needs and available resources, within a priority framework that emphasised the reinforcement of informal care, with minimum intervention, targeted to those with greatest needs, with local authorities acting to manage and consolidate the system, rather than as major providers of care. Such an approach was financially attractive to a government beset with economic difficulties, and fitted neatly within the emerging central government policy framework of reducing public provision, minimising intervention, emphasising individual responsibility and increasing public accountability through clear managerial responsibility, while encouraging and co-ordinating a diverse mixed economy of care.

BOX 1. MAIN RECOMMENDATIONS OF AGENDA FOR ACTION

- The appointment of a Minister of State with clear responsibility for community care, including issuing a statement of Government community care objectives and priorities; outlining standards of services; distribution of a specific grant to local authorities for community care services, and ensuring the necessary match between policy objectives and resources; and establishing an effective system for reviewing local authority community care plans and performance.
- Local authorities to assume lead responsibility for community care, and within available resources to be responsible for assessing the community care needs of their localities; establishing priorities and service objectives and developing local community care plans in collaboration with health authorities, voluntary and private agencies.
- Local authorities to be responsible for the identification and assessment of individual needs for community care; for devising packages to allow individuals to live as normal a life as possible, and for delivering such packages of care by building on existing support networks of informal and neighbourhood care.
- Local authorities to become designers, organisers and purchasers of non-health services care, and not primarily direct providers, making maximum use of voluntary and private agencies to widen consumer choice, to stimulate innovation and encourage efficiency.
- Finally, central government to arrange the transfer of the necessary resources to local authorities through a specific grant, subject to being satisfied of the existence of effective local arrangements for community care.

Source: Griffiths (1988, pp.1-2).

Although widely welcomed, and taken as a significant vote of confidence in local authorities, the Griffiths recommendations fundamentally shifted the emerging concept of the enabling local authority, especially for personal social services, much further towards a market economy than any previous proposals, and not all were convinced that a move to more community-based care would necessarily lead to the anticipated cost reductions (Davies et al., 1990).

Despite the popular response to *Agenda for Action*, the Government remained strangely silent, while income support payments to independent sector residential and nursing care homes continued to rise. The major problem was the government's understandable reluctance to transfer greater financial resources and responsibility to local authorities, at a time when a central feature of economic policy was ever more effective control of public expenditure, and reduction in the powers of local government.

THE WHITE PAPER

For almost two years the policy hung in the balance, while the pressure of social security expenditure increased remorselessly. Eventually, in November 1989, 22 months after the publication of the Griffiths report, government accepted the inevitable and responded with the White Paper *Caring for People*: Community Care in the Next Decade and Beyond (Secretaries of State, 1989b). By this time the monolithic DHSS had been split into its two component Departments of Health and Social Security, and Kenneth Clarke had become Secretary of State for Health. This included parliamentary responsibility for personal social services, although the financing of local authorities, including social services, continued to remain the responsibility of the Department of the Environment.

The government had also recently published its proposals for the reorganisation of the NHS in Working for Patients (Secretaries of State, 1989a) following the long-awaited internal review. This outlined the establishment of the NHS Management Executive; creation of new health authorities of executive managers and non-executive directors; and a move towards clear capitation funding. More importantly, the White Paper also outlined the creation of an internal NHS market by the separation of purchasing health authorities from provider hospitals and community units, with resources following patients across health authority boundaries. The White Paper also included proposals for hospitals to apply for self-governing status as NHS Trust hospitals, and the opportunity for large GP practices to apply to become budget holders.

Under the circumstances, the emphasis in the *Caring for People* White Paper on creating a similar market framework for community care was hardly surprising, with its focus on consumer choice, quality and individual care provided through care managers with decentralised budgets. Although not accepting the Griffiths proposals for specific community care grants, nor the setting of explicit national objectives and priorities to form the basis for an annual activity programme, the White Paper largely followed the broad thrust of the Griffiths recommendations, and established the Government approach to achieving better care, by:

- enabling people to live as normal a life a possible in their own homes or in a homely environment in the local community;
- providing the right amount of care and support to help people achieve maximum possible independence and by acquiring or re-acquiring basic living skills help them to achieve their full potential;
- giving people a greater individual say in how they live their lives and the services they need to help them to do so (Secretaries of State, 1989b, para. 1.8).

BOX 2. KEY COMPONENTS OF COMMUNITY CARE

- Services that respond flexibly and sensitively to the needs of individuals and their carers;
- Services that allow a range of options for consumers;
- Services that intervene no more than is necessary to foster independence;
- Services that concentrate on those with the greatest needs.

Source: *Caring for People* White Paper, para. 1.10.

BOX 3. KEY OBJECTIVES FOR COMMUNITY CARE

- To promote the development of domiciliary day and respite services to enable people to live in their own homes whenever feasible and sensible.
- To ensure that service providers make practical support for carers a high priority.
- To make proper assessment of need and good case management the cornerstone of high quality care.
- To promote the development of a flourishing independent sector alongside good quality public services.
- To clarify the responsibilities of agencies and so make it easier to hold them to account for their performance.
- To secure better value for taxpayers' money by introducing a new funding structure for social care.

Source: *Caring for People* White Paper, para. 1.11.

The White Paper clearly identified the major components of community care (Box 2), and outlined six key objectives for community care (Box 3). To achieve these objectives, the White Paper proposed a number of changes in the way in which social care was delivered and funded (Box 4).

The White Paper therefore provided a comprehensive framework for the future operation of community care services for all major client groups, based on local authority social services taking lead responsibility for managing and co-ordinating services, using the mechanism of care management proposed in the Griffiths report (1988). The transfer of responsibility for income support for community care also provided central government with a way to control social security expenditure on residential and nursing care through the phased transfer of cash-limited resources to local authorities. Thus the two central imperatives of financial control and more efficiently managed services were brought together in a single policy framework in the White Paper. This general framework may be summarised as follows:

BOX 4. KEY POLICY CONTENT

- Local authorities to become responsible for assessing individual need, designing care arrangements and securing their delivery within available resources.
- Local authorities to produce and publish clear plans for the development of community care services.
- Local authorities to make maximum use of the independent sector;
- Local authorities to take responsibility for financial support for people in private and voluntary homes.
- Applicants with few or no resources of their own to be eligible for the same level of income support and housing benefit, irrespective of whether they live in their own homes or in independent residential or nursing homes.
- Local authorities to establish inspection and registration units at arm's length from the management of their own services, responsible for checking on standards in both their own homes and independent sector residential care homes.
- The introduction of a new specific grant to promote the development of social care for seriously mentally ill people.

Source: Caring for People White Paper, para. 1.12.

- New organisation structures based on the separation of purchaser and provider functions, the promotion of a mixed economy and the creation of new providers operating in an open external market.
- Service delivery to be effected through systematic arrangements for assessment, care management, devolved budgeting and some degree of decentralised purchasing.
- More effective inter-agency working through clearer allocation of responsibilities for health and social care, combined with strengthening financial incentives for collaboration, with a focus on achieving effective outcomes rather than concentrating on structures or processes.
- Financial control effected through cash-limited budgets accessed following individual assessment of need.

Again it is worth re-emphasising that the White Paper drew no clear distinction between the major client groups, although there was a separate chapter on mental illness, including a proposal for a specific grant to local authorities for the development of mental health services.

The publication of the White Paper was swiftly followed by the introduction of the NHS and Community Care Bill. This rapidly passed through its various parliamentary stages, and received the Royal Assent on 29 June 1990, a process that was in marked contrast to the slow process of deliberations which characterised the parallel development of the 1989 Children Act.

The 1990 NHS and Community Care Act is itself an interesting document, and stands in marked contrast to the 1989 Children Act, the other major item of social services legislation during this period. The Children Act provides a very detailed statutory framework drawing together a wide range of previously scattered family and child care law into a single and coherent new legal instrument. The NHS and Community Care Act, on the other hand, allows all previous adult and social services legislation to remain, scattered through a variety of individual statutes, and indeed of its 67 clauses and ten schedules only nine clauses relate to community care in England and Wales, and a further eight clauses to community care in Scotland, with a number of these being of a technical nature. The most important was Section 50, requiring social services authorities to exercise their functions in accordance with any specific directions from the Secretary of State: the new era of advice, guidance and regulation was about to begin in earnest, further blurring the distinction between central and local government relationships and responsibilities.

The two 1989 White Papers and the 1990 NHS and Community Care Act broadly completed the new central policy vision for health and personal social services that had been gradually evolving through successive Conservative administrations from 1979. While uniquely British in origin and emphasis, the new policy imperatives have some similarity of approach if not of detail with general policy developments elsewhere, particularly in the United States and Australia. The next, and more crucial, phase was to be the transformation of this policy vision into operational reality at a local level. Unlike the 1989 Children Act which had evolved from a gradually emerging consensus among policy-makers, practitioners, managers, academics and the media, the NHS and Community Care Act was a centrally derived initiative, largely devised by Department of Health officials, within an economic and ideological framework that formed the basis for the later Thatcher administrations. The broad parameters set out in the two White Papers and in the 1990 NHS and Community Care Act gave little clue to the transformation in local organisation and practice that would be necessary to achieve effective implementation. The long haul from policy vision to service reality was about to begin in earnest.

4   National Implementation, 1990-1993

With the passing of the NHS and Community Care Act in June 1990, the stage was set for a major national policy implementation programme. In many ways, implementation of the new vision became as revolutionary as the policy itself, with considerable central direction and some notable innovations, such as the eventual establishment of the Community Care Support Force in September 1992. Central control of the process became more sophisticated in the months immediately prior to formal implementation in April 1993, but in the early stages it was largely ad hoc and non-directive. In retrospect it is possible to distinguish a series of distinct phases in the implementation process, to which *Agenda for Action* and the *Caring for People* White Paper provided the context:

- overture;
- Chief Inspector's letter of January 1990 and establishment of SSI Development Groups;
- publication of policy and practice guidance in 1990/1991;
- introduction of monitoring in 1991/1992;
- formal involvement of NHS with publication of the Foster/Laming letter in March 1992;
- establishment of the Community Care Support Force in September 1992;
- introduction of special transitional grant mechanisms in 1992/93; and
- post-April 1993 implementation phase.

OVERTURE

The start was not propitious. On 18 July 1990, only three weeks after the Royal Assent, it was announced that although implementation of the NHS components of the Act would go ahead as planned on 1 April 1991, the community care elements would take place in three stages up to April 1993. It has been suggested that the main reason for this delay was the need to ensure there was no confusion in the public mind between the transfer of income support responsibilities to local authorities and the new community charge (poll tax), introduced at the same time (Henwood et al., 1991). The principal consequence was that transfer of resources from social security to local authorities was delayed until April 1993.

The announcement argued that postponement would ensure more time for local authorities to prepare for implementation (Wistow et al., 1994). The delay provoked considerable anger among local authorities, especially from the Association of Directors of Social Services (ADSS) and the Local Authority Associations (LAAs), who saw this as yet further evidence of central government's reluctance to transfer new responsibilities to local government. The revised implementation timetable sent out by the Department of Health is given in Box 5.

Given the magnitude of the community care changes, it is clear in retrospect that few if any local authorities would have been in a position to cope effectively with the new income support responsibilities in April 1991, nor indeed would the Department of Health have been in a position to develop appropriate distribution mechanisms for the new resources by that date.

Whatever the reason for delay, the additional time did allow better preparation for implementation, albeit at the price of some further turbulence and confusion. More important, it gave the Department of Health an opportunity to launch a major programme of development work with an increasing flow of guidance, advice, regulations and performance targets to local authorities on implementation. This was reinforced by the introduction of national monitoring of local authority progress on implementation. As a result, the community care reforms became one of the most carefully stage-managed and centrally controlled policy implementations of what are essentially new functions and responsibilities of individual local authorities. But to talk of stage management implies knowledge of both text and plot. The director has the text in advance. But the White Paper provided only the outline of the plot and not its detail, nor those all-important lines without which the most gifted and committed actors are likely to flounder, fluff their entries, and pull in opposing directions. In the case of community care, the actual dialogue and characterisation had to be made up, not just at rehearsal, but often in front of the public audience.

BOX 5. KEY EVENTS IN COMMUNITY CARE IMPLEMENTATION

Feb. 1988	Griffiths Report *Agenda for Action* published
Nov. 1989	White Paper: *Caring for People* published
Jan. 1990	Utting letter (CI(90)3) issued and establishment of Development Groups
June 1990	NHS and Community Care Act
July 1990	Announcement of phased implementation
Nov. 1990	Policy guidance on community care implementation (LAC(90)12) published
Various 1991	Practice guidance on specific topics (e.g. care management and assessment) published
April 1991	Inspection units and complaints procedures introduced
May 1991	Price Waterhouse guidance published on purchaser/commissioner and provider roles
Sept. 1991	First SSI/RHA monitoring exercise
Feb. 1992	Second SSI/RHA monitoring exercise
March 1992	First Foster/Laming letter (EL(92)13)
April 1992	First community care plans published
May 1992	Audit Commission report *Cascade of Change* published
June 1992	Audit Commission report *The Community Revolution* published
Sept. 1992	Third, and more formalised, SSI/RHA monitoring exercises
Sept. 1992	Establishment of Community Care Support Force
Oct. 1992	Outline of total special transitional grant (STG) resources by Secretary of State
Dec. 1992	Joint health/social services agreements to be completed in order to qualify for STG
Dec. 1992	SSI guidance on assesment and resources (CI(92)34) published
Jan. 1993	Fourth SSI/RHA monitoring exercise
March 1993	Langland/Laming letter (EL(93)18) published
April 1993	Formal implementation of NHS and Community Care Act
May 1993	Winding up of Community Care Support Force

THE CHIEF INSPECTOR'S LETTER (JANUARY 1990)

With the advantage of hindsight it is possible to see that both social services managers and Department of Health officials significantly underestimated the magnitude and complexity of the required changes. This is perhaps reflected most clearly in the letter to directors of social services from the

Social Services Chief Inspector at the Department of Health in January 1990. This letter, issued six months before the NHS and Community Care Act completed its parliamentary passage, and little more than a year before the anticipated implementation in April 1991, outlined the key objectives of the changes stressing that, while certain clear steps needed to be taken by 1 April 1991, many of the White Paper objectives were much longer term. The letter concluded:

> [T]he community care changes do not create totally new demands: your staff are already familiar with elements of needs assessment, collaboration with other agencies, and the purchasing of services from outside the department ... so while the direction of the changes required is not entirely new, the imminence of social security changes gives them a new urgency (Utting, 1990).

The letter indicated that by 1 April 1991 social services departments needed to have in place:

- an initial set of community care plans, with monitoring and review systems for these plans;
- arrangements for assessing care needs and for securing the provision of care;
- financial arrangements for people receiving residential and nursing care, including the reassessment of all present residents in local authority homes;
- subject to consultation, the introduction of arm's-length inspection units; and
- complaints procedures.

The letter went on to suggest that other aspects of the White Paper proposals, including the establishment of case management (sic), the promotion of a wider role for the independent sector and the development of innovative purchasing and contracting arrangements, were likely to take longer to become fully operational, and needed to develop from good practice, as well as from operational experience and from staff training and development.

The letter also suggested that there was no need for local authorities to rush to reduce their stock of directly-managed residential provision, or the direct provision of other services. Rather, initial concentration should be on identifying the needs of the local population, and how best to ensure provision was available to meet those needs, particularly for new applicants who but for the changes would have been supported in independent sector homes via the existing social security system (Utting, 1990, pp.1-2).

The letter also outlined a series of development projects being mounted by the Social Services Inspectorate over the next twelve months, involving a range of representatives from local authorities, the ADSS and the local authority associations. Each project was intended to:

- collate existing experience and information;
- contribute significantly to departmental advice and guidance;
- undertake development work with SSDs;
- identify and commission training materials; and
- disseminate the outcomes of its work.

Projects were set up in the following areas:

- assessment and case management;
- inspection (including quality assurance);
- purchasing and budgeting;
- community care plans;
- monitoring the mental illness specific grant; and
- training for social services staff.

In addition, an existing SSI-led project on complaints procedures initiated as part of the Department of Health's response to the report of the Wagner Committee (1988) on residential care services would also be doing work in this area. Finally, and perhaps most significantly, the letter indicated that the community care changes were largely a continuation of existing developments, although the imminence of the change in social security responsibilities was likely to create a new sense of urgency, ensuring a substantial increasing number of clients for social services departments over time (Utting, 1990).

In response, local authorities readied themselves for a busy twelve months, gearing up for community care implementation in parallel with training and development work for the introduction for the 1989 Children Act in November 1991. As a first stage, many authorities established similar working groups to those being run nationally by the SSI as a way of identifying the key issues that needed to be understood and addressed. It is now clear that, with few exceptions, local authorities were still seeing community care as more a development of existing responsibilities, coupled with a move away from their current levels of direct service provision (especially local authority residential care for elderly people), rather than as a fundamental revolution in organisation and operation. This view was reinforced by the focus of the special project groups, which inevitably concentrated on developing practice guidelines within their discrete areas of responsibility, by building on existing knowledge and practice. This approach had the effect of ignoring both the over-arching new managerial vision elaborated by Sir Roy Griffiths, as well as the essential complementary linkages between the various specific activities.

The highly generalised policy outline in *Agenda for Action* and the White Paper also tended to reinforce this response. As a result, management thinking was dominated by structural issues, particularly a growing recognition of the need to begin to move away from departments mainly organised along generic and functional lines, towards a specialist structure, split essentially between adult and children's services. While a number of departments had already moved to reorganise in this way (see Challis and Ferlie, 1986, 1987, 1988, for example), the issue was still being hotly debated, and represented a continuation of the argument over the Barclay model of community social work (Barclay, 1982). However, the introduction of the 1983 Mental Health Act, with a requirement for specialist approved mental health social workers, had given important impetus to the move to specialisation. A second factor dominating early implementation debates remained the focus on the future level and role of in-house residential care, and its relationship with the rapidly growing independent sector provision.

Local authority attention was also increasingly engaged in the development of new financial systems for the transfer from rates to the community charge or poll tax throughout this early period, as well as with decentralisation resulting from the local management of schools initiative, so there was little spare capacity available to assist social services departments with community care developments.

POLICY AND PRACTICE GUIDANCE (1990/91)

The next significant event was the publication on 20 November 1990 of *Policy Guidance on Community Care Implementation* (Department of Health, 1990b), which set out:

> what is expected of health and local authorities to meet the Government's proposals on community care. It provides the framework within which the delivery of community care should be planned, developed, commissioned and implemented locally. It leaves maximum scope for innovation and flexibility at local level, while being sufficient to enable ministers to monitor and review progress towards national policy objectives (para. 1.4).

The guidance was specifically addressed to both health and social services authorities, and particularly emphasised the need for partnership and collaboration in implementation. Six main areas of activity were covered in some detail (para. 1.5), to form the basis for the development programmes being undertaken within individual local authorities, and these were largely based around the original SSI topic groups:

- community care plans
- assessment and care management
- purchasing and contracting
- complaints procedures
- inspection units
- mental illness specific grant.

It was becoming increasingly clear that the Department of Health was taking the implementation process very seriously. The Caring for People programme now had its own logo and headed stationery; a regular flow of newsletters (*Caring for People*) began; and a series of major national conferences on key implementation topics was organised. In the meantime, local authorities proceeded with the establishment of their arm's length inspection units and complaints procedures, and these appear to have been in place, at least in embryonic form, in all local authorities by April 1991 as required by the implementation timetable.

The policy guidance was reinforced throughout 1991 by a series of practice guidance publications, which set out clearly specified advice on *how* local authorities might best implement their new community care responsibilities locally. The main early items in this series were:

- inspecting for quality (Department of Health, 1991g);
- the right to complain (Department of Health, 1991e);
- purchaser/commissioner and provider roles (Department of Health, 1991a);
- purchase of service (Department of Health, 1991f);
- care management and assessment — practitioners guide (Department of Health, 1991c); and
- care management and assessment — managers' guide (Department of Health, 1991d).

This practice guidance was largely produced by the Social Services Inspectorate on the basis of the special project groups, using teams of representatives of key agencies, co-ordinated by the SSI. It was during this period that the real complexity of community care implementation began to be more clearly seen within both health and local authorities, and major anxieties about the organisational complexities and the financial implications started to arise. Probably the most important of these early documents was that on *Purchaser/ Commissioner and Provider Roles* (Department of Health, 1991a), prepared by Price Waterhouse, which emphasised the crucial importance of creating clear organisational separation between purchasing and providing activities within social services, and outlined a number of potential models. The debate over the need or logic for such separation was to rage within local authorities for the next two years and more (Wistow et al., 1994).

INTRODUCTION OF MONITORING (SEPTEMBER 1991)

As part of the implementation programme, the Department of Health commissioned a number of research projects to look at specific areas of preparation for community care (for example, Wistow et al., 1994). The Audit Commission also undertook regular reviews of progress, either directly or in individual authorities, through the District Audit Service, and drew attention both to anxieties about the speed of progress, particularly on collaboration between health and social services, in *The Cascade of Change* (Audit Commission, 1992a), and to the complexity of the implementation process itself in *The Community Revolution* (Audit Commission, 1992b).

The Department of Health, already anxious about progress, now introduced what were to become regular reviews of progress on implementation through national monitoring exercises undertaken jointly by regional health authorities (RHAs) and regional SSI inspectors. The first such exercise was undertaken in September 1991, and was followed by further reviews in March and September 1992, and January 1993. These early exercises were very crude, and the September 1991 and February 1992 exercises were simply meetings of respective health and social services senior managers within individual local authority areas, attended by the locality SSI liaison inspector and RHA representative. The SSI clearly had some checklist of questions, but these were not circulated to authorities. Later monitoring became more sophisticated, with a national checklist requiring papers and responses to be prepared by authorities in advance. This joint work was the beginning of the really active involvement of health authorities in community care implementation, which until then had been seen largely as a local authority responsibility, with the NHS concentrating on its own major reorganisation.

FOSTER/LAMING LETTER (MARCH 1992)

Information in SSI reports from the early monitoring rounds began to trigger alarm bells at the Department of Health, especially the apparent lack of engagement of health authorities, so that implementation responsibility, which had been largely the responsibility of the Department of Health Community Services Division and the SSI, was extended to include the NHS Management Executive. As a result, the Department of Health issued the first in a series of joint letters from the new Chief Social Services Inspector (Herbert Laming) and the Deputy Chief Executive of the NHS Management Executive (originally Andrew Foster and subsequently Alan Langlands). The first of these Foster, Andrew/Laming letters (EL(92)13) was issued to health and local authorities on 11 March 1992 and, while acknowledging that the monitoring reviews in September 1991 had shown that the statutory authorities were making largely satisfactory progress, emphasised the need for health authorities to engage more energetically in developing community care through closer collaboration with local authorities.

More significantly, the letter (Department of Health, 1992a) set out clearly eight key tasks that jointly needed to be achieved by April 1993. These can be summarised as:

- agreeing the basis for required assessment systems for individuals;
- clarifying and agreeing arrangements for continuing care for new clients in residential and nursing homes, including arrangements for respite care;
- ensuring the robustness and mutual acceptability of discharge arrangements;
- clarifying the roles of GPs and primary health care teams;
- ensuring that adequate purchasing and charging arrangements were in place in respect of individuals who would be receiving residential or nursing home care;
- ensuring that financial and other management systems could meet the new demands after 1 April 1993;
- ensuring that staff were suitably trained, whenever appropriate on a joint basis; and
- informing the public of the arrangements made by the authority for assessment and the provision of care.

Given the central importance of this document in outlining the main agenda for action, and the way in which it focused attention in both health and local authorities on the key activities needing to be achieved, it is interesting to speculate on its genesis, and the central importance of Andrew Foster (previously director of social services in two local authorities, as well as a former regional general manager, so providing an important bridge between the two cultures of health and social services). Given the other important activities being undertaken by the NHS during this period, it is hardly surprising that community care tended to remain somewhat peripheral to the main NHS agenda, but there can be no doubt that Andrew Foster was able to raise the profile of community care significantly in the NHS at a critical time in its development, by ensuring that community care issues became part of general performance management and corporate contract arrangements in the NHS, rather than as some optional extra activity.

The positive effect of the Foster/Laming letter was that it focused immediate joint attention on the eight key tasks which formed the essential underlying infrastructure for community care in individual localities. However, this very specific focus also had the inevitable consequence of drawing attention away from other important issues, particularly the development of a longer-term strategic vision of the way departments would need to develop over the medium term, as well as from other crucial requirements such as the development of care management and decentralised financial arrangements. Therefore, although the letter put assessment at the top of the list, care management almost dropped from the development agenda during 1992, although it had been the central pivot on which *Agenda for Action* had been based. Also, it did not encourage a sufficient participation of health personnel in the collation of material for assessment, or their participation in the assessment itself. In the event, the eight key tasks were seized upon with enthusiasm by both health and social services authorities as providing a clear action agenda for joint working. They also formed the basis for the more detailed joint RHA/SSI national monitoring exercise undertaken in September 1992. This was also the broad conclusion of a joint monitoring study (Department of Health, 1994a).

In the meantime, during the spring of 1992 as required by the phased implementation timetable, all local authorities (with only one recorded exception) published their first community care plans. Inevitably, these were very varied, but represented a significant attempt not only to produce plans in collaboration with other key health and local agencies, but also to involve users, carers and the public more generally in the process of planning and developing services. Because of the wide variety in the plans, it proved difficult to undertake any systematic analysis, although the Department of Health did commission the Nuffield Institute to undertake a review of a representative sample of 25 community care plans. This review (Wistow et al., 1992a) emphasised that the existing guidance did not set out a standard format for community care plans and that, in addition to preparing and publishing a plan, there were only three specific requirements placed on local authorities by the guidance:

- that they consult widely over its preparation;
- that they involve joint working as far as possible; and
- that it be as accessible as possible.

The review concluded that the great majority of plans could be considered joint documents, and appeared to have acted as an added stimulus to joint working. On the other hand, consultation arrangements appeared to be much more varied, and tended to relate to consultation on prepared drafts, rather than involvement in their preparation. Finally, accessibility appeared very varied, with some plans being much more readable than others. Only a minority of authorities had produced summary plans, or plans in different languages or other formats. Overall, the report concluded that these first plans were much more position statements on which future activities could be based than formal plans in their own right (Wistow et al., 1992a). The development of community care planning, on the basis of the Nuffield review, was the subject of a number of joint Department of Health/SSI seminars and workshops during the autumn of 1992, in an effort to improve the process.

THE COMMUNITY CARE SUPPORT FORCE (SEPTEMBER 1992)

The second Foster/Laming letter (Department of Health, 1992b) issued on 25 September 1992 (EL(92)65) also had a section on community care planning, and outlined specific additional topics and information to be included in the 1993/94 plans. This second letter also confirmed the eight key tasks for attention during the remainder of 1992/93, while emphasising the need for progress in the longer term on issues such as care management. More importantly, this letter contained a requirement that all health and local authorities reached agreement by 31 December on:

- agreed strategies governing health and local authority responsibilities for placing people in nursing homes and the likely numbers to be involved during 1993/94; and
- how hospital discharge arrangements would be integrated with new local authority assessment arrangements.

The letter indicated that such arrangements also needed to take account of the cross-boundary flows of patients between authorities, and should be included in 1993/94 NHS contracts. The letter also reinforced earlier requirements to ensure that no resources were withdrawn from community services by either health or local authorities without mutual consent, and stressed the need for FHSAs and GPs to be actively involved in community care planning.

Finally, the 25 September 1992 letter formally announced the establishment of the Community Care Support Force, under the joint leadership of Andrew Foster (Deputy Chief Executive of the NHS Management Executive) and Terry Butler (Director of Social Services for Hampshire County Council). The Support Force was intended to offer practical support to local and health authorities in implementing *Caring for People* through:

- wide dissemination of good practice relating to key implementation tasks and development of practical guidance;
- support in resolving across-the-board implementation issues;
- reporting back to Ministers on implementation issues; and
- work, by invitation, with individual local and health authorities and other organisations which might be experiencing difficulty with particular aspects of implantation.

The Support Force was established in early September 1992 as a multi-disciplinary team with members drawn on a secondment basis from a wide variety of backgrounds in health and social care, all with a wide range of practical experience, supported by a small group of Department of Health officials.

Despite some initial anxiety as to its role by many directors of social services and the SSI, the Support Force began work immediately, and throughout the winter and spring of 1992/93 organised a wide range of conferences and seminars, issued a regular newsletter (*Communiqué*), and produced a stream of well-received publications. Perhaps more importantly, small groups of Support Force members also became involved in working with those local authorities identified as having difficulties with implementation by the joint SSI/RHA monitoring in September 1992.

One further innovation in September 1992 was the issuing of a joint circular by the Department of Health and Department of Environment (LAC(92)12) on housing and community care, which set out guidance to housing authorities on their role in implementing and developing community care. This was the first formal attempt to extend responsibility for community care within local authorities more widely than social services departments (Department of the Environment, 1992).

SPECIAL TRANSITIONAL GRANT (AUTUMN 1992)

Meanwhile, on 2 October 1992 at the annual Social Services Conference held that year on the Isle of Wight, Health Secretary Virginia Bottomley outlined the global resources to be transferred from the Department of Social Security to local authorities under the new special transitional grant (STG) arrangements (Department of Health, 1992c):

	Cumulative amount	Annual increase
1993/94	£ 399 million	£ 399 million
1994/95	£1050 million	£ 651 million
1995/96	£1568 million	£ 518 million

In addition, in 1993/94 a further £140 million was also to be made available to assist with development of the necessary community care infrastructure.

Despite claims from the local authority associations that this was still inadequate to support known requirements, the ADSS broadly welcomed the announcement, and appeared genuinely surprised by the relative generosity of the settlement. More anxiety was expressed about the distribution mechanisms, which had been the subject of fierce discussion between the Department of Health, ADSS and local authority associations during late 1991 and early 1992 in the so-called 'Algebra Group'. In 1993/94, 50 per cent of the STG was to be distributed on the basis of the local authority standard spending assessment (SSA) and the remainder on the level of residential and nursing home placements in individual localities. This had the immediate effect of reducing STG resources in areas with low levels of independent care, such as central London, while being overgenerous in the initial year to some county authorities. The use of this hybrid distribution formula would lead to significant problems for these latter authorities when the formula reverted to an SSA-only basis in subsequent years. A further surprise was a requirement that 85 per cent of the grant must be spent on independent sector care, although not necessarily residential care. Later guidance clarified that this latter could also include community services provided by NHS Trusts.

For the first time, however, individual social services authorities now had a clearer picture of the likely amounts of additional resources they would be receiving, even though final figures for individual authorities would not be available until the annual autumn financial statement later in 1992. As a result, local authorities were at last in a position to begin planning in earnest for the new arrangements.

Two final conditions for STG emerged at the same time. One was the requirement for individual health and local authorities to sign joint agreements by 31 December 1992, as set out in the September Foster/Laming letter. The second was a statutory instrument to ensure that individuals requiring residential or nursing care received adequate choice of placement (Department of Health, 1992e).

While it was clear from the September 1992 monitoring exercise that a good deal of work was already in hand, there is no doubt that the announcement of the overall settlement level, and the requirement to conclude 31 December Agreements, focused attention on the need to make rapid progress on the key elements of community care, and a good deal of concentrated effort went into these activities throughout the autumn of 1992, largely supported by a stream of very effective material emerging from the Support Force. As a result, all local authorities produced 31 December Agreements, and the January 1993 joint RHA/SSI monitoring demonstrated that significant progress had been made in many areas, although information systems, staff training and general publicity about the proposed local changes were still in need of attention (Department of Health, 1993).

One further area of concern emerged quietly just before Christmas 1992, with the issue of new guidance from the Department of Health (1992d) on needs assessment. This caused increasing anxiety in some quarters as to the legal responsibility of local authorities to respond to explicitly identified needs. The guidance drew attention to the important distinction between the statutory requirement to undertake assessment and any decision about services to be provided in response to that assessment, which must be made on the basis of available resources. This is still a contentious topic in many local authorities, and the balance between needs, resources and choice remains a delicate issue.

POST-APRIL 1993 IMPLEMENTATION

The broad conclusions of the January 1993 joint monitoring were reinforced by a third Langlands/Laming letter (EL(93)18) of 15 March 1993 (Department of Health, 1993), which outlined the continuing joint health and social services development programme required beyond April 1993, and identified a number of issues needing specific attention: in particular, ensuring that the arrangements being put in place for assessment and securing care and for the management of budgets worked effectively. In addition, authorities were expected to make progress during 1993/94 on six further tasks (EL(93)18):

- *Care management and assessment*: the development of assessment and care management systems, including progress on management and information systems.
- *Users and carers involvement*: increasing the involvement of service users and carers in the planning and delivery of community care services.
- *Shifting the balance of care*: beginning to shift the balance of resources towards non-residential care, and the provision of more respite care and support for carers.
- *Purchasing and commissioning*: further development of joint planning and commissioning between health (including GP fundholders) and social services, building on the progress already made in preparing for implementation.
- *Provider development*: the further development of a positive relationship between purchasers and providers which enabled the potential of all providers to be exploited fully and which challenged them to increase the service options available.
- *Housing*: improving collaboration with housing authorities and agencies.

In late March and early April 1993, the Community Care Support Force produced a final series of documents. It was wound up at the end of April 1993, and was subsequently replaced by a new Community Care Unit within the NHS Management Executive. In the meantime, quietly and seemingly imperceptibly, in April 1993 community care slipped into place and became a reality.

This chapter has outlined the way in which the implementation of community care has been systematically stage-managed by central government — and particularly by the Department of Health Community Services Division, the SSI and the NHS Management Executive — through a variety of mechanisms. With hindsight it is possible to impose some order on the various activities, but at the time many of the broad themes and developments were much less clear than it has been possible to indicate in this brief description.

The March 1992 Foster/Laming letter, and the agreements required to be concluded by health and local authorities by 31 December 1992 in order for social services authorities to qualify for the first allocation of the special transitional grant, were probably the two most significant events which ensured the creation of the minimum foundations for community care in all local authorities by April 1993.

It is not clear how far this implementation process was based on some explicit strategy, and how much it was simply the result of an ad hoc response to emerging circumstances and events. Circumstantial evidence suggests much more of the latter, and this may provide an important clue to ensuring more effective top-down policy implementation. If so, what seems clear is that the centre requires clear and regular information about progress in individual local agencies, and in this case that requirement was achieved with great effectiveness through the regular SSI/RHA monitoring exercises and by the involvement of the Community Care Support Force. What remains less clear is how these imperatives have impacted on individual local authority implementation activities at a local level.

In order to explore this aspect further, Part Two looks in some detail at a small sample of local authorities, and explores some of the emerging implementation themes at this level.

PART TWO
THE LOCAL RESPONSE:
INTRODUCTION TO THE STUDY

Introduction

The Monitoring of Social Care of Elderly People (MSCEP) Project was undertaken by the PSSRU on behalf of the Department of Health, and followed the process of implementation of the changes required by the 1990 NHS and Community Care Act in four contrasting local authorities in England, specifically in relation to services and activities for elderly people. Inevitably, however, the general principles underlying community care implementation in individual local authorities relate to the full range of adult services, and indeed to the more general operation of local government as a whole, and not just to those for elderly people,

The four local authorities were chosen to represent a variety of political/structural and rural/urban characteristics at the time of the initial fieldwork, as shown below:

- *Authority A*: an Outer London borough with a stable Conservative council;
- *Authority B*: a northern metropolitan authority with a stable Labour council;
- *Authority C*: a northern metropolitan authority with a hung council; and
- *Authority D*: a shire county with a hung council.

The MSCEP team has long-standing links with all four local authorities, who also participated in the mid-1980s Domiciliary Care Project data collection (Davies et al., 1990), which followed 589 new recipients of community-based services over a 30-month period in order to establish the main production of welfare framework of who gets how much of what resources and services, at what cost to whom, and with what effects, as well as why the answers to these questions differ between different localities and have changed through time. This major study is being replicated in 1994-1996.

The immediate objective of this small present study was to assess the impact of the community care changes, and to monitor the progress of those changes in four of the original study local authorities during the early period of the new community care policy implementation up to mid-1992, both to act as a comparative study of progress, but more importantly to provide a deeper understanding of the developing circumstances in each local authority for use during the 1994-1996 replication project.

Monitoring of the four authorities was achieved through regular discussions with key contacts in each authority, together with the systematic collection and review of a wide range of documentary evidence being produced in each locality. A week was spent in each authority in the period between April and July 1991, in which twenty people from the Director downwards were interviewed in each of the four authorities, together with one or two people in each of the associated district health authorities (DHA) and family health services authorities (FHSA). Formal monitoring in all four authorities was continued at least until the summer of 1992 when the project formally ended, but more informal monitoring of relevant documentation (such as community care plans) continued until early 1993.

Part Two of this short monograph looks in greater detail at the emerging key areas of community care implementation, both in a wide sense, and then more specifically at particular activities being undertaken in each of the four local authority areas. The specific issues covered in Part Two are organised around the following themes:

- planning for community care implementation;
- developing the mixed economy infrastructure;
- regulation and quality assurance;
- assessment and care management;
- development of home care services; and
- residential care strategies.

Inevitably, these themes are not mutually exclusive and have a tendency to overlap, but they do provide a useful framework within which to discuss developments in individual authorities.

Finally, we round off Part Two with a more detailed case study of the implementation process in a fifth local authority, also part of the original Domiciliary Care Study, based on a range of material collected up until April 1993.

5 Planning for Community Care Implementation

This chapter reviews the planning undertaken by local authorities for becoming lead agencies for community care in April 1993. Since 1979, policy change by central government has largely been pursued through fiscal means rather than by formal planning mechanisms (Webb and Wistow, 1982, 1986), but the community care legislation reintroduced a formal requirement for social services departments to plan services locally, although in a significantly different way to the more traditional guideline-based planning of the 1970s.

This new form of planning is consistent with new forms of management. It is oriented towards researching, managing and monitoring markets, and is less bureaucratic and centralised than previous planning. Authorities must now build up population profiles identifying demand, need and supply; collaborate closely with the NHS; and produce community care plans showing how they intend to implement the various aspects of community care. It is important that by giving local authorities the crucial role of planning to meet need, and of rationing demand by need assessment, the *Caring for People* White Paper stops short of committing social services to reliance only on unregulated markets for the allocation of resources.

Also, the ideas underlying the new planning concepts reflect the assumed decentralisation of decision-making for allocations. The DH has consistently encouraged authorities to associate the development of care management with the devolution of budgets which would finance the consumption of services to a level at or near the care management team, while arguing that this could not be done without appropriate information and control systems. Figure 7 of the White Paper had shown all the SSD financing of services being directed thus. The combination of budget devolution with the argument that care management teams should provide information about shortages and gaps in provision suggested the use of planning models at the level of the care management team or close to it.

In addition, the White Paper was much clearer about the expectations that users who could afford to do so should pay for services: a principle implicit in the post-war settlement, but only being worked through as the pressures on local social services budgets mounted during the 1980s (Davies et al., 1990). Though need was expected to override demand, it could not be imagined that either the decision to consume or the quantity a consumer would demand would be completely unresponsive to prices in all circumstances. Indeed, evidence suggested the opposite (Davies et al., 1990; Evandrou et al., 1990). Again, the assumptions were radically different from those of the 1970s, when local planning was last in vogue in the social services, and the era during which some of the methodologies of needs-based planning were developed.

Since the mid-1970s, successive governments have introduced mechanisms to exert financial control over local government expenditure, and the combined effects of these measures have created problems for the expansion of community care in many authorities, particularly those in which total expenditure is being cut through the impact of the standard spending assessment and charge-capping. The financial context of the four authorities participating in this study was an important issue determining their approach to implementation.

Authority A started its planning process by identifying an additional £3.2 million to be used by social services before the end of 1994 for the implementation of community care, but the other three authorities all had to make large cuts in 1991/2 to avoid charge-capping. In all four authorities there was anxiety over the adequacy of the special transitional grant, especially in the longer term. This general climate of financial uncertainty created a poor context for change, but one in which authorities nevertheless had to struggle to make progress.

INFORMATION FOR PLANNING, PURCHASING AND PROVISION

Information on demand, need and existing supply are basic requirements for a planned service, regardless of the development of any form of mixed economy, since such information will identify the gap between existing provision, including that in the health and independent sectors, and the volume, mix and distribution of services required to meet identified community and user needs.

Hoggett (1990) suggests that the more complex organisational environment being introduced in public sector organisations — involving the decentralisation of production and the centralisation of command — was made possible in the private sector by computerised management and financial information systems. He notes that fragmentation and disintegration may result from a devolved structure in the absence of effective information systems to hold the organisation together. In future, social services managers will need to know how much it costs to deliver a package of services from various providers to a client; total costs for all clients; and whether they are within budget (Streatfield, 1992). Providers will equally need to know just what commissioning authorities are likely to purchase. Writing on the NHS, Fitchett comments that:

> As purchasers and providers are linked through the common duty to make services available to patients as well as through the NHS information network, collaboration is likely to produce much better results for the public, both in health care and value for money, than a unilateral approach. Furthermore, purchasers will need to collaborate to avoid the risk of purchasing fragmentation (Fitchett, 1991).

Whittingham (1992) outlines the wide range of information needing to be exchanged across organisation boundaries, and suggests that information management, especially across agency boundaries, is as important as the technical aspects of information collection. A strategic information system is required, giving as complete a picture as possible of the environment in which the authority is operating, including crucial information links with external agencies.

But social services start from a very low information base. Local authority information system development throughout the 1980s and early 1990s was dominated by the need to develop large mainframe systems to collect the community charge and later council tax, as well as the implementation of local management of schools. As a result there was little or no spare capacity for social services system development. An ICL survey in 1991 found that only 28 per cent had fully computerised client indexes. Streatfield (1992) identifies four particular issues that need to be addressed in implementing information strategies:

- creating information awareness among staff and managers is important since they are the people who must collect and use the information;
- the purchaser/provider relationship places complex demands on information systems, as noted above;
- problems will arise over the ownership and control of information, compounded by the reluctance of many treasurers' departments to devolve budgetary control; and
- the costs of IT implementation are likely to run well ahead of existing capital allocations.

The Audit Commission criticised poor financial management systems in Managing the Cascade of Change (1992a), and the Department of Health promptly announced a £93,000 increase in individual local authority capital expenditure approval for developing new technology. A further issue is whether information strategies should be top-down or bottom-up. Most such strategies currently appear to be led by resource management issues and as a result tend to be top-down. However, a more bottom-up approach may be necessary to ensure better-quality data collection. Clearly, both are needed, but effectively integrating systems that are developed separately in the short term will be difficult, and possibly may be more expensive in the long run. It is likely that while local authorities can adopt a number of strategies in the short term to provide information on demand, need and supply, such information can only be generated effectively, and regularly updated, by local systems, linking into assessment and care management procedures.

Such systems were still at an early stage of development in all four study authorities at the time of the study. Problems included the difficulty of getting all the players to work together to agree what information was needed, by whom and for what purpose, and to devise workable systems for collecting and aggregating such information. The key players — including computing, information, finance, planning and field people — tended to be working separately, and the different terminologies, priorities and attitudes of each group presented barriers to effective communication and decision-making. Independent sector agencies and health authorities also need to be involved.

Some of the major structural decisions (such as how assessment and case management will work, and who will hold budgets) still had to be made in all four authorities before systems could be designed. The lack of any suitable computer packages was also presenting problems. Authorities were looking for systems to use, but in the main felt that none of the existing commercial packages or systems developed in other authorities would suffice, nor would any one system provide for all their needs. Authorities were therefore inclined to develop their own systems.

At the time of the study, all four authorities still lacked the information and computing systems required to map demand and need. However, the requirement to produce community care plans in April 1992 led to more systematic assembly of data than in the past, with authorities pulling together existing information, however crude. There was also encouraging evidence of authorities working more closely with health agencies to secure epidemiological data which might then suggest a strategy for improvement over time. The development of management and financial information systems were being given priority in 1992/3, in line with Department of Health guidelines.

The mapping of supply, on the other hand, was generally receiving a lower priority. Authorities had good information on their own resources, but lacked comprehensive data on activity levels and the nature of clients. Local authorities also had insufficient information on the existence and activities of independent providers outside the residential care sector. A number of examples of activity to map demand, need and supply deserve a mention.

Authority D, with a mix of rural and urban areas, had brought in consultants in 1990 to conduct a study to give them an overall picture of the distribution of demand, need (using socio-economic characteristics) and supply, broken down by area. However, the authority was having difficulty adapting this for more detailed use, to answer such questions as 'What would happen if we closed residential home X in area Y?'

Authority C was piloting an anti-poverty strategy in two social services areas. Home care staff had been trained and been given resources in order to give advice on benefits, and to monitor take-up, which it was hoped would generate information on need as well as demand for home care. Authority B was conducting an audit of independent sector services. This was absorbing a large amount of time and was still underway in May 1992, but it was not clear how the database would be updated in future. Finally, the health authority in locality C had developed a market research strategy, identifying typical control groups (such as women of child-bearing age) to survey on particular issues, and had also conducted a survey of GPs' views on local health services, which had generated an agenda for discussions with providers.

COLLABORATION WITH HEALTH AUTHORITIES

More effective joint working, particularly between health and social care agencies, has been a central feature of policy since the early 1970s (DHSS, 1985, for example), and is an explicit requirement in the *Caring for People* White Paper and subsequent policy guidance (Department of Health, 1990b), but there have always been difficulties in achieving such collaboration. In *Making a Reality of Community Care*, the Audit Commission (1986) noted that a major obstacle was organisational fragmentation and confusion. *Caring for People* sought to achieve better collaboration by improved clarification of roles (relying on the distinction between health and social care), a simplification of collaborative machinery through the production of planning agreements, and shifting the emphasis of collaboration away from process towards the achievement of desired outcomes.

Wistow and Henwood (1991) expressed concern that, although the White Paper claims to offer a better framework for joint working 'based on strengthened incentives and clearer responsibilities', it was unclear whether this could be achieved. They suggested that the difficulty of distinguishing between health and social care might create incentives for service differentiation and boundary defence, rather than collaboration. The different priorities of the two agencies might also provide potentially fertile ground for conflict.

The MSCEP study identified a number of opportunities and barriers to improved collaboration, brought about by implementation of the community care legislation. The first was the potential for planning primary health care through FHSAs. This was at an early stage of development at the time of the study, but FHSAs can apply incentives for GPs to do certain types of work. They can tap into GP knowledge of local communities and they can represent GPs in setting up projects jointly with health and local authorities. However, the role of FHSAs in joint planning is often restricted by their small size. Three of the FHSAs in the study reported that they had too few staff available to make an effective contribution in joint planning, especially since in the early stages of implementation during 1990/91, local authorities were tending to set up large numbers of working groups dealing with issues such as assessment and case management, information systems, and client group planning.

Second, confronting joint problems can encourage joint solutions. For instance, in Authority D, recognition that health and social services were both experiencing budgetary restriction led to monthly meetings of the directors of the health and local authorities and FHSA who agreed not to reduce levels of provision during 1991/2 until better information on demand, need and supply was available. To do this, joint financial reviews and a joint review of acute and community hospitals, nursing and residential homes were both established.

Because of its location at the interface of health and social care, the service for elderly mentally ill people was a particular area of concern, in which there was increasing evidence of joint agreements. In Authority C, an agreement had been reached between the social services, psychogeriatricians, community psychiatric nurses and GPs regarding who was responsible for people with differing degrees of dementia. In Authority D, a 'joint policy and action schedule' had been drawn up for elderly people with disturbed behaviour, clarifying respective boundaries of responsibilities, and with an agreed policy and referral pattern. The authority was also planning to use this schedule as a model for agreements in other service areas.

Unlike the local authorities, health authorities had already implemented a purchaser/provider separation as part of the 1991 NHS reforms, and this was causing some problems in joint planning groups. On the whole, both health purchasers and providers were still growing into their new roles, and there were early signs of conflict as to who should be involved in planning and at what level. In Authority A, NHS providers sat on joint planning teams, while purchasers sat on the joint strategy group to which they reported. In the other three authorities, purchasers and providers sat together on working groups, and these were sometimes the only places where they did come together collectively. This uncertainty about roles caused difficulties for local authorities, who had no such split as yet, as well as for health authorities who wanted to know whether they were talking to a social care purchaser or provider. Social services were watching these developments in the NHS purchaser and provider functions carefully, with a view to how their own split might best emerge, if at all. Health authority D, which emphasised partnership between purchasers and providers, had found it vital for providers to be very closely involved in planning, through identifying problems and gaps, and suggesting creative ways of overcoming them.

Two health authorities, C and D, noted the imbalance of decision-making power between their own officers, who could make fast decisions, and social services staff, who constantly had to refer back to their members and who were constrained by political decisions which might suddenly change the planning parameters. For instance, in Authorities B and C, plans to transfer residential care to independent trusts had suddenly been abandoned. All four local authorities reported that NHS staff were taken up with implementing their own changes, as well as engaged in managing crises, so they had little time or inclination for collaborating in community care planning.

There were some early examples of joint purchasing service was established in April 1992 following the closure of an old geriatric hospital. Authority D expected the community care plan to become more of a service-commissioning document in future, and thought that joint commissioning was likely to be developed. There were also some examples of experimentation at the local level. For instance, Authority C was piloting the placing of social services case managers with budgets in GP practices, to bring the purchase of social and health care closer together at local level, and to facilitate referral.

There were also some hopeful signs of joint provision, including a number of examples of the adaptation of Part III residential homes into resource centres providing a wide variety of services for elderly people, in which health personnel could also be based (although such initiatives existed before Griffiths and the White Paper were published). Specialist EMI resource centres were also being discussed in Authorities C and D, while Authority A was considering developing a joint home care and district nursing service. There was also evidence that independent providers were beginning to be involved in planning and development, and it is worth noting that they may hold the key to bridging the boundary between social and health provision, since they are not so constrained by artificial boundaries.

There seems to have been some confusion about the order in which decisions needed to be made to ensure the implementation of community care. This was partly to do with the change in the timing of implementation, and partly because neither central government nor the local authorities initially realised the degree of interdependence of certain key decisions. Consequently, all four authorities in the study began their planning exercise by setting up separate working groups along the lines of the SSI development agenda (Utting, 1990), such as assessment and case management, purchasing and contracting. These working groups got as far as they could on paper, but it soon became clear that decisions about how case management would work had be linked to arrangements for devolving budgets and the design of client-based information systems. As a result, all four authorities moved to a more experimental approach, piloting new arrangements on a small scale,

adding new elements as more was understood about how the new arrangements would work, and adapting them to local circumstances, in preparation
for 1 April 1993.

CONCLUSION

The planning task for local authorities in introducing the community care
changes and ensuring a supply of appropriate and effective services to meet
the demands of users and their care managers was complicated by a number
of factors, not least the financial uncertainty which faced all four study authorities at the beginning of the process. Establishing management and financial
information systems is a huge and complex task which has generally received
too little attention but is vital to the success of the whole venture. In particular,
a joint information strategy is required to cement together the different parts
of the organisation both geographically and functionally: the centre with the
decentralised units, the purchasing and providing functions both at a macro
and micro-level, and the different agencies involved in purchasing and provision. The slow development of such strategy and systems is a major problem,
but if implementation continues without sound information there is a danger
of organisational fragmentation which will have serious consequences for
service users as well as for organisational efficiency.

While there is clear evidence of much more contact between senior health
and social services managers, achieving effective collaboration continues to
be difficult. The problem of distinguishing between health and social care
may promote conflict rather than collaboration, and it is unclear whether the
current balance of opportunities and barriers represents an improvement on
the past. There were some interesting examples of collaboration in planning
and provision at both authority and local level at the time of the study, and
some evidence of joint purchasing emerging.

Faced with such uncertainty, local authorities were wise in moving to an
experimental approach to implementation. Discontinuous change and un-
predictability make planning difficult. Risk-taking, choice, and learning by
mistakes are all catch-phrases of 'new managerialism' (Handy, 1985), but are
not easy to achieve within a public service environment. So, while implementation of the new policy was happening slowly, it was nevertheless occurring,
and providing opportunities for all involved to learn about how the new
policy might work in practice. However, authorities must not lose sight of
the fact that these new systems are only a means to an end: the provision of
a choice of good quality services to enable people to continue living at home,
and to enable them to lead independent, fulfilling lives.

6 Assessment and Care Management

At the time of our visits to the four project authorities during the spring and summer of 1991, Department of Health policy guidance on community care had been issued, but the more detailed practice guidance had not yet appeared. It was very early days, so this chapter is no more than a first glance at a time when events were moving rapidly and authorities faced the problem of which activity to prioritise. It has little detailed analysis of systems or processes as few had yet reached that stage.

The Department of Health guidance (SSI, 1991c) identifies the core tasks of care management as:

- publishing information;
- determining the level of assessment;
- assessing need;
- care planning;
- care plan implementation; and
- monitoring and review.

The post-assessment stage can be viewed as a set of complementary tasks comprising care planning, care implementation, monitoring and review to be undertaken by the assessor or by some other individual. The four authorities were understandably more concerned with basic assessment issues and the various general models of care management they might adopt than with developing the post-assessment stage activities in more detail, so this chapter focuses on the first three of these core tasks before going on to discuss care management arrangements more generally.

PUBLISHING INFORMATION

Access to services will be improved if users and carers have good information. The dilemma for local authorities is what kind of information to provide, and how to ensure that it gets to, and is assimilated by, the appropriate people. Information can help empower individuals and their care networks, making them better able to come forward for referral and to express their own perceived needs. People need information if they are to take control and responsibility for themselves, attend to their own well-being and make choices about their lives (Steele, 1991).

Previous attempts by social service departments to provide information have not been noticeably successful, and have tended to be service-specific (SSI, 1991e). The challenge for both assessors and service providers is to think in a non-service-specific manner. Unless this happens, there is potential for users' demands to clash with more traditional professional working patterns. The key question is therefore what kind of information is needed. Studies have shown that older people make the most effective use of information when it is given directly to them (Silverstein, 1984) and verbally (Tester and Meredith, 1987; Allen et al., 1992).

A linked issue is how to ensure that information gets to the appropriate people. The GP surgery is often the first and only point of call for many older people, and GPs now have a ready-made framework for accessing older people and ensuring that they are aware of their facilities. Local authorities have no such obvious route to older people in their community unless they can link in with GP assessments of the population aged 75 and over. Sensory impairment may render more traditional methods of information inappropriate, and this may also be the case for ethnic minority communities. The need for advocacy for people suffering from dementia represents one of the most challenging areas for care agencies.

In the four authorities there was a thin spread of posters and leaflets, all advertising specific services. Authority A had a comprehensive booklet listing all voluntary organisations in the area, and Authority D had a draft of a policy and procedures manual which included details on eligibility, the assessment process and so on. Several authorities had leaflets on, and often put together by, carers' organisations or about specialised services. Distribution of information in all four authorities often relied on carers or potential service users already being in contact with social services, or at least being mobile and having opportunities to visit places where leaflets were available. Information was invariably in written form only.

Authority C had translated information into several ethnic minority languages, while Authority D had an innovative carers' scheme which was a good meeting point for local carers and so for the distribution of further information to those who had found their way to the scheme. Authorities B and D were committed to consulting with the public, although apart from the existence of user forums in Authority B, it was not clear how this would progress after the completion of consultations around the drawing up of community care plans. Authorities A and D were more concerned with dealing in a more efficient manner with the cases for which they were already providing services than improving case finding, and there was a general feeling that the authorities would not be able to cope with the increased demand better information might provoke.

Social services departments need to develop a presence in the community that will aid case finding. This will involve reaching out to unearth unmet needs, and responding more positively to enquiries. Accessibility can be helped by physically moving contact points to more appropriate places, and making them more user-friendly. Physical and environmental factors play a significant role in improving access to services and reducing stigma. Reception staff are often responsible for making major decisions about whether a particular referral sounds like it should be directed to one service or another, or indeed whether it should be turned away. With little training or formal recognition of this function, the receptionist in a local office acts as a powerful gatekeeper to information and access.

How questions are asked and with what level of privacy and confidentiality also affect a person's likelihood of coming forward for help. One obvious outreach activity is to collaborate with contact points used by other agencies, such as GP surgeries, health centres and Age Concern premises. This will require close collaboration with colleagues and formal acknowledgement of common goals.

Several of the authorities had plans to refurbish local offices and saw improving the image as important to attracting people. Authority C in particular identified the need to relocate local offices to buildings more conveniently placed for the public. All authorities recognised the key role of the receptionist or switchboard operator, and three authorities had plans to review the role of receptionist. Authorities A and C also aimed to extend the role of reception staff to include initial basic assessment with each new referral. Authority B was less clear about developments concerning reception staff, but had been recently told by a users' forum that having to answer the same, often very personal, questions over and over again to different people was both unnecessarily invasive and often distressing.

Improving case finding for older people poses several challenges for social services departments, not least to existing cultures and assumptive worlds. Work with older people has been neither high-priority nor particularly popular in the past, but demographic trends will require more commitment in the future. Social services staff need to be encouraged to see the advantages of proactive case finding and not to view a well-informed public as a threat to their autonomy. This means training, re-education and a review of many existing assumptions. Fear of ever-increasing demand is a poor response to evidence of low horizontal target efficiency.

DETERMINING THE LEVEL OF ASSESSMENT

Good information and clear referral systems are the two complementary faces of case finding. Referral systems must provide clear pathways and decision points on who will be assessed and at what level of assessment. Practitioners require unambiguous guidelines of both screening and eligibility criteria for assessment. The way services are organised has an impact on referral patterns, particularly whether services are organised under specific client groups or whether an authority employs specialist workers within generic teams. The type and form of duty and referral systems are also important. Although there is no definitive research comparing the relative advantages of the variety of potential organisational forms, Black et al. (1983) concluded that the organisation of social work can both implicitly and explicitly endorse some kinds of activities and not others.

Even before the publication of the guidance, all four authorities had defined the need for either a revised referral form or a standardised assessment form. Authority A piloted a single referral route during the spring of 1991, and had asked reception staff to take more details about each referral regardless of the referral source. There was then a daily meeting to discuss the appropriate route for new referrals in the light of the increased amount of information gathered. This process revealed considerable idiosyncrasies. For example, professionals such as GPs were often unwilling either to spend time giving out details or were reluctant to give these details to the receptionist, preferring instead to be put straight through to the home care manager or social worker.

Where they were obviously short-term (which could mean up to a year or more), elderly referrals in Authority C went to the only elderly specialist social worker, who was part of a short-term intake team. Long-term elderly referrals went to social work assistants in the long-term team. There seemed little internal logic to this system, and there was little liaison at the referral stage with community nursing colleagues. Home care, on the other hand, was newly organised on a patch basis, which brought home care staff much closer to surgeries and the district nurses. Referrals to home care occurred in a variety of ways, which could involve considerable repetitious form-filling if a referral had already gone via social work. As a result, a multidisciplinary group was set up to produce an 'access to service form', which was seen as separate from the assessment form. They aimed to produce both a request for access to services (referral) form, and a new standardised assessment form.

A restructuring plan in Authority C proposed changes along client group lines, to create a split between a care management team (who would be social workers) and a resource management team (concerned with home care). The home care service had recently become patch-based, and was proving to be more expensive as it required the development of senior home care assistants as an extra tier.

In Authority B, referrals passed through the duty team to a social work team meeting (where they might or might not receive an assessment from a social worker, depending on resources and apparent urgency), before being passed on to home care. Referrals could also go direct to the home care manager, and the home care organiser would still make an assessment regardless of whether a social work assessment had recently been undertaken. Only one local office had a specialist elderly team, and even in this office duty was generic, with non-specialist social workers regularly taking elderly referrals.

Authority D was organised both geographically and on a client basis, with five geographical divisions. Elderly services were separate from disability services. This was a new structure in which the elderly services team manager managed the heads of homes, the home care service, social workers and occupational therapists. A multidisciplinary assessment working group set up at the end of 1990 had produced a core referral/early assessment document to which all agencies could add their own assessments, designed in such a way as to trigger other professionals to the need for them to carry out a further specialist assessment.

Once a potential client has been identified, authorities need systems for determining the level of assessment required. Authorities must give priority to those whose needs are greatest and they cannot offer a full or complex assessment to every referral (nor would this usually be appropriate). The guidance (Department of Health, 1991c) suggests a system to trigger different levels or types of assessment, and outlines six possibilities (as set out in Box 6), and the use of a standardised referral form.

BOX 6. TYPES AND LEVEL OF ASSESSMENT

The guidance distinguished six levels:
- simple
- limited
- multiple
- specialist simple or specialist complex
- complex
- comprehensive

Source: Department of Health (1991c).

This will ensure a minimal requirement for referral information from the variety of agencies that refer to social services. Systems must be able to cope with the simplest request (such as for a disabled parking badge) as well as the most complex assessment involving multidisciplinary co-ordination and communication. Early draft guidance (Department of Health, 1990a) referred to 'graduated systems' to initiate the appropriate response in terms of type and level of assessment and personnel, and the subsequent practice guidance (Department of Health, 1991c) broke these down into a set of interrelated functions (Box 7).

BOX 7. MAIN ELEMENTS OF ASSESSMENT

The practice guidance identified seven functions:
- receive enquiries;
- give and gather information;
- encourage the full participation of the appropriate people;
- develop triggers for identifying other significant needs;
- designate responsibility for the allocation of the assessment response;
- set criteria for decision-making; and
- identify levels of assessment and agree priorities for allocation.

Source: Department of Health (1991c).

The practice guidance advises authorities to set criteria for decision-making and agree priorities for allocation (Department of Health, 1991c). In the past, criteria have tended to refer to individual services and a person's apparent eligibility for them, not to the eligibility of an individual's needs to be met by social services. At this stage there was little evidence of effective criteria being established in the four authorities, and where they did exist it was under the heading of individual services such as home care, day care or social work. In other words, needs were not yet being looked at as a whole, only a person's eligibility for an existing service. Similarly, there was little evidence of formal targeting, except for those shifts that had been occurring in the home care service since the mid-1980s.

All four authorities had some form of prioritising criteria for home care managers, although the information was for internal use only, and represented a formal attempt to target home care services. Authority D had relatively new home care eligibility criteria in a draft policy and procedures document. The criteria were threefold. They included a 'client dependency rating', a calculation of 'support already available' and one indicating 'risk factors of no intervention'. The dependency rating had been introduced in an attempt to re-target home care away from clients receiving two hours of help a week or less and on to 'medium' and 'high' dependency cases.

In Authority C there was clear evidence in one area of home care being targeted. Recent statistics showed only 3.5 per cent of the weekly home care budget was spent on cleaning, whereas 35.7 per cent of the weekly budget was being spent on clients who received six or more hours of home *help* a week. This authority also had a policy statement on personal care which included a guide for home care workers on issues such as the division of duties between the district nursing services and home care. Authority A had a vast home *help* service as well as a highly-targeted and small (that is, 30 cases in total) home *care* service, and was looking at ways to enable individual workers to operate more efficiently doing several people's shopping rather than many workers doing many people's shopping. A useful indicator of change was the home help job description which still made little reference to personal care and emphasised domestic tasks.

Other targeting mechanisms in evidence across all four authorities were assessment panels controlling demand for residential care. Three authorities also had multidisciplinary panels to review applications for residential, day and respite care, and generally required social workers presenting a client to the panel to have exhausted every other option first.

More informal targeting occurs as practitioners and their managers interpret policy and face the realities of providing a finite resource to an insatiable demand. Indeed, the SSI practice guidance recognises that staff with responsibility for assessments have to be trained to use their discretion in targeting assessments on relevant areas of need (Department of Health, 1991c). Informal targeting or street-level discretion, as it is increasingly being labelled, is so entrenched in the public sector that it can almost be viewed as formal practice (Lipsky, 1980). This suggests that the success or otherwise of targeting strategies is determined more by the enthusiasm and energy of individual staff than by explicit policy and detailed documentation. The rigours and realities at field level are key, and neither new procedures nor urgent directives from managers will change entrenched working patterns.

Only Authority D had seriously started working on a new training schedule, which included a board-game where practitioners were allocated finite budgets and required to devise packages of care with their community nursing colleagues. Perhaps one of the most striking issues identified here is the need to address thoroughly the factors that affect practitioners daily, such as what they do with clients who no longer fit the criteria and how they manage during a stressful time. None of this can occur unless a certain threshold of concordance is reached, for many staff work in these agencies primarily because they believe in what they are doing. Taking part in action research and having access to research findings and literature as well as seminars and training is another starting point.

For 'determining the level of assessment', one must read the broader 'targeting care management inputs'. That it was called the former reflects the excessive weighting on assessment, and the failure to work through the perception of care management as an essentially long-term model, with a continuing cycle from assessment to other tasks and back to subsequent re-assessments.

By 1991, there were a number of British studies on which managers could have drawn. Between them, they provided a great deal of discussion about the targeting of care management, and the fitting of care management arrangements to the varying needs of users in different circumstances, the priorities of the authorities, and the characteristics of the local systems of health and social care. Argument had been extensively supported with reviews of practice and outcomes in British experiments and programmes in other countries. The logic of a managerial approach to designing the matching of care management arrangements to user circumstances had been presented. Indeed, it had been published in summary in at least one of the professional weeklies. However, there was little sign in the authorities visited that the managers were familiar with the concepts and argument, far less that they were applying them.

Indeed, there was evidence that in the authorities which were best endowed with managerial and field-professional talent, there was a great deal of re-invention of wheels taking place. That is, the task forces (of which one of the authorities had so many on the community care reform that it established a task force to ascertain the nature and number of its task forces) did not start from the state of knowledge as described in the literature, and then build and adapt for the local situation. They started from the skeletal frameworks provided by the central government documents; necessarily less full in their discussion, more exhortatory and directive in style.

Two features emerged clearly. One has later been commented on by the Social Services Inspectorate, and need therefore not be further discussed: a focus on paper, rules and procedures, not on practice content and skills (SSI, 1993).

The other remains neglected, and has not been discussed by the SSI. We did not encounter any authorities which started from the principle that some needed much care management like they needed "an 'ole in the 'ead" — the expression used by a senior manager of care management in one of the pioneering American programmes and quoted in the British literature; that the provision of an unnecessary level of care management was likely to be efficiency-reducing, as was argued in later studies; that it was as important to match users to care management arrangements on such factors as the skill mix and resources controlled by care management teams as on the level of intensity of that care management. Instead, what seemed to be evident was a tendency to standardise the input (providing too much to many; too little to others), to be unimaginative in the organisational locus of teams in the pathways through care (argued to affect target efficiencies) and organisational locus in the sense of the auspices and agency or area setting of the team (found in Australia to affect the acceptability of flexibility and innovation). One way of describing what was observed was managerial responsiveness mainly to local contingencies and expectations. Another description would be 'aparadigmatic innovation'; because it was aparadigmatic, important possibilities for the long-run improvements in outcomes were ignored.

It is therefore unsurprising that the targeting of care management was to emerge by 1994 as a major concern of the SSI. However, it would be complacent to suggest that by late 1995, there were sufficiently great improvements in managers' intellectual basis for targeting care management inputs that progress in it would be fast (Davies et al., 1997).

ASSESSING NEED

Proper assessment of need to identify how best to help each individual is central to the community care reforms. Such assessments need to focus positively on what each individual can and cannot do, and might be expected to achieve, taking account of his or her personal and social relationships. Conventional assessment tools tend to be descriptive rather than analytical, making assumptions about the nature of dependency, and being schematic rather than multidimensional, with many interrelated aspects. Isaacs and Neville (1976) devised three categories of needs which were adopted by Davies et al. (1990) as: 'critical interval needs' specifically relating to self-care (for example, toileting); 'short interval needs' which include food preparation; and 'long interval needs' which tended to occur less often than daily (shopping and laundry, for example).

Williams (1986) identified three 'social performance levels' (with the specific purpose of improving the assessments that GPs carried out of their older patients) which he illustrated as interacting like three concentric circles. The three levels were 'ability to relate to the outside world'; 'ability to undertake domestic tasks'; and 'ability to undertake personal tasks', the latter two being measurable using activities of daily living scales. In practice, however, less concentration has usually been given to identifying such dimensions or levels. The practice guidance (Department of Health, 1991c) recommends that a comprehensive assessment should include a range of details, as outlined in Box 8.

Authorities will also have to decide how they are to delineate and interpret need. In other words, what kind of measurement instrument helps the case management role and will it be a single all-purpose instrument? There are two basic methods for collecting assessment information. Broadly, these are qualitative and quantitative mechanisms. Qualitative methods encourage and facilitate less formal discussion with a client and can produce a colourful and very individual picture of a person's life. They often rely on interpretation of the information being divulged in a less formal setting, with form-filling taking place separately after the interview. Such assessments can be criticised for lacking objectivity. However, this is the standard method by which social workers and home care managers glean information (Hudson, 1991) and may often be the only sensitive and appropriate method.

BOX 8. INFORMATION REQUIREMENTS FOR ASSESSMENT

The practice guidance identified information necessary in order to carry out an assessment:
- biographical details
- self-perceived needs
- self-care
- physical health
- mental health
- use of medicines
- abilities, attitudes and lifestyle
- race and culture
- personal history
- needs of carers
- social network and support
- care services
- housing
- finance
- transport and risk.

Source: Department of Health (1991c).

On the other hand, quantitative assessment techniques such as functional scales have advantages in that, if used appropriately, they can help ensure equity, standardised measurement and aid in evaluation, although the individuality of need can more easily be lost. To encourage the gathering of valid and useful assessment information, the practice guidance recommends adopting standardising procedures for the case management process (Department of Health, 1991c). Standardising data collected during the initial assessment stage should also ensure better compatibility between agencies. This would both facilitate joint computer systems and avoid a user having to answer the same basic details to a potentially large number of people.

Quantitative and qualitative approaches both contain useful elements. The real issue is how to combine the two perspectives (Allen-Mears and Lane 1990; Hudson, 1991). They are not inherently incompatible, but producing a form which is both user- and computer-friendly may raise questions of compatibility. A principal officer summed it up by saying, 'We need to bridge the gap between the stream of consciousness common to social work assessments and the rigid structure of (functional) scales.' Many assessment scales record information at a particular time and do not allow for 'best' or 'usual' performance and are frequently criticised for being crude. Occupational therapists and physiotherapists regularly use their own specialist scales, which inevitably give only a part of the picture. There are dangers in reducing an assessment (even if it is only an initial assessment) to a row of ticked boxes or a column of figures which still require translation into needs to be met. Indeed, the particular needs of older people living with dementia, or suffering from severe sensory loss, may make functional scales particularly inappropriate (Thompson, 1987; Askam and Thompson, 1990).

Risk categorisation is increasingly being incorporated into assessment forms as a useful assessment of individual needs. Risk is frequently used by social services departments to justify intervention or service input (Davies et al., 1990; Lutz et al., 1991). It is also used where a practitioner feels obliged to offer something rather than nothing, or where it can be used to justify services to make a person appear safe, even if it is not clear what is 'unsafe' about their situation. Meals-on-wheels and day care are often offered on this basis, and often have high subsequent drop-out rates (Bebbington and Charnley, 1985). Risk categorisation can too easily lead to standardised service responses. Davies et al. showed the degree to which the field personnel's assessment of risk simply reflected other needs-related circumstances which can be directly embodied in targeting guidelines (1990, chap. 3). The field personnel's thinking about risk seems not to be accompanied by estimates of the probability of the feared outcomes; and when these are pressed for, they often emerge as low even for non-catastrophic events, though used to justify allocations (Davies et al., 1997).

Unlike insurance companies, social services departments do not have an 'equivalent technology of risk measurement and management' (Alaszewski and Manthorpe, 1991), and such categories are often ill-defined, such as: 'elderly confused, elderly dementia, elderly at risk' (Lutz et al., 1991). Far from being useful determinants of need, it has been argued that risk assessments for older people can be both patronising and even a denial of civil liberties (Norman, 1981; Wynne-Harley, 1991). Much will need to be done to operationalise risk categories as a form of eligibility criteria, and before they can be used sensitively and uniformly practitioners will require enhanced supervision, clearer lines of accountability and better training. Vagueness at field level has been seen to lead to thin, unimaginative and often inappropriate allocation of standardised services (Audit Commission, 1986). Consequently, the use of risk categories requires careful consideration (Salter, 1992).

In practice, authorities were responding to the challenges of producing new instrumentation in a variety of ways. Authority B had produced a new assessment form which had been brought into practice over a year ago as a replacement for a wide variety of different existing forms. There was no evidence of formal training relating to its implementation, and introduction had not been monitored or evaluated. As a result, there seemed to be some disenchantment with it, particularly its appropriateness to both home care and social work in an authority where these two services had no integration, and old forms were still in use in some areas. Despite these difficulties, this was an important attempt to introduce client and carer perspectives into the assessment process, and had it been piloted as a draft many of these problems could have been overcome. Whether or not introducing a new form alone can shift the paradigm from service to needs led assessments remains to be seen.

Authority D also hoped initially to devise a standardised front page that all client groups and all sectors would adopt, but dropped the idea of a basic assessment/referral form with bolt-on assessment forms for different specialist assessments for all client groups after it became obvious that this was too contentious. The initial form was to be sophisticated enough to trigger the need for particular specialist assessments. Again, a task group had been set up to develop a comprehensive assessment instrument and, in common with working groups in other authorities, several small but significant problems were encountered early on, particularly failure to agree on common terminology. Different professional groups also appeared unwilling to relinquish their own assessment procedures, despite their enthusiasm in principle for procedures to facilitate the smooth transfer of users from one sector to another.

It is a common misperception that a single comprehensive needs assessment by a care management agency such as social services will make it unnecessary for each service provider to make its own assessment (Kane and Kane, 1981; Steinberg and Carter, 1983). An example was offered by a home care development officer who, faced with the prospect of home care moving over to the provider side, believed that they would still have to assess for health and safety matters, at the very least. It is also unlikely that a fully comprehensive assessment can be obtained on a single visit. The assessment process probably involves several related activities to detect variables including 'understanding, listening, observing and relating, and tuning-in with ears, eyes, nose and heart, not to mention good timing' (Neill, 1989).

CARE MANAGEMENT ARRANGEMENTS

All authorities were at a very early stage in deciding systems of care management, seeing this as a longer-term development than the initial establishment of more effective screening and assessment systems. There are many models available, including those with a split between the assessor and provider, or models where differently qualified personnel carry out different levels of assessment. The general assumption is that social workers will normally become the care managers, but there is no obvious reason why this need always be the case. Authorities will need to consider whether social workers have the appropriate skills in the light of the new community care requirements (Hunter and Judge, 1988). Although social workers may appear to be the obvious choice, no particular professional background has so far been seen as a prerequisite, and other professions may also feel they have appropriate skills: for example nursing, occupational therapy and home care management (Fisher, 1991; Wintersgill, 1991).

Authorities were at very early stages in deciding who would carry out which task, and whether and how to introduce a split between purchasers and providers. Splitting purchasing and providing was of low priority for several authorities unconvinced by the role of markets in the provision of social care. They were happy with the concept of separating out assessment from resource management, although some had flirted with models that also appear to split all tasks of care management from provision.

In Authority C, it was envisaged that the care management team would primarily consist of social workers, with the care manager as team manager. Home care would be primarily on the resource management side, although it was recognised that this ignored some of the skills the home care service had developed over the years. In the process of restructuring, the authority had come up with plans to introduce a split between care management and resource management at area level. The care manager was, on paper, at team leader or area officer status. They would be separate but of equal status to resource managers. Both would be line managed by the same area elderly services manager. The care manager would have a care management team (from social work backgrounds) carrying out assessments, care planning and care plan implementation. The home care services, together with the residential and day care services, would form the resource management team. Limited assessments within the care management system would go to social work aides. Comprehensive and multidisciplinary assessments would go to social workers.

The authority had also specified the circumstances in which a qualified social worker would be essential for older people, despite the fact that social work with older people was currently unpopular, with only one (elderly) specialist worker in the whole authority and less than 13 per cent of all social work time spent on older people.

Authority D did not feel able to predict who would be care manager or assessor. They had recently restructured into geographical divisions, abandoning the division between residential, field and domiciliary care, and introduced a team manager responsible for the full range of services to a client group within a geographical area. If necessary these teams could split into purchasers and providers, rather like Authority C. However, as in Authority C, both purchasers and providers would have the same line manager at area level. This authority had a strong tradition of qualified social work, although they had not been organised on a specialist model. This meant in reality older people were far more likely to be referred to home care. It was felt that the home care service could now introduce its own assessment/resource management split as the newly implemented post of assistant home care organisers could take over the personnel side, and the home care organisers could carry out assessments.

Authority B had still to decide whom the care managers would be, but it was thought likely to be a social worker or a district nurse. This authority had planned to introduce care management alongside more traditional services, with a view to comparing and evaluating the benefits of the two before being stopped in its tracks by large expenditure cuts. They also had a strong social work tradition, although with only one specialist elderly care team. There was some anxiety about social workers having the time to assess all referrals, especially in the light of child care commitments. In more complex assessments, home care staff would be required to do a follow-up assessment for anyone assessed by a care manager as needing home care. Basic details at least were needed, such as health and safety, and financial assessments.

In all four authorities there was anxiety about the ability of social workers to carry out complex assessments for older people, and the potential loss of the home care role as a relative expert in ascertaining (if not assessing) the practical needs of elderly people (regardless of the usual criticisms of this service). One option suggested in several authorities was that home care could split in half, with managers with the Certificate of Social Services qualification becoming assessors, and those without remaining on the provider side.

Authority A piloted their care management plans between Christmas and Easter 1992, building on an earlier pilot of the referral and assessment procedures in one area office where, rather than referrals being processed to separate services, they were all to involve a standardised amount of problem-orientated (rather than solution-orientated) information. This was then discussed by the team at a daily meeting before being allocated to various sectors for assessment. The care management system built onto this, so that more complex cases needing creative care packages would pass to a care management team. A proportion of existing service budgets was being transferred to care managers who could either buy back internal services or purchase care from the independent sector. Care management teams were being established in each of three local offices and managed by a new principal officer for assessment and care management. They would be purchasers only. Care managers would be recruited from community social work and community care scheme posts. A purchaser/provider split was to be created by separating care management from the two existing principal officers posts, with one principal officer now managing social work and home care, and the other all rehabilitation services, including occupational therapy, social workers for the visually and hearing impaired and day care.

An assumption in all four authorities was that the role of home care would continue to some extent alongside care-managed services. No one had seriously addressed the issue of the role of home care, or the practical problems of interweaving two apparently separate services. The Kent Community Care Scheme has shown that good relations with 'hands-on' staff are important, and one of its most effective features was the relationship the case manager was able to establish with both home helps and community care workers (Challis and Davies, 1986). This allowed for good matching of carer to client, direct feedback about client progress to the care manager, and for the development of initiatives among innovative and experienced home help staff.

CONCLUSION

Although at an early stage of development, all four authorities were clear about the crucial importance of more effective needs-focused assessment systems for the implementation of community care, and all were addressing seriously the development of such systems. Care management was increasingly being seen as the mechanism by which this might be achieved, but again was only at an early stage of development. Authorities were perhaps inevitably still confronting issues of organisation and structure, but there seemed a somewhat surprising lack of recognition of the equal importance of training and development for front-line staff in changing attitudes to the way in which services are perceived and delivered in the future. This aspect will need to be addressed with some urgency.

Already social workers were being seen as the main focus for care management activities, but while they may possess many of the necessary skills, in many authorities they start from a low threshold in working with elderly people. On the other hand, more and more home care managers have now completed Certificate of Social Services or other in-service management courses, and frequently have the most knowledge and experience of working with older people and their families and of their intimate personal care needs.

As a result, home care may be both better placed and more willing to work with district nursing and other primary health care agencies, especially where home care is patch-based (Payne, 1979). That, after all, is where the service first started. Sinclair et al. (1988) found home care referrals were more likely to come from members of the primary health care team than through social workers or occupational therapists.

There are no easy answers as to how best to move from a service-based to a needs-led multidisciplinary, multi-agency service, and little guidance or illumination is available from previous research. Nonetheless, it is increasingly clear that these issues and questions lay at the heart of effective community care implementation, and the manner in which they are being addressed in these early stages is likely to be an indicator of the degree to which services become more user responsive in the future.

Finally, care management — particularly the budget-devolved care management which is advocated by the SSI — requires gap-filling and other improvement in skills, aids (like information systems and support systems) and the development of checks and balances in the framework in which care managers work. Perhaps most obviously, it requires the more systematic application of the knowledge and analytic frameworks assembled in the international literature. Care management is one of the new elements of the community care reforms. There must be the prerequisites for effective learning from within each programme, and learning from the outside world.

7 Developing the Mixed Economy of Care: Enabling, Purchasing and Contracting

Having established a picture of demand, need and supply (and any discrepancy between them), and come to agreements with health agencies about who is going to do what, local authorities must arrange for the provision of services, and are called upon to consider what they might usefully purchase from independent providers to generate a mixed economy of supply. This requires the development of purchasing and contracting functions at the macro level in which local authorities make arrangements with providers for blocks of provision, and also at the micro level where case managers make arrangements for services to be provided to individual clients. Purchasing at these two levels must be linked. This chapter is primarily concerned with macro purchasing and contracting arrangements.

Two structural changes are of particular importance in fostering a mixed economy: first, the devolution of management and budgets to bring purchasing and provision decisions closer to individuals and communities and so yield more responsive services which allow choice through local purchasing decisions; and second, the distinction between purchasers and providers in order to foster accountability, and create more opportunities for voluntary and private providers to supply services on behalf of local authorities.

DEVOLVED MANAGEMENT AND BUDGETS

Flynn and Common (1990) argue that the degree of choice and flexibility in provision is related to the extent to which purchasing responsibilities are decentralised, since only decentralised budgets and negotiations with a range of providers will produce genuine flexibility and responsiveness. The four sample authorities were all at various stages of thinking about what to devolve, but budgets and finance, property management, personnel, contract and grant giving, as well as administration, were all mentioned as possibilities.

In 1991/2 devolved budgets were at an early stage of development, in terms of who would hold budgets, what form budgets should take (money, hours, personnel), and what associated systems would be needed, such as financial information systems (for example, costing, pricing and invoicing). There tended to be an emphasis on retaining central control over purchasing, with Authorities B and C saying they would allocate budgets to case managers in the form of hours of in-house care, or numbers of staff, with perhaps a small cash element to purchase from elsewhere as the need arose. This suggested that the social care market would have a monolithic purchaser (the local authority), rather than many purchasers (case managers) at local level, which would restrict the flexibility of local purchasing decisions on behalf of clients, and of responsiveness to local community needs.

In general it had become clear to authorities that devolved budgets had to be linked to the development of information systems covering both service and financial information, and that these could not be developed in the absence of decisions about case management. In April 1992 Authority B began piloting the devolvement of EMI budgets, from the Mental Illness Specific Grant, to two area directors. These budgets were to be used for services over and above the standard allocation. Authority D was planning to devolve budgets to team manager level, with guidance for further devolution below that level.

The devolution of management responsibilities and control raises fundamental questions about the future role of the centre. All senior managers foresaw a contraction of the centre arising from the need to devolve management and finance, leading to flatter organisational structures. However, assistant directors tended to feel uncertain whether they could trust people in the localities to discharge their new duties effectively. There was also uncertainty about how to manage a devolved structure, especially as management information systems were so underdeveloped. In all four authorities, structural change was being implemented which would make the incorporation of care management and a purchaser/provider separation possible. In Authorities A and B, at the time of the study, structural change and contraction of the centre were being speeded up by the transfer of residential homes to trusts, although the transfer scheme in Authority B has since been abandoned.

THE SEPARATION OF PURCHASING AND PROVISION

In mid-1992 authorities had still to make decisions on the purchaser/provider relationship, and it was not seen as a high priority to do so in any authority, the emphasis being on letting a split evolve if and when it became necessary.

The need for a separation was becoming clearer in one authority because the transfer of residential and some community care services to a trust was creating divided loyalties for managers who had both purchaser responsibilities (through managing social work) and provider responsibilities (through managing the provision of home care).

Health authority D found it easier to develop constructive relationships between parties with separate roles and identities (although often common aims). Where the division is unclear, disparate elements of the organisation may be forced to pretend to share aims. Their experience was that contract managers worked closely with small provider units, both in constructing the contract and in deciding on what indicators of quality and performance should be chosen. The providers were very creative in generating ideas, and this was also found to be true by an inspection and quality assurance manager in local authority B, when working with residential home staff to identify and improve on quality.

During 1992 authorities appear to have given up trying to make decisions about the purchaser/provider split on paper, and were relying more on thinking about this in the context of changes that were actually happening: for instance, the transfer of residential homes to trusts of various types, and care management pilot projects. This suggests an incremental, learning process, through experimentation, evaluation, extension and replication, which seems more likely to achieve success in the context of emergent knowledge, and financial and political uncertainty, than large-scale change. Indeed, the March 1992 Foster and Laming letter (Department of Health, 1992a) announced that 'the progress of SSDs towards becoming enabling authorities will be an evolutionary one'. As with devolved management and budgets, the purchaser/provider split might be facilitated by information systems that were as yet underdeveloped.

DEVELOPMENT OF A MIXED ECONOMY OF SUPPLY

In the 1989 *Caring for People* White Paper and subsequent guidance, developing a mixed economy was intended to increase the variety of services available, and therefore the choice for users. It was suggested that pluralism would give rise to greater flexibility and innovation, while competition would promote increased value for money and efficiency. Local authorities were expected to stimulate the development of independent supply while reducing their own direct role as providers, and to take on a new role as purchaser, enabler, standard setter and regulator.

The concept of a mixed economy incorporating informal and formal care was outlined by Griffiths (1988), although the purchase of care from a variety of voluntary and private sources by local authorities was not new. The Association of Directors of Social Services, while supporting the Griffiths report, emphasised that supply was already more diversified than was often appreciated, and that the enabling role should be seen as an extension of their existing activities rather than a break with the past (Association of Directors of Social Services, 1989).

The expanded use of voluntary and private providers, except in relation to residential care, has been one of the slower developments of community care. There are a number of reasons for this. First, there was, and remains, scepticism about the sufficiency of the voluntary sector, in terms of their numbers, distribution and capacity to take on a larger role (Johnson, 1990; Wistow et al., 1994). It was also unclear that a private sector market would emerge for non-residential services. A survey of all English local authorities concluded that there was no sign of a competitive market developing in domiciliary services, and that the existing contribution of private domiciliary agencies was insignificant (Booth, 1990). Furthermore, the relationship between expansion in variety of providers on the one hand, and the range, flexibility and innovatory capacities of provision on the other, is not a clear one (Wistow, 1989; Pfeffer and Coote, 1991).

There was a strong commitment to in-house services in all four study authorities, arising from a belief in their intrinsic value, a desire to avoid redundancies, and a recognition that independent sector pay and conditions are usually not as good as those offered in the public sector. The view was expressed in several authorities that choice, flexibility and the more efficient use of resources could be achieved without a full-blown competitive mixed economy. Rather than by changing the culture of staff at all levels, placing greater emphasis on the individual client, introducing assessment based on need and the more flexible use of resources by devolved care management, more responsive, individualised local services could be achieved. However, there was also a commitment to providing more choice for users which, coupled with the realisation at senior management level that they were a long way from achieving such an ideal system, was leading to an acceptance that some degree of mixed economy, over and above existing arrangements, was inevitable and possibly desirable.

In general, there was more support for increasing the involvement of independent providers among managers, while front-line staff placed more emphasis on the public service ethos. For instance, in Authority B unions had backed the transfer of transport services to an independent trust but strongly opposed such a move for residential and other forms of care; the national body of one union had appointed a full-time officer to block the initiative.

In all four authorities there was an underlying anti-private sector stance because of the perceived incompatibility of the profit motive with social care. This was reported to be particularly strong among elected members, regardless of their political allegiance, although they were not interviewed as part of the study. Wistow et al. (1994) report similar findings. While the voluntary sector was generally viewed more favourably, there was a common view that, with few exceptions, existing voluntary organisations were too few and too small, and still lacked the managerial and technical ability to play a major role in community care. There was little emphasis on enabling them to develop the required skills and systems, except in relation to achieving registration and inspection standards in residential care.

In general, it was reported that independent sector providers would only be used in the following circumstances:

- where they represented financial advantages, such as was the case in selling residential homes, or transferring them to independent management;
- where they represented better quality;
- in areas complementary to LA activity, such as day care for less dependent elderly people;
- in areas supplementary to LA activity, such as the provision of home care during the evening and at weekends; and
- where the LA was withdrawing from certain types of service or client, such as cleaning for less dependent elderly people.

This suggests that authorities were pursuing a *planned* rather than a *competitive* service, in which any division of tasks between sectors was based mainly on complementarity. The belief that social care is somehow different and should not be subject to competition transcended political boundaries (Wistow et al., 1994). However, senior managers were beginning to think about competition, if only because some degree of competition in residential care would be inevitable after April 1993.

It has been suggested that competition is more important than ownership (public, voluntary or private) in achieving improved efficiency (Millward, 1982; Letwin, 1988; Hartley and Hooper, 1990). However, a competitive mixed economy is expensive, and is difficult to organise and regulate, leading to higher transaction costs which may cancel out or even exceed any efficiency savings (Bartlett, 1991). This may encourage reliance on one or two large providers who, in competing to survive, may cut quality and choice. For example, in the early 1990s when many private residential homes were struggling to survive the combined effects of economic recession, high interest rates and the freeze in income support levels for residents, an ADSS survey revealed that many home owners were seeking to reduce their costs by shedding staff and reducing choice of food, leading to less flexibility and choice for residents unless they or their families paid for 'extras' from their own pockets (Association of Directors of Social Services, 1992).

The views expressed in the four study authorities indicated that thinking on competition was still at a relatively unsophisticated level. However, authorities were clearly 'learning by doing', particularly in the field of residential care. For example, the director of Authority A felt that competition was only relevant where a market with a number of suppliers existed. He believed there would never be an effective market in services for elderly people outside of residential care, and that it was not his job to generate competition. He conceded, however, that the contracting out of residential care for people with learning difficulties over the last few years had generated a market. His authority had recently put the renewal of such a contract to tender and received a number of good bids, whereas the original provider had been selected simply on recommendation. This suggests that for competition to be relevant a number of suppliers must exist in the area, and that contracts can be used to stimulate supply. Taking this point further, a health authority manager in Authority D commented that competition is more relevant in large urban areas where there is some potential for cross-boundary buying and selling, whereas in more rural areas contracts are more about forging partnerships and improving accountability than fostering competition.

Areas that were thought to be suitable for competition, because of their intrinsic nature or because a market already existed, included transport, information technology, research, training and laundry services. However, there was a desire to give plenty of time and effort to improving the performance of in-house services and reducing unit costs or improving quality before there was any question of exposing them to competition from outside the organisation. An alternative approach was to ring-fence a portion of purchasing budgets for use only with in-house services, at least in the early years of exposure to competition. Similarly, internal markets were being established in three of the four authorities, for services such as personnel and finance, which would have to sell their services to other parts of the organisation in order to generate income.

The director of social services in Authority B reported a popular misconception among staff that competition was purely about cost-cutting, whereas it was also, and perhaps more importantly, about improving quality. This could be demonstrated in the field of residential care. Unit costs for in-house services tended to be higher than independent sector costs in both residential and home care, due largely to the better pay and conditions of LA staff. This was identified as a major barrier to the introduction of competition in the short term. However, local authority residential homes would be faced with competition after April 1993, and would either have to reduce costs, or work to compete by quality. Authority B was concerned that private residential homes might increase prices to the LA level after April 1993, unless the latter could prove that the higher costs were justified by better quality. Consequently, it had recently invested time and resources in setting up quality assurance systems in one of its homes to be used as a model to get all homes to the required standard by 1993. This authority believed that quality was as important as cost, and could be improved by a consumer-led approach.

The preceding sections indicate that the four study authorities were adopting a rather passive role in relation to independent providers, simply using what was already there if it met their requirements. They did not yet see themselves as playing any significant part in strengthening the organisations for a greater role in future, nor was there any emphasis on stimulating the development of new organisations. This was perhaps understandable, since all authorities still had so much to do in establishing other community care changes. There were, however, some developments in contracts, which the White Paper considers to be an important means of stimulating supply. Authorities A and D were in the process of turning existing grants into contracts and service agreements, with an emphasis on improved account-ability through specifying the service to be provided more fully, and including indicators of performance or outcome. There was a move away from simply renewing grants on a historical basis. However, Authority C had sought legal advice on contracts, and had decided to stick to grants, since this gave the LA more control. The argument was that contracts placed obligations on the contractor as well as the service provider, whereas the LA was free to with-draw or change the terms of grants at will, although it was emphasised that they would not do so without prior consultation with the grant-holder. Having noted the development of contracts, however, there was little evidence of any increase in the amount of grant aid, and local authorities are largely sticking to existing arrangements. In other words, contracts were being used to improve accountability rather than to stimulate supply. Authorities A and D said they were likely to introduce block contracts with the voluntary sector in future, but this was as yet merely a statement of intent.

In terms of other types of enablement, an Independent Care Forum had been set up in Authority A, attended by a mix of in-house, voluntary and private providers. This grew out of social workers' desire to be able to offer a choice of alternatives for home and day care. The Forum had produced a code of practice, enabling providers to be placed on an approved list. Regular meetings were held, with speakers, and the possibility of access to LA training for independent sector staff was being discussed. There were other examples of this kind of active support in the field of registration and inspection, with authorities often giving private residential homes time to improve their stan-dards, and providing advice on setting up quality assurance systems. This might prove to be an important area of enablement, since the costs of meeting registration and other regulatory requirements may force some smaller homes out of business, leaving the field to large corporate companies.

In the USA, contracts are used both to stimulate supply, to make explicit the outcome of planning in terms of what services are required, and to enhance the credibility of the purchaser with regard to fairness, efficiency and accountability. Other means to stimulate supply include bidders' con-ferences, technical assistance, independent managerial advice funded by the public agency, aid in the creation of new agencies, and capital subsidies to cut set-up costs (Kramer and Grossman, 1987). There was little evidence of such active attempts to stimulate supply in the four authorities at the time of the study.

Baldock and Evers (1991) described how the UK community care reforms have their counterparts in a surprising number of other European countries. However, European experiences of mixed economies in social and health care give some cause for concern. The Netherlands has a mixed economy of both provision and financing (through social insurance), which exhibits many of the features the British Government would like to see in its welfare services (Baldock and Evers, 1991; Baldock, 1993). The Dekker Committee was set up by the Dutch Government in 1986 with a remit to advise on 'strategies for volume and cost containment against the background of an ageing population', but found that it was the very pluralism of the Dutch system which was the source of rigidity and inflexibility, since the diversity of finance and supply meant that there was little substitution between one part of the care system and another. Elderly people found it difficult to change provider, and there were particularly tough barriers to 'substitution down' towards cheaper forms of care. The Dekker report (1987) indicates that there is no necessary relationship between competition and socially desirable outcomes, and seeks to devise a regulatory environment that will make competition improve welfare rather than detract from it.

The German experience, where there is also a mixed economy of supply and finance, is that five big voluntary organisations have come to dominate the provision of personal social services, controlling it in a corporatist manner without expanding choice. However, the problems of rigidity experienced in the Netherlands and Germany derive partly from their diversity of funding as well as provision. Since April 1993, UK local authorities have become the major purchasers of community care, and should be in a position to ensure substitution, and so prevent corporatist restrictive practices from taking root.

CONCLUSION

The genesis of a mixed economy of supply in the four study authorities was occurring slowly. There was general support for the need to offer increased choice to users, but all authorities were still at an early stage of thinking through the implications of moving to a mixed economy. There was also a reluctance to reduce their own direct provision and some fear of losing control over the totality of the service system. However, the transfer of LA residential homes to independent management or ownership was forcing the pace of change in two of the authorities, and was providing opportunities for learning about, for instance, the purchasing role, negotiating and managing contracts, and the potential benefits of competition. Other examples of a more market orientation included turning grants into contracts, the specification of services and the setting of more explicit standards, and the establishment of internal markets.

An ideological shift is required if change is to be implemented effectively. Brunsson (1982) argues that organisations periodically jump from one predominant ideology to another, and radical changes need to be preceded by and initiated by ideological shifts. He contends that periods when ideological shifts are in process, 'when the dominant ideology has not yet been debunked and when any aspiring new ideology still lacks a critical mass of support', are poor contexts for action. There was widespread support for the new community care policy in the four authorities, especially the need to offer choice and flexibility, together with a growing recognition that monolithic public bureaucracies cannot easily provide this, but there was not yet a critical mass of support for an effective move towards a mixed economy of care.

8 Regulation and Quality Assurance

A central feature of community care is the requirement for local authorities to ensure the availability of a range of local services flexible enough to meet diverse needs and circumstances, by the encouragement of innovation and the introduction of market forces. This in turn requires local authority staff to learn new skills in purchasing and contracting, as well as in regulation and quality control. For this purpose, there is much to learn from trade and industry policy, formulated and implemented by governments to intervene in markets to ensure they work efficiently and equitably towards social as well as economic goals.

REGULATION

Regulation is one aspect of trade and industry policy, designed to compensate for lack of (or weak) competitive forces and to ensure a range of good-quality products at low price, thereby protecting consumer interests. Lessons from the regulation of industrial product markets will be highly relevant to local authorities as they begin to purchase more services from independent sources. To understand why intervention is necessary requires an examination of how markets work. A market exists where there is an opportunity to buy and sell goods and services. In essence, a market is a self-regulating, self-correcting system in which supply and demand, and profit and loss, are said to allocate resources more efficiently, and therefore solve the perennial economic problem of scarcity, better than any known alternative. In the real world, markets rarely resemble this ideal. For instance, there are industries in which certain producers, through the control of vital resources, can reduce output and raise prices to secure monopoly profits. Similarly, there are certain public goods such as defence, clean air, or law and order which, if provided, cannot easily be restricted to some beneficiaries, and so cannot be priced by the market, which are seriously undersupplied (if at all) by voluntary exchanges (Barry, 1987).

There are also arguments that state intervention itself can lead to market failure, and that companies can manipulate the systems designed to regulate their activities. But it seems clear that without perfect information and perfect competition, markets will inevitably fail to provide efficiency and social justice without some degree of intervention (Barr, 1987). A recent Dutch Government study of their mixed economy of social care found that pluralism *within* the system was the source of rigidity and inflexibility, and recommended a regulatory environment in which competition will improve welfare rather than detract from it (Dekker, 1987). The issue is therefore *how* can local authorities best achieve effective regulation of the developing social care market.

The purpose of regulation is to ensure a choice of good-quality products at low price, so as to protect consumer interests. 'If the customer is to be protected, competition will have to be fostered where it is feasible and regulation relied on where it is not' (Stelzer, 1989). The important point about regulation is to find a level and type that is affordable and effective, both for the regulator and the provider agency. The danger is that regulation can become so costly and complex that it leads to fewer providers entering or surviving in the market. This in turn drives up prices unnecessarily, and means that providers are unable to afford research and development so innovation is regulated out of existence.

The Department of Health has provided some general guidance on purchasing and contracting (1991f) and on standards for residential care (1990c), but as yet there is little information on what aspects of service are being regulated by local authorities, or of the impact of regulatory measures, although some evidence is now emerging about residential care regarding levels of regulation.

Patel (1991), reviewing future prospects for the long-term care industry in the UK, offers a word of warning on overregulation, predicting that costs will in future be driven by the regulation process rather than commercial and marketing considerations. He also foresees a reduction in the number of new organisations entering the market due to barriers to entry presented by tough regulatory requirements, combined with price and other financial constraints. The market may therefore be left to the big corporate provider organisations, who will pursue mergers and acquisitions to increase their market share. Unless this process is controlled it can lead both to fewer providers and to loss of services due to restrictive practices such as the formation of cartels.

The costs of responding to market requirements and constraints are called *transaction costs*, and include any significant expense involved in arranging and conducting trading, and may play a major role in determining efficiency (Friedman, 1985). Robinson (1991), studying the development of internal markets in the NHS, also drew attention to transaction costs, noting that the early rhetoric for free market competition has had to be watered down to a concept of 'managed competition', as the need for regulation to ensure equitable access to services and good quality through contract specifications and standards has been recognised. He suggests that rising transaction costs as a result of regulation will be a key issue in future, and will lead to purchasers adopting policies of limited competition between fewer providers, with longer-term, more settled relationships with the purchaser. Efficiency in this context could be ensured through yardstick competition (setting yardstick indicators of price for instance, for competitors to work around), and ensuring that markets in health care are contestable; in other words, that new competitors can enter the market through, for example, franchise arrangements.

Lawson (1991) suggests that local authorities as purchasers have to find a way of balancing users needs against their own requirements and those of providers in order to reconcile the need for flexibility and choice on the one hand and continuity, security and economies of scale on the other. This requires the continued contestability of the market once large areas of work are taken up in contracts, such as providing some short-term and small contracts, and ensuring a flexible approach to contracting and payment mechanisms to suit different kinds of provider.

REGULATION IN THE FOUR STUDY AUTHORITIES

Issues relating to transaction costs were already beginning to emerge in all four authorities, for instance the balance of costs borne by providers as opposed to purchasers. In the shire county, which was developing a three-part inspection process involving a certain amount of work by the providers themselves, there was already concern among independent homes at the cost of meeting standards and the amount of administrative work involved in the inspection process. This suggests the need for specifying an affordable set of minimum acceptable registration standards, and to simplify the inspection process. In Authority A, one of its homes lay outside its boundaries, and although it retained responsibility for inspecting it, there was a potential problem in the 'host' local authority having different standards. A similar problem will occur wherever an authority purchases a significant proportion of the beds in any home outside its boundary. There is likely to be increasing difficulty for individual authorities to keep track of the wide variety of placements that can be expected after April 1993 if users are given real choice.

Existing registration standards cover staff ratios, staff qualifications, physical fabric and so on. There is a relationship between quality of care and quality of employment, and Deming (1982) argues that staff should be enabled to work smarter, not harder, suggesting that a major issue affecting care and innovation is the morale of staff and how they are treated. As a result, social services departments may consider including pay and conditions of staff as well as equal opportunities in their standards and specifications. While this may be more costly — and, indeed, at least two of the participating local authorities had uncompetitively high unit costs in residential care because of levels of pay and conditions of service — a balance needs to be established between cost and quality. The costs involved in a residential home being deregistered are high, and are borne not only by the home owner but also by the residents and their relatives who suffer disruption, as well as by social services. There is an incentive, therefore, to avoid deregistration by ensuring effective systems are established to prevent problems from occurring, and to remedy existing shortcomings.

To avoid problems of deregistration and to keep communication channels open over issues such as transaction costs, it is important to involve voluntary and private providers in discussions about the level and type of regulation to be used. Indeed, Juran and Gryna (1980) suggest a law of diminishing returns, with an optimum point of quality beyond which conformance is more costly than the value of additional quality obtained. This is clearly a matter for discussion with local service providers. The Department of Health also recommends provider participation in service specification (1991f). There was some degree of independent provider involvement during planning and implementation in at least three of the study authorities, including membership of working groups on inspection, and attendance at workshops and seminars. Authority D had local forums, pre-dating the new legislation on inspection, where homes proprietors and their staff met local inspectors, as well as an annual meeting of all homes with the director of social services.

Membership of the new Inspection Advisory Committees should also include representatives of registered homes (Department of Health, 1991g), and although developing relationships with individual independent providers may be straightforward, achieving collective agreements and finding individuals to represent the sector may become more difficult when large numbers of homes are involved. The establishment of both local and national associations for care home owners is likely to be helpful in addressing these difficulties.

A similar problem was being encountered in all four authorities in identifying truly independent people to sit on complaints review panels, and in deciding who should chair them. The difficulties included voluntary sector anxieties about being judged by their local peers, doubts also about local authority staff judging voluntary services, as well as the fact that voluntary organisation staff generally lack the time to sit on panels. In addition, there was uncertainty over whether 'independent persons' should be knowledgeable about the specific area of the complaint (for example, child care) or simply be experts on handling complaints. The response included building up a pool of independent people with a variety of skills/areas of knowledge who could be called upon to sit on panels; the inclusion of regional representatives with, for instance, experience of advocacy, a social work background, or involvement with pressure groups. No clear policy had yet emerged as to whether represent-atives attending advisory committees or complaints panels should receive payment, or in some cases even expenses.

There was some evidence of authorities providing training to independent agencies in inspection and complaints. This included how to handle com-plaints; the circulation of published information and guidance to staff; develop-ment of quality statements for independent homes so that they could train their staff and prepare for registration and/or inspection; offering places on local authority mainstream training courses to independent sector residential, day and domiciliary providers; seminars on specific issues, such as the manage-ment of shortfall in benefits; and a local residential care homes association providing training and advice to one of its members.

At least three of the authorities allowed independent residential homes to conduct part of the inspection themselves. In Authority B, which had a strong quality assessment bias, staff of homes were to check their own work, super-visors were to check that requirements were being met, and providers were to conduct periodic reviews of their homes. In Authority D some home owners and heads of council homes wanted a role in inspection, such as talking to residents, and it had been agreed that such people might be seconded to conduct a pilot of new inspection procedures. The same authority was about to pilot a self-evaluation scheme in its own and two independent homes. In Authority C, the local residential care homes association employed its own inspector (who had previously worked for a local authority), and also provided an insurance package against deregistration. Understandably, all four auth-orities had been concentrating their regulatory activities on the registration and inspection of residential homes, and the development of basic standards in contracts and service specifications. This process needs to improve in both range and sophistication as local authorities become increasingly involved in contractual relationships with independent providers after April 1993, and new areas of control, for example in day and domiciliary care, also need to be developed.

QUALITY ASSURANCE

Quality assurance (QA) is one of the central elements of new managerialism, but is often more in evidence in policy statements than in practice. Initial thinking on quality assurance developed in the US soon after the Second World War. Juran and Gryna (1980) in particular developed a statistical quality control methodology which was more influential in Japan as it struggled to rebuild its economy after the war. More recently, it has been picked up in the USA and parts of Europe to the extent that Oakland (1990) now argues that, having had the computer revolution in the 1980s, Western industry is undergoing a quality revolution in the 1990s.

Quality assurance and total quality management (TQM) are ways of achieving and maintaining competitive edge in the manufacturing sector. TQM 'aims to understand and deliver precisely what the customer wants, at the same time meeting any internal cost or return-on-investment goals' (Burke and Moss, 1990). It means producing the right thing at the right time in the right place at the right price. Oakland provides another definition:

> TQM is an approach to improving the effectiveness and flexibility of business as a whole. It is essentially a way of organising and involving the whole organisation: every department, every activity, every single person at every level. For an organisation to be truly effective, each part of it must work properly together, recognising that every person and every activity affects and in turn is affected by others (1990).

The QA buzz words are 'getting it right first time', 'zero defects', and 'total conformance to specifications'.

The value of QA and TQM is that it gives firms competitive edge. The theory is that as quality improves so costs fall through reduction in failure and appraisal costs. Satisfying the customer in terms of quality as well as price will clearly benefit market share. The absence of quality problems also removes the need for the resources devoted to dealing with failure and waste, so increasing output and productivity (Oakland, 1990). QA techniques clearly have important potential for social care, particularly in improving responsiveness to users, and by emphasising that issues of quality cannot be divorced from issues of efficiency, value for money and effectiveness.

The increasing importance of quality in the social policy agenda has arisen primarily from the collision in the US, UK and other industrialised countries between the rising costs of public services (health care in particular), and the desire of purchasers to restrict expenditure by developing measures of cost-effectiveness and quality which indicate value for money (Pollitt, 1987; Opit, 1991). This has meant an encroachment into areas of professional judgement and competence, as managers seek to influence the activities of professionals which carry significant financial consequences (Pollitt, 1987, 1990), and to make them more accountable for the economic consequences of their decisions, particularly in medicine, social work and teaching. More recently, the introduction of market forces into public services has been carried out in the belief that it is a major means of improving quality, efficiency and accountability.

Within personal social services, work on standards, inspection, specification and contracts for residential care is more advanced than in any other area due to past registration and inspection requirements and the significant level of private and voluntary residential provision. Considerable progress in developing standards was achieved through the publication of *Home Life* (Centre for Policy on Ageing, 1984) and *Residential Care: A Positive Choice* (Wagner, 1988), which identify and discuss a range of fundamental principles of residential care, and offer a clear foundation on which to build quality assurance programmes and develop relevant monitoring standards (Gibbs and Corden, 1991).

Homes Are For Living In (SSI, 1989) builds on these two earlier reports, presenting a theoretical model and practical guide for assessing quality in residential care, based on the six basic values of privacy, dignity, independence, choice, rights and fulfilment (Gibbs and Corden, 1991). In 1990 the Department of Health also published *Caring for Quality* — guidance on standards for residential homes for elderly people — which aimed to provide a way of thinking about standards and their management, clarifying the difference between standards for management, standards for care and for a good quality of life. It also offered a compilation of the standards developed by the SSI in recent years.

The Department of Health placed specific emphasis on QA activities as part of the implementation of community care, and published three guidance documents on the issue during 1991:

- *purchase of service*: practice guidance and practice material for social services departments and other agencies (1991f);
- *inspecting for quality*: guidance on practice for inspection units in social services departments and other agencies: principles, issues and recommendations (1991g);
- *the right to complain*: practice guidance on complaints procedures in social services departments (1991e).

Other important government publications concerning quality include *The Citizens Charter* (Cabinet Office, 1991a), and *Competing for Quality* (Cabinet Office, 1991b). The first introduces principles of public service, such as openness, choice and accessibility, while the second places quality in the context of greater competition and fundamental management reform in the public sector.

While the measures introduced by the *Caring for People* White Paper are important, they represent a rather restricted view of QA. In the US a far wider repertoire of measures is used: for example, financial incentives in the form of performance payments to providers (Davies, 1986b). Pfeffer and Coote (1991) identify four approaches to quality which are currently in use in the public sector, all of which have been borrowed from commerce. They are:

- the traditional approach: to convey prestige and positional advantage;
- *the 'scientific' or expert approach*: meeting standards set by experts;
- *the managerial excellence approach*: to measure customer satisfaction (TQM, customer relations, market surveys, and 'getting closer to the customer' are all features of this approach); and
- *the consumerist approach*: to empower the customer, through complaints procedures, redress and customer groups.

Pfeffer and Coote (1991) are dissatisfied with each approach on the grounds that none acknowledges the differences between commerce and welfare. Nevertheless, each approach features in *Caring for People*, with the managerial excellence approach, and particularly TQM, predominating. Oakland describes quality as 'the most important competitive weapon' (1990), arguing that its application is wider than simply assuring product or service quality. Rather, it is a way of managing the whole organisation to ensure complete customer satisfaction at every stage. The SSI apparently supports this view, recommending that inspection, complaints and so on 'are part of a wider management system aimed at ensuring the quality of care provided, and the quality of life of users' (Department of Health, 1991g).

QUALITY ASSURANCE IN THE FOUR STUDY AUTHORITIES

Authorities A and B were adopting a quality assurance approach/model, emphasising the need to build good quality in, rather than inspect bad quality out, and aiming to sell QA and inspection to staff and independent homes as a positive and attractive proposition. Both were using BS5750 as a basis for ideas, although one felt this emphasised the identification of failure and removal of faulty goods rather than preventing faults and noting successes. Both rejected the use of checklists and merely inspecting for conformity, and wanted a continuous, questing search for improvement. Authority A hoped to achieve this through the development of codes of practice which were in place for residential care by summer 1992. Authority B wanted homes to have their own quality assurance systems in place and to get BS5750 accreditation. The role of inspection units was to work with homes to develop specifications, codes of practice and quality assurance systems, as well as to conduct inspections. By summer 1991, Authority B had one of its own homes accredited as achieving BS5750, and this was being used as a model for other homes. By the summer of 1992 this authority had also started to experiment with QA in home care.

Authority D had established a QA programme with a management emphasis on staff taking responsibility for their own work. While the social services approach to inspection was innovative and participatory, it was not part of the QA system of the local authority as a whole. Authority C was adopting a more straightforward approach, concentrating on inspection visits in excess of their statutory obligations. The aim was to ensure that services were meeting clients needs as well as meeting the standard of quality expected by clients.

Department of Health guidance recommends that 'units will only be effective if they are properly resourced' (Department of Health, 1991g, p.6), and although all four inspection units were hoping to expand, activities were focusing mainly on the fulfilment of statutory obligations. Financial limitation had forced at least three (B, C and D) to slow down the pace of development other than in the obligatory areas of registration and inspection of residential homes. Authorities C and D in particular commented that they lacked resources to undertake development work beyond their inspection responsibilities. In Authority A the head of inspection had a 'specific remit to undertake practice reviews and development work', and the head of inspection in Authority B had sufficient staff to undertake the day-to-day work, and so he was able to devote time to developmental pursuits. In these two authorities, therefore, inspection staff did have the potential to contribute to the establishment of a QA ethos. An alternative way of ensuring that resources went as far as possible was that of Authority C, which had seconded staff, who would go back into the field after a couple of years, to spread and share their knowledge and experience. This authority had also adopted a generic complaints system, with a named officer in each establishment or office. They reported monthly to their appropriate assistant directors, who reported twice yearly to the director of social services. The inspection unit could also take on complaints.

Three of the local authorities also planned to begin work outside their statutory obligations by involving other staff, such as specialist principal officers, in work on standards and specifications in home care, for instance. Work on community-based services was less developed. Authority B had completed its residential care work by the end of summer 1991 and was planning to start work in community services, while in Authority D a day care development group was working on standards and specifications. Authority C intended to establish clear eligibility criteria for all services, to be linked to service specifications and quality standards.

Inspection units and complaints are required to be at arm's length from operation and financial parts of the local authority to retain their impartiality, and the guidance recommends that the head of the unit should be a senior manager with responsibility for preparing the annual report and determining the annual programme of the unit. As part of a wider quality assurance system, guidance also emphasises that 'good communications and information flows need to be established between the units and other quality systems within the social services department' (Department of Health, 1991g). This raises questions about the structure and remit of units within the wider local authority responsibilities.

At the time of the review, Authorities C and D were both considering relocating their inspection units away from headquarters to emphasise the 'arm's-length' nature of their work. In all cases the head of the inspection unit was one or two stages removed from the director of social services. With the exception of Authority D, the head of the unit was also the designated complaints officer, reporting indirectly to the social services committee.

Two other structural changes will have an impact on the effectiveness of QA: the separation of purchasing from provision, and the process of decentralisation. Gaster (1991) suggests that 'quality needs decentralisation, but decentralisation does not in itself lead to quality', and recommends that decisions about what should be decentralised should depend on 'which services — or parts of services — would be improved by going local'. The four authorities were at various stages in thinking about devolution, but budgets and finance, property management, personnel, contract- and grant-giving, and administration were all mentioned as possibilities.

It is also important that inspection is linked to purchasing and contracting, to ensure feedback on individual services and that any gaps in services or contracts are identified. Given that the purchasing and contracting functions were as yet relatively undeveloped in each of the authorities, links to inspection and complaints were at the stage of supposition rather than plans. Ideas included the possibility of units taking on a role in inspecting contracts, the unit providing accreditation of providers prior to the letting of contracts to them, and the feeding of standards and QA requirements into contracts.

Links between care managers and inspection and complaints will also be important. The guidance on assessment and care management (Department of Health, 1991c) notes that QA systems are one of an important range of supports to the assessment and care management process, and that care managers should feed back into QA information about deficiencies in type, volume and quality of services provided to their clients. Links reported in the four authorities between inspection and care management again tended to be anticipatory, since final decisions on organisation had yet to be made. However, inspection units suggested they could offer information about homes or provide an accreditation service to give care managers a measure of confidence about homes in which they made placements. In return, they anticipated information being fed back on levels of client satisfaction and any problems in the care provided.

Finally, the development of information systems, and effective management are important requirements for integrating the various functions and geographical units of an organisation, and are vital for an effective quality assurance system. Hudson (1983) points out that the impact of QA policies is dependent on three elements:

- the information system employed to identify deficiencies in care;
- the management system developed to make corrective actions; and
- the system of incentives that influenced the formation of the information and correction system.

These systems were still at a very early stage of development in all authorities, but it will be important to ensure that they remain a high priority as community care implementation progresses. A further indicator of a TQM approach is an emphasis on consumerism, particularly an ability to deliver precisely what the customer wants (Burke and Moss, 1990). Gaster (1991) agrees that the definition of quality in relation to social care must be influenced by consumers and be meaningful to them. However, there are problems in applying consumerism to social care. Hambleton and Hoggett (1990) contend that consumerism requires the option of going elsewhere when dissatisfied with a service. This is not normally the case in social care, either because no options exist, or because an individual lacks the information, physical strength, or mental capacity to exercise choice. Yet the whole purpose of a mixed economy is to ensure such a choice in future, and one of the objectives of care management is that people will be enabled to exercise choice. There will often be a third party — in the form of a GP or care manager — purchasing services on behalf of a user, and their valuations will also have a bearing on perceived quality. Indeed, Donabedian (1982) contends that the valuation of benefits and risks of a procedure or service must be shared by client and practitioner in defining the quality of care.

These arguments make it paramount that user wants and needs can be effectively expressed, so it is encouraging that both getting information to service users and decentralising services are being promoted by the Department of Health in the community care legislation and guidance. Within the four participating authorities there were positive signs in relation to publicising complaints procedures and the various documents covering standards and specifications in residential care which could be made available to residents as well as staff. However, Gaster (1991) and Pollitt (1990) both found that standards, specifications and inspection schema tended to be drawn up by professionals, with little or no consultation with users or local staff, and that user wants were poorly defined.

With the exception of Authority B, work on standards and specifications was being carried out by the operational parts of the Department, and although inspection staff expressed an interest in this field of work, they tended to lack the time to get involved. There was no evidence of users being involved, although they may have been in individual homes. In Authority B former carers of residents were being involved in conducting audits, while the inclusion of user representatives on at least two Inspection Advisory Committees should ensure that the consumer voice could at least begin to be heard.

Having noted the extent to which social services authorities appear to emphasise consumers wants and needs, Hambleton and Hoggett (1990), Pollitt (1990) and Gaster (1991) all comment that a solely consumerist approach, as put forward by the TQM measures designed for industry, omits the major requirement of public services of both collective and public accountability. Gaster contends that local authorities need policies on quality, and that all standards must be based on these, with definitions of quality being capable of assessment and review so that the political leaders can be informed clearly about findings on quality. Department of Health guidance (1991g) also incorporates such concern. Within the four study authorities, the advisory committees were the key means of achieving accountability for inspection, although the way in which these fitted into the wider local authority committee structure tended to be less clearly defined. One authority suggested it might be a subcommittee of the social services committee, another planned for it to report to the client group subcommittee of the social services committee and so on.

The guidance recommends that as a general rule reports should be open to the public and that only exceptionally should material be withheld (Department of Health, 1991g). This research suggested that local authorities intended to comply with this recommendation, which requires that reports are written clearly, and that outcomes are measurable. In addition to the involvement of service users, TQM writers consistently recommend the involvement of staff at every level in the organisation in the pursuit of quality, together with employee participation in decision-making. Guidance has already picked up this point, and is promoting the involvement of staff and providers in general (Department of Health, 1991g). In all four participating authorities there had been some degree of involvement during planning and implementation. This included residential staff membership of working groups on inspection, and attendance at workshops and seminars on the subject. Local authority residential staff were only directly represented on the inspection advisory committee in Authority C.

Department of Health guidance (1991g) also recommends that service providers, like users, should participate in the specification of services and their evaluation, although Gaster (1991) and Pollitt (1990) found in social services and health respectively that specifications and inspection schema appeared to be drawn up with little or no consultation with local staff or users. In three of the four study authorities, work in this area was being carried out by the operational parts of the department with little involvement from inspection staff, but it was less clear whether staff in homes were being consulted. However, there was a good example of staff involvement in developing standards and evaluating services during inspection in Authority D, where the inspection unit had set up a standard inspection development group with representatives of its own private and voluntary homes plus, at some meetings, national representatives of large independent providers. As a result they had developed a three-part inspection process:

- *Part 1*: a computer generated schedule for the head of home to complete;
- *Part 2*: to check details of the self-completion schedule and pick up on financial changes and establishment policies; and
- *Part 3*: to focus on quality of life by talking to residents, relatives and staff.

A day care development group was also working on standards and specifications in Authority D, including day care staff as members.

In Authorities A and B, work on standards and specifications in residential care had been led by the need to develop contracts for the transfer of homes to independent management or ownership. The kinds of instruments that had been developed included good practice guides, a handbook for care staff, and guidebooks on implementing standards for each client group to ensure that staff were aware of standards and specifications, even if they were not involved in drawing them up.

Three of the authorities had provided an induction programme of some sort for their staff, including workshops on QA, the development of training packs, and training provided by a regional group of inspection units. It was also recognised that all staff needed to be aware of the role of quality in their work, and it was hoped to achieve this through training packages, involving staff in the development and use of codes of practice, and by the effective use of supervision and team meetings.

CONCLUSION

There is good theoretical evidence to suggest that industrial and commercial quality assurance systems are transferable to organisations involved in social care, providing that allowance is made for public accountability, as well as an emphasis on the individual consumer. This study indicates that in two of the four participating authorities the heads of inspection were adopting an overtly TQM approach, and in all four authorities there was evidence of work going on outside the inspection units to suggest that quality issues were now firmly on the agenda. An emphasis on prevention, consumerism, involving and valuing staff and decentralisation was also apparent to varying degrees. What was less clear was whether information systems and management systems were adequate either to pick up information about quality or to ensure it was acted upon. More attention may also be needed to ensure that staff have adequate support from management to build a positive attitude towards quality assurance; and that identified problems are seen as opportunities for learning, improvement and change, rather than sources of punishment. The market regulatory activities of local authorities will need to improve in both range and sophistication as they become increasingly involved in contractual relationships with independent providers after April 1993 in a wider spectrum of services. Authorities will need to find the optimum level of intervention in the social care market to balance the needs of service users for choice and quality with the need of purchasers and providers to limit transaction costs and reap the benefits of economies of scale. Despite this being a very new area of activity for social services authorities, there was encouraging evidence of an increasing enthusiasm to develop this area of work in all four authorities.

9 Developing Home Care Services

Home care, formerly the home help service, is the backbone of formal support to older people in their own homes, and this is reflected in the high percentage of local authority resources it consumes. The *Caring for People* White Paper laid the foundation for the new community care ideal that older people should be enabled to live in their own homes for as long as possible with the support of domiciliary, respite and day care services. However, neither the White Paper nor subsequent documentation give much guidance as to the nature or scope of these developments, only that they must be 'targeted on those whose needs for them is greatest'. Anxiety over the new funding arrangements for residential care also compounded the problems facing social service departments in developing home-based services. Authorities are not expected to offer a spectrum of home-based services single-handed but should be encouraging the independent sector to complement social services provision. The level of frailty of an ageing population requires local authorities to collaborate with nursing, medical and paramedical professions to secure community care arrangements that can effectively substitute for residential or nursing home alternatives.

The community care changes require home-based services not only to substitute for residential care, but also to diversify to meet an expanding range of needs, and to offer choice and flexibility (Griffiths, 1988; Audit Commission, 1992b). Since 1985, pressure has increased on social service departments to make changes to their home help service. A 1986 Audit Commission report illustrated how in three particular authorities half the people in residential care could potentially have been maintained in the community, and that in four authorities half the community services expenditure was allocated to those who did not need it. Successive SSI reports have called for more personal care and increasing flexibility and co-ordination with other service providers. Evidence suggests that clients tended to receive what was available at the time or what was the standard in service provision — two hours help per week, for example — while the amount of service available and allocated to individual clients was often sacrificed to spread services across a larger number of clients at any given level of resources (SSI, 1987). Hunter et al. (1988) concluded that the level of service received often depended on its availability at the time, and this could change daily.

Home care has generally been neglected by social services departments. Its pre-war origins were in the voluntary sector, and the provision spread sporadically across England as a service keeping house for the frail, the sick and for women during confinement. Over time it evolved into a diverse set of responses to the basic requirements of the incapacitated and the frail at home. Originally conceived as a support to community nursing services, it was increasingly attacked for dealing with non-nursing needs, such as housework and laundry, and between 1946 and the Seebohm reforms of 1970 the service operated within the health departments of local authorities. Consequently, it has developed in a pragmatic and unco-ordinated manner in response to changing circumstance rather than as deliberately planned initiatives.

The major requirement of home care in the future is flexibility and an ability to affect target efficiencies and marginal productivity. Home-based services will be under a considerable amount of pressure from the increasing demands of an ageing population. With the substitution of residential care for home care, and reduced length of stay in hospitals (Victor et al., 1992), the needs of older people at home will diversify and intensify, and existing service delivery structures are unlikely to be able to cope with increasing demands. As a result, both *horizontal* and *vertical target efficiencies* (i.e. the extent to which people who need a service receive care, and the extent of targeting by degree of dependency) could easily remain low, with resources failing to reach those people who most need them.

In outlining the potential development of new responses, a number of aspects of care need to be considered. Recognition of the size of existing informal care networks is one such issue. Ungerson (1987) identifies a number of pressures for caring labour to take on a 'quasi-kin' model of care. Informal care is often provided one to one, and is more likely to meet the requirements of the individual as it has developed around them and over time. Formal in-home care services need to align themselves more with the natural rhythms of individual life if they are more fully to meet individual needs. There is also a need to bridge formal and informal care organisations and this could be facilitated by more innovative patterns of staff employment practices and modifications to agency organisational systems (Audit Commission, 1992b).

Many of the current conditions of service exist to protect a low-paid, part-time and predominantly female workforce and would be heavily defended by workers and unions alike. Getting rid of rotas, time sheets, guaranteed hours and uniforms, for example, may not appear to be very obviously in the best interest of staff. Ungerson (1995) identifies a range of problems with the development of 'quasi-kin' caring models. They include the identification of boundaries between 'public' and 'private' domains (that is to say, paying for tasks hitherto regarded as part of the traditional female role); and the question of whether cash relationships are incompatible with care relationships.

British home care services have traditionally been burdened with an image of inflexibility and overbureaucratisation. Reflections on the development of home care suggest that this may have been a more appropriate model in the early days when distributing a standard domestic service over the largest population possible was a main aim, and the service still retains some of these traits. Concentrating on administration and efficient rotas may well be an obvious focus for a manager's energy when the task of intensive assessments and intervention becomes far more than the job ever promised to be. But perfecting paperwork does not equate with better matching of resources to needs, and it may be that the only way to promote better targeting will be the dismantling of traditional structures which currently impede progress, despite recent practice guidance recommending a level of standardisation both in referral routes and in assessments (Department of Health, 1991c).

HOME CARE IN THE FOUR AUTHORITIES

Structurally, the home care and home help services in all four authorities remained segregated from other services, despite some restructuring to create sections embracing all community care services and functions, such as field work, day care, residential and respite care, often on a geographical basis.

In Authorities A and D, restructuring meant that home care was line-managed by the same principal officer as fieldwork services, while in Authorities B and C the separation remained. Indeed, in Authority C the proposed new structure left home care entirely on the resource side of the department and even further away from its field work colleagues than it was already. In this authority, however, the home care service had managerial responsibility for sheltered housing residents and wardens, and residents of sheltered housing appeared on individual managers' caseloads.

Although all authorities were attempting to standardise paperwork, different recording and computer systems existed. Problems were caused in Authority B because, although a joint social work and home care client would initially be known to both services, there was currently no way of updating social work records if the home care input altered. This authority, like Authority D, was in the process of piloting and testing the social service database SOSCIS for home care records, which aimed to give spreadsheet information on helper and client hours, travel, personal care input, and so on to the home care managers. The overall emphasis was on the development of a computer system that could replace longhand administrative tasks. The creation of a system for care packaging, care planning and care prioritising seemed of lesser importance. Hence a system was being piloted based on existing information needs and structures, not designed to address the new requirements of an advanced and flexible set of in-home care services.

In all four authorities, referrals tended to arrive at home care by a range of different routes. Practice guidance on care management has highlighted the need for standardised systems that can be publicised (Department of Health, 1991c), but this raises the issue of home care services being able to bridge the formal and informal worlds to create a system that does not eliminate the benefits of flexibility and individuality. Formalising referral routes could lead to a loss of individuality to the detriment of both users and their carers, because friends or neighbours may not have the means to channel concerns through the formal route.

Another structural anomaly for the home care service is that of client group specialisation. Local authorities are becoming increasingly client group orientated. Authority B had not yet structured around client groups, and staff worked with a variety of different types of users. In the past individual home helps were selected for training for work with children with physical disabilities. However, the home care development officer commented that there was no provision for maintaining these workers as specialists, so they often ended up with full caseloads of other types of cases, while the needs of children would be dealt with by untrained workers. Work with abused children was becoming more and more common among home care workers, with a general fear that it was unfair and unrealistic to ask workers to work with such a range of needs.

In three authorities home care has tended to respond to demographic pressures and become increasingly focused on older people. In Authority A the home help service was described as serving principally older people, with over 90 per cent of clients aged over 65, while in Authority D — which includes a university city — a considerably higher proportion of home care resources were spent on the younger people with physical disabilities in the case study area than in other parts of the authority.

HOME CARE PERSONNEL ISSUES IN THE FOUR AUTHORITIES

Employment structures within the home care and home help service generally followed traditional lines, and did not promote flexible responses to user needs, although they did give basic conditions of service to employees. Some upgrading of home care workers and the introduction of extra tiers of management had occurred. These issues are so crucial to the development of more responsive home care services that the position in each of the four authorities is considered individually.

Authority A

In 1991 the home help service was serving 2,716 clients, of whom 87 per cent were receiving two hours service a week. Of these, 44 per cent received domestic support only and the remaining 56 per cent received a mixture of domestic and personal care. Caseloads were as high as 270 clients per manager. Each area was headed by a senior home care manager, with two or three home care managers. There were 370 home helps across the local authority employed on an hourly rate, and three senior home care assistants also on an hourly rate. Each area also had at least one whole-time equivalent clerk.

During the late 1980s, transforming the whole of the service into a home care service had been considered. The aim would have been for care workers to complete a week's training and receive a certificate of competence. However, this did not happen. The home help service covered the hours of 7 a.m. to 8 p.m. which included several different shifts and different teams of workers. There was some cover at weekends and a night service for terminal care cases. There was no out-of-hours service for back-up. This authority had created a small intensive home care service serving 30 highly dependent clients on the verge of needing residential care. However, there appeared to be some tension remaining, despite the fact that the department had recently restructured to bring all domiciliary and fieldwork services under one line manager. The home care workers on the small intensive scheme were split between being accountable to their home care manager and to the co-ordinator (often a social worker) of the home care scheme.

Authority B

This authority had its fair share of difficult negotiations over personnel issues, with unions keen to protect existing work patterns. It had taken several years to extend the working hours from the traditional 9 a.m. to 1 p.m. By 1992 hours had been extended to 8 a.m. to 10 p.m., seven days a week. Each area was headed by a senior home care manager although, following a merger of six areas into four, one senior found herself managing two whole areas. An average senior managed five home care managers with up to 250 home care workers: that is, approximately 45 home care workers per manager. With an average of five clients per worker, caseloads for home care managers could once again be up to 225.

The authority was aware of the need to review home care budgets and, after drastic expenditure cuts in 1991, introduced a new weighted system for calculating home care resources across the authority based on three age bands (under 65, 65-80, over 80). Cutbacks meant the loss of 80 home care workers. There had also been pressure on managers to offer one week on and one week off and not to offer cover at weekends in order to make savings.

However, this was increasingly difficult to achieve as overall client dependency continued to rise. Home care workers had been offered a wide range of training, especially relating to the needs of older people, and a number of home care managers were Certificate of Social Services-trained.

Authority C

The home care service had six tiers of management including an assistant director. Each area had a senior home care manager who managed a team of home care organisers. The service worked on a patch system and each home care organiser managed several patches. A patch would often be headed by a senior home care worker whose role was to organise a team of home care assistants. The introduction of senior home care assistants had caused some resentment and consequent management difficulties. In some teams they facilitated the management role and took over programming and co-ordinating holidays and sick leave. They might also become involved in assessments with the home care organiser, and potentially could release the time of the organiser who often had a total caseload of 300 or more clients.

The service formally only covered until 9 p.m., when a night care aide was supposed to take over. However, as any one area might only have one night care aide, home care workers often did work after 9 p.m. When the patch system had been created contracts were not updated and, according to one area home care manager, this meant that some prevailing inflexibility had not been eradicated. The night service was small, but night care aides could also be 'borrowed' from other sectors such as residential homes. Reasons for providing a night care service varied, and it was not used as a matter of routine. Such inconsistencies in the provision of in-home night care services highlight the dilemma facing local authorities when attempting to be both 'good' employers as well as user and efficiency led.

Home care assistants were on a variety of fixed and flexible contracts. All staff were contracted for a minimum of twenty hours and, where possible, out-of-hours work was planned as part of the contract. However, since the introduction of flexible contracts, the unions in this authority had been concerned about the potential for exploitation. Many home care organisers had gained the Certificate of Social Services qualification or an in-service certificate of management (CMS). Senior home care assistants were required to complete a two-week course before being upgraded. Although home care managers had some flexibility over budgeting for home care assistants, the budget for senior home care assistants had been fixed at the centre, so relief for senior home care assistants, for instance, had to come out of the home care budget, preventing the home care manager from having total freedom to manage flexibly. There was also a separate budget for night care aides.

Authority D

A recent restructuring brought home care, social work and occupational therapy under a single team manager along client group lines. The home care teams were headed by a home care officer who managed assistant home care officers. A recent modernisation had introduced senior home care assistants who were salaried rather than paid hourly, aimed at producing flexibility and to increase the mobility of workers. They had the same job description as home care workers and covered the hours of 7 a.m. to 10 p.m. However, the introduction of salaried workers was said to have made budgeting more difficult for managers because of dealing with increments and overtime. Non-salaried staff still received guaranteed hours on a two-weekly cycle and, on the whole, home care workers had chosen which system suited them best. Full-time clerks were employed with the introduction of senior home care workers. Senior home care workers also helped with some of the day-to-day administration and development of the teams.

Profile of Home Care Clients

Even without conscious targeting, the dependency of the average home care user is likely to increase as the numbers of very old people rises. However, there is considerable evidence that caseloads remain in the region of 200 to 300 per manager. In some authorities, management of such large caseloads is facilitated by extra tiers of management. Regardless of the actual numbers involved, it is the need of the user that remains critical, but there is little clear evidence as yet to describe the specific characteristics of home care service users.

Authority A has had criteria for the assessment of need since 1990, with clients' ability assessed under nine headings. Anything above a certain score qualifies for help, and a weekly allocation of time in minutes is determined by whether the requirement is standard, medium or high allocation. The home help service has fixed allocations of time taken to complete a task. This authority had considerably more private domestic agencies than the other three in the study, and home care managers indicated a commitment to transferring 'domestic only' clients to private providers. The authority also offered to put independent agencies on a list that could be given to clients if the agency could meet the requirements set out in a code of practice.

Authority D had recently introduced a client dependency rating score, which together with an assessment of 'support available' and 'the risk factor of no intervention' was used to calculate eligibility for home care. The aim had been to move away from the low dependency clients, categorised as needing only domestic support and monitoring. Managers were still keen to preserve what they considered to be the preventive aspect of the service, and were prepared to increase the number of hours a client received, thus moving them into a safer category. The 1992 community care plan calculated that the average client received 3.8 hours per week.

In Authority C the service had very much gone over to personal care. During a particular week in 1991 of 3,703 allocated hours, 1,400 hours (37 per cent) were spent on 'very intensive interventions', while only 100 hours (3 per cent) were spent on cleaning.

Innovations in Standard Home Care

Innovations or developments in 'standard' home care often occur to save money (or prevent money being unnecessarily wasted) or following decisions to meet client needs more intensively.

Shopping. Authority A had developed a dedicated shopping and pension scheme in the last few years. The shopping scheme involved 33 specifically trained home helps and in 1991 served over 700 clients in the local authority. It was calculated during 1991 to have saved £160,000.

Cleaning. The home care development officer in Authority D reported how she had created a 'cleaning only service' to supplement existing home care services because, in one particular locality, people with heavy packages were not getting their house cleaned at all. This authority was not keen to contract with the independent sector.

Laundry. Authority A had realised that time was being wasted doing individual clients' washing, and a special scheme was set up in one area. It involved six designated home helps taking clients' laundry to modernised laundry units in the authority's own residential homes, and working early evening hours Monday to Friday. The laundry tended to consist of items soiled by incontinent clients. The scheme saved £8,000 and it was originally intended that, as it had been a success, it would be introduced across the authority. However, a further area office claimed they had no demand for a laundry service and it would not be used were it introduced. There was no evidence that this area had more private washing machines, but to introduce such a scheme could potentially cost the authority money rather than save it.

Meals. Modernisation to meals services appeared to have daunted authorities considerably. In some cases this might have been due to the nature of the service and the reliance on the goodwill of volunteers. However, Authority B had a standard in-house meals-on-wheels service providing over 700 meals a week. Anyone over 65 requesting the meals service would be granted it. Those in receipt of the meals service could be referred from various sources, often as part of a home care package, although traditionally requests for meals were social work referrals.

Authority A had invested in freezers and freezer meals for a wide range of users with some success, while Authority C had a range of options for clients requiring meals, including frozen meals that could either be cooked by the client or by the home care worker; fresh meals cooked by the home care worker on an individual basis; and hot meals delivered by WRVS or an old people's welfare luncheon club. Alternatively, a home care worker might even deliver fish and chips. Many of the small patches in this authority had freezers based in residential homes or sheltered housing blocks.

Innovations in Enhanced Home Care
Personal care tasks within the home care service have frequently developed more out of compassion for individuals than as a defined function of the home help service and, until recently, were considered to be 'beyond the call of duty'. Informally, however, home helps have often cooked meals in their own homes to give to clients, and taken clients' washing home with them. There have always been recorded incidents of home helps socialising with clients and visiting on their day off, reflecting an awareness that human relationships and interactions do not fit neatly between working hours and defined tasks. It is rare to find explicit operational styles or formulated philosophies as these tend to evolve over time from the grassroots and embody the aspects of human caring which can rarely be categorised. Formal examples of services attempting to meet explicit needs can more frequently be seen in smaller specialised schemes, often where there is extra or enhanced care.

As early as 1986, Authority B had considered splitting the service into a more intensive home care service and a larger home help service undertaking mainly domestic tasks. Latterly, such innovations as managers and workers being selected to work in the patch in which they live, often dedicating their service entirely to a number of tower blocks or a single street, had emerged. Although predominantly an 8 a.m. to 10 p.m., seven day a week service, the lack of night support had led to a proposal to set up special houses for older people with senile dementia, where home care workers could provide support between 8 a.m. and 10 p.m. and a private agency be paid to provide sleep-in services.

Since 1989 in Authority A, a more intensive home care service was formed in addition to the large army of home helps. This operated across the local authority, and enabled up to 30 people to be kept at home on a joint social service and health authority initiative. Clients who were eligible generally had to require up to 23 hours help a week (although the average was twelve hours a week), and there was priority over hospital beds for regular respite and emergency admission. It was reported that the hospital social work team made most intensive use of this scheme, although they sometimes felt that when there were no more places available they were having to construct care packages themselves.

Authority A also had another enhanced care scheme devised entirely for older people with mental health problems which encouraged clients to apply to the Independent Living Fund for support to pay *quasi-kin* style carers direct, who then took over much of the responsibility and pressures from relatives. The intensity of the commitment required a different kind of worker, perhaps a neighbour, who often worked almost exclusively with one user for long periods of time. It also relied on clients' own benefits and the use of the Independent Living Fund to pay such carers directly, and not through the local authority.

Authority C also had a small scheme in one area called *integrated locality care* which involved home care workers being based in health centres with occupational therapists and physiotherapists. The scheme had found that home care was better able to support frail older people at home because of the early involvement of therapists. Therapists were also on hand to help teach home care workers how to manage aids and adaptations, such as lifts and hoists, more successfully for clients.

Home care schemes to facilitate discharge from hospital and to respond quickly to emergencies are essential. Authority D had a rapid response team involving a system of staff on rota, often working until needed in day centres or meals services. Such teams are often able to provide a very intensive initial response. However, overall success is very dependent on the communication and co-operation between these special teams and the home care teams who have to take over in the longer term. This has been known to cause serious breakdowns in continuity, especially where a rapid response team received instructions direct from a hospital social work department and the community team might be unaware of the case.

Home Care and Health Care Interface

As home care has evolved and adapted to changing demands, the interface with health care has presented an increasingly prominent set of issues. The home help service began by working alongside general practitioners and district nurses to assist frail elderly people in their homes, but the division of roles and responsibilities for personal care tasks is increasingly emerging as an issue separating the health and social care domains.

Discussions between home care and community nursing have centred on the need to retain professional domains and hence jurisdiction over parts of the body. The Royal College of Nursing and the National Union of Public Employers have drawn attention to the problems that periodically arise concerning the lack of skilled nursing input and the burden placed on unskilled manual grade workers such as home helps and home care workers. There is a desire by both health and local authorities to eliminate the grey areas between health and social care tasks and, while authorities are often well able to define those tasks that belong to their own 'professional' jurisdiction and those that do not, this generally leaves room for considerable debate over potential overlaps, with mutual responsibility still unresolved.

The aim of a recent National Association of Health Authorities and Trusts working group (1992) was to produce a report on definitions of health and social care in order to establish responsibility and accountability for the provision of particular services. Their approach was task-based and led to an

---

BOX 9. SOCIAL CARE TASKS

NAHAT distinguished the following as social care tasks:

- house care
- laundry
- fetching (shopping, pensions, etc.)
- preparing and cooking meals and drinks
- personal care, such as bathing and washing (but with certain exceptions, such as diabetic care)
- assisting in mobility (but not lifting)
- respite care (other than in hospitals)
- adaptations and 'straightforward' management of appliances/prosthesis
- encouraging practical and employment skills
- executive functions
- advocacy
- educational psychology services and provision of day centres, lunch clubs and environmental health

Source: NAHAT (1992).

---

advisory document primarily concerned with presenting professional domains rather than addressing individual holistic needs. The domains, or tasks within domains (because many domains have 'shared' responsibility), that fall exclusively to social care are set out in Box 9.

Areas where either or both service might be involved are shown in Box 10. The teaching of clients, carers and relatives is generally seen as a health care responsibility, even where the responsible authority for the task is the social care authority. The definitions produced by NAHAT were intended to refer to both residential and community settings. However, hospital nurses carry out all the delineated tasks in all three categories, while carers in their own homes will often be carrying out the bulk of these tasks unaided and untrained.

NHS commissioning teams are faced with the need to calculate budgets and labour utilisation, and there has been considerable discussion on the skill mix of district nurses, with a desire to minimise numbers of highly-skilled staff attending to very basic care needs. Qualified nurses are therefore being encouraged to develop as facilitators and trainers, spending less of their time on hands-on tasks. This may lead to health and social care agencies having different agendas.

Three of the local authorities were currently addressing the issue of overlaps and gaps between the home care and the district nursing services. Interestingly, such initiatives appeared to occur at grassroots level rather than at headquarters. Authority D had piloted a joint code of practice with district nursing colleagues in one area designed to be extended across the whole

---

BOX 10. JOINT HEALTH AND SOCIAL CARE TASKS

NAHAT distinguished the following as joint health and social care tasks:
- joint aid services
- washing and dressing (because if this is replacing a carer it is a social care responsibility and if it is for a severely disabled person it is a health care responsibility)
- escorting to GP, hospital, etc.
- help with getting up and going to bed
- toileting (excluding assisting with evacuation, promotion of continence and management of incontinence)
- medicine administrations of tablets, eye drops and applications
- advice on equipment (as long as 'straightforward')
- encouraging emotional and social skills
- individual, family and life crisis counselling
- bereavement counselling and protection from self-harm

Source: NAHAT (1992).

---

authority. As in the NAHAT document, tasks had been divided into three categories: health, social or joint. This authority was happy to emphasise 'jointness,' and joint assessments and joint working were being encouraged, the promise being, as with the NAHAT document, that if care involved 'severe disability' it would automatically be a health care responsibility, whereas if it was to replace a carer it would be a social care responsibility.

Nurses may be more able to undertake holistic assessments than they are to provide holistic care in the community. However, any gap (or overlap) between their assessment and that of the home care service could potentially be better filled if home care and community nursing merged further, as does occur in a few specialist innovatory schemes. In the main, however, the services in Authority D had decided to maintain their own paperwork and assessment instruments, although district nurses would maintain their own records even if they were not currently involved with a client. District nurses had also agreed to train home care assistants, but social services were concerned that this might not actually materialise in reality, as district nurses' priorities could change from day to day.

Authority A planned to launch a pilot project on home care and district nurses in 1992 to look at role designation. This had arisen out of earlier discussions between senior home care managers and district nursing officers on the appropriateness of referrals to each service. The problem stemmed from a feeling by both services that ward sisters were incorrectly referring patients on discharge. Joint assessments would become policy unless the needs were obviously at one end of the social/health care continuum. These general agreements were to be written up and given to ward sisters. However, the general opinion of the project officer was that both services would have been happier if tasks could have been divided into health or social care domains, so avoiding the proverbial 'grey' area.

In Authority A, community nursing services such as the twilight and bathing services were being gradually reduced by the health authority, although this was not made explicit to social services. Since 1988 Authority A had extended the role of the home help service to include areas of personal care, such as help with washing, bathing and using the toilet. These guidelines had not been jointly set with the health authority at the time and potentially crossed the lines demarcated in the NAHAT report.

Authority B had no explicit documentation dividing personal care tasks between agencies, but the introduction of incontinence training had been carried out jointly with the health authority. In 1992 district nurses seemed to have stopped all bathing services unless explicitly medical. Such measures rarely take place in an atmosphere of joint negotiation or consultation, and one sector is often left feeling that the other has acted unreasonably.

Authority C had produced guidelines for the home care service, establishing a framework within which personal care could 'appropriately, safely and effectively be delivered'. It stressed the benefits of joint working between district nurses, physiotherapists, occupational therapists, health visitors and general practitioners. And indeed in one locality therapists and home care workers were reported to have developed ways for clients to be maintained at home more effectively and for longer than would normally have been possible. This had not been extended to other parts of the authority, which highlights the way innovation may occur quite independently of policy at field level but not necessarily be replicable. These personal care guidelines did not attempt to designate tasks as either a health or social care responsibility, but rather to outline the 'dos' and 'don'ts' of various tasks such as washing, bathing and undressing, as well as more intimate activities such as toileting, and dealing with incontinence and medication. The guidance outlined good and bad practice, and made explicit whom to ask for help where a task should not be attempted.

Medication
The administration of medication is an interesting example of discrepancy and conflict in meeting client needs. Medication is a very contentious area because, although it is most obviously a medically related task, daily administration is usually carried out by individuals for themselves or by their lay carers. In Authority D the joint agreement between home care and district nurses indicated that where there was medication a district nurse must be involved, even if it was only to put the medication in the dispenser for the home care worker to then hand to the client. However, the task of 'promoting taking of medication' was designated as a social care task. In Authority C home care was responsible for reminding people to take their medication,

collecting prescriptions, recording and monitoring what medication was taken and reporting obvious non-taking or abuse. However, although medication must not be 'put out' in its required dosage for a client, after joint assessment and 'where medication is needed several times per day', the guidelines state that home care may be involved in providing at least part of this task. In Authority A, district nurses were refusing to visit just to fill up dispensers, and a pilot was being set up to look at improving co-ordination between home care, general practitioners and pharmacists. The hope was for pharmacist to agree to deliver the trays each week. In Authority B, district nurses' refusal to fill dispensing boxes for home care staff to administer was currently an issue. Home care workers had been taking the initiative and asking pharmacists to fill the boxes. However, pharmacist were often refusing, saying that home care workers were 'untrained to be involved', thus leaving the needs of the client unmet by three different but overlapping services.

CONCLUSION

On the basis of existing developments, it is difficult to escape the conclusion that the real future of home care lies with primary health services. There are already trends in this direction: for example, fundholding GPs were being encouraged to provide for all the health care needs of the population they serve from community resources. Many social service departments also appeared to be toying with the idea of aligning care managers with their GP counterparts, and one or two pilots around the country (including in Authority C) were planning to align budgetary resources for health and social care by locating care managers in surgeries.

Evidence of increasing innovation, diversification and flexibility remained sporadic and somewhat unconvincing in the four authorities. Home care was almost entirely provided by in-house services, structures tended to remain rigid and rarely did home care appear as part of an interdisciplinary team. Repetitive assessments still occurred between home care, social work, hospital and district nursing, and communication links seemed random and weak. Caseloads remained unmanageably large, while average hours of service received still seemed low. Yet home care once again came out as the service most dedicated to the needs of older people at home. There were few examples in our authorities of variety in staff employment terms and conditions, and several examples of rigid rota and inflexible guaranteed weeks were evident.

Successful innovation was on a very small scale, and had usually developed from grassroots initiatives. Although several authorities were consciously trying to work out and agree useful operational guidelines between themselves and their nursing colleagues, time and again the first stumbling block seemed to be the failure of agencies to see the client's need first, and the issue of how to actually meet that need as second. In the example of administering medication, the idea of a 'quasi-kin' model is probably the most helpful. From outside professional boundaries, the issue of organising and administering medication is one that most individuals or their kin would usually learn to manage for themselves. The gulf between the formal care services and informal care worlds still remained perhaps too wide for an innovation of this sort.

Ultimately home care suffers from being all things to all people, and to better serve the needs of older people it must determine its own typology, and collaborate across all sectors to decide which levels of in-home care the population needs. Re-merger with primary health care may be one such alternative, but a range of other options is possible and needs to be encouraged so that the impact of the various models can be evaluated. Health and local authorities should be looking to jointly commission cross-boundary services of this kind if they are to make the concept of a seamless in-home service meaningful for users and carers alike.

10 Residential Care Strategies

The role of residential care has been central to the development of the community care reforms, particularly the massive and sustained growth of independent sector residential and nursing care homes fuelled by income support benefits between 1980 and the early 1990s (Wistow et al., 1994), and remains crucial to the way in which implementation is developing. Increasing numbers of elderly people are making demands for care, and this has highlighted the need for a shift towards community care, which is often (naively) seen as a preferred and lower-cost alternative to residential care, as demonstrated by such innovatory schemes such as the Kent Community Care Project (Davies and Challis, 1986). Residential care, on the other hand, is often regarded as inefficient in terms of investment, since it benefits only a relatively small proportion of elderly people, and on the grounds that it is institutional rather than homely. Hence there is increasing pressure on local authorities to change the balance of resources away from residential towards community alternatives, and to target any remaining residential care on those who 'cannot be sustained in the community and only (on) those who would not benefit from other methods of support' (Audit Commission, 1985, p.26).

In addition to shifting the balance of care and targeting resources, residential care is expected to change in a number of other ways. Considerable attention has been given to the size and design of residential homes over the years (Willcocks et al., 1987), and in clarifying the philosophy and objectives of residential care, improving its quality, and making homes less institutional and more homely (for example, Wagner, 1988). The integration of residential homes into the community by increasing the range of services provided by them, such as day and respite care, has continued to be seen as one means of making homes more homely (ibid; SSI, 1989). However, the UK lacks argument which relates the characteristics of alternative forms of congregate living to

user circumstances, and the benefits which each characteristic or form of congregate living contributes. Therefore we lack the knowledge necessary for
good targeting argument.

Despite attempts to change the balance of care in favour of community-
based services, and to integrate community and residential services, policies
for residential care are still too often being developed separately from community care, perpetuating the division between them (Willcocks et al., 1987).
The *Caring for People* White Paper is no exception. It proposed the pursuit of
good-quality residential homes through the development of standards and
specifications, the establishment of arm's-length inspection units, and recommended the further development of respite care, but said little about the role
of residential care within a comprehensive service except as a last resort.

Residential care remains at the forefront of change in personal social services, particularly in relation to the implementation of community care, which
requires the stimulation of a mixed economy, and the development of contracts, regulation and other quality control mechanisms. And it is through
residential care services that local authorities began to learn of the opportunities and pitfalls of a mixed economy. Furthermore, given the continuing
problems of local authority finance, residential care was seen as one of the
few sources of resources available to fund community developments, and a
number of authorities pioneered the transfer of their in-house residential care
homes to independent ownership or management in order to release resources
to finance community alternatives. Strategies for residential care, therefore,
and transfers in particular, play a crucial role in many local authorities in
determining the future of community care.

The incentives for a mixed economy in residential care fell into two
categories: the policy incentives outlined in *Caring for People*; and financial
incentives created by differences in the way in which residents of public and
independently-run residential homes were funded prior to April 1993.

Under the new community care policy objectives, local authorities were
expected to stimulate the development of independent supply, while reducing
their own role as providers, and developing new roles of purchaser, enabler,
standard-setter and monitor of services. All four participating local authorities
remained strongly committed to public provision, but the potential of an
extension of the mixed economy to provide greater choice was acknowledged,
and senior managers were beginning to think about competition, if only
because some degree of competition in residential care was inevitable after
April 1993.

The growth in private and voluntary sector provision, and the transfers of
local authority homes to independent management or ownership in the early
1990s, were stimulated largely by the financial incentives created by central
government, since residents in independent homes could claim benefits at a
higher rate than residents in local authority homes. This situation led many
authorities to plan to transfer or sell homes to independent management or

ownership in the early 1990s. However, the Department of Social Security (DSS) quickly pulled the financial rug from under local authorities by issuing new regulations which came into effect in August 1991, with all residents transferred after this date being considered as still under council care and therefore ineligible for income support. This led to the abandonment of transfer plans by a number of local authorities (including two of our four study authorities), although some authorities continued with their plans on the basis of the potential longer-term advantages.

This change of heart was almost certainly the result of concern at the potential cost of widespread transfers before the DSS lost control of income support for residential and nursing care with the implementation of the NHS and Community Care Act in April 1993, although the reason given by the Secretary of State for Social Security was that:

> While government favours a mixed economy of care, the balance between voluntary, private and public ownership should be determined by the long-term needs of those needing care, rather than short-term financial considerations (Cervi, 1991, p.3).

This was followed by guidance that local authorities should retain *some* residential care, and that they should establish a 'balance of provision between statutory and independent sectors which will ensure that a full range of care is provided' (Ivory, 1991, p.3). The central message still seemed to be that local authorities should continue to review the scale of their own provision and transfer services to other providers, but that they should follow the Department of Health rules, get good legal advice, and make sure there was a well thought out strategy for residential care services rather than an 'unseemly rush for the social security gold' (Phillips, 1991, p.17).

The benefit system had also caused a boom in private nursing home care and, like local authorities, many health authorities were busily transferring their continuing care activities to the independent sector. Since benefit rates were higher than for people entering residential care, there was an added incentive to place people in nursing home beds, when perhaps they could be catered for in cheaper, residential care, or even in their own homes (Victor et al., 1992). Concern was expressed that health authorities were reducing their direct provision of continuing care for older people, in many cases with little evidence of how alternatives had been planned, and who might require such provision in future. These fears were allayed somewhat by the letter to health and local authorities from the Department of Health in March 1992, which indicated that health authorities could continue topping up private nursing home fees to enable very frail elderly people to leave hospital and keep waiting lists down (Downey, 1992), but required health and local authorities to make no changes to existing levels of residential and nursing home provision without prior agreement. RHAs and regional SSI were required to identify any instances of unilateral withdrawal of service in the course of their regular community care monitoring activities. Transfer of a home to independent management or ownership did not necessarily reduce the total amount of long-term provision available, so those transfer plans which survived the August 1991 benefit changes could still go ahead.

The Department of Health guidance indicated that, although the closure of homes would not be tolerated in the immediate future, sales and transfers might still be viable options. And indeed, a number of longer-term financial incentives remained. The potential costs of refurbishing local authority homes to reach registration standard by April 1993 were also particularly important, since transfers could help either to raise or to free capital for refurbishment of retained homes, or else housing associations and private companies were able to raise capital in the marketplace to fund refurbishment of transferred homes. Other concerns involved the need to control the unit costs of local authority accommodation in order to compete with private and voluntary homes, and concern at the proportion of total SSD budget that would be swallowed up by residential care from April 1993, unless money could be freed to develop community-based alternatives, so reducing demand for residential care in the long term.

As a direct result of these issues, residential care paradoxically continued to dominate the community care implementation agenda, despite current policy imperatives being designed to achieve better community alternatives.

THE SIGNIFICANCE OF LOCAL AUTHORITY HOME TRANSFERS

The policy directives suggest that a number of elements need to be included in local authority strategies for residential care, in order both to change the role of residential care and to extend the mixed economy. In particular, the strategy should link residential and community care in some way, and demonstrate a shift in the balance of care towards community services, as well as incorporate choice and flexibility. Criteria also need to show how residential care will be targeted, how a refurbishment programme will bring retained homes up to registration standard, and how alternatives to residential care are to be developed. There should also be indications of the anticipated future balance between direct provision and independent sector care, and how this might change over time, particularly through the transfer of homes to independent management or ownership. Finally, there should be signs of collaborative discussions and activity between local and health authorities regarding the provision of continuing care.

The approach adopted by each of the four studies was markedly different. Authority A had leased five of its nine homes to a housing association on a ten-year basis. Authority D was in the process of replacing five homes with five sheltered housing with care units in an arrangement with two housing associations; and plans to transfer a proportion of its remaining 25 homes to voluntary organisations were abandoned following the change in benefit regulations in August 1991. Authority B developed a scheme whereby the majority of its homes would be sold to staff and management in an employee shared ownership programme (ESOP). Although this scheme was abandoned following the August 1991 benefit changes, it is included in the discussion as an interesting theoretical model which may be replicable in other settings. Finally, Authority C decided against transferring any of its 28 homes after consultation with staff and residents.

Targeting and the Balance of Care
The transfers in both Authority A and B were intended to free resources by maximising access to income support for residents of transferred homes. Although the transfers would mean no reduction in the quantity of residential care, except in relation to a reduced number of beds in reaching registration standards, the freed up resources could be used to fund additional community based services, so ultimately changing the balance of provision.

For those authorities which retained all or most of their residential homes, the main responses were the development of at least some homes into resource centres offering a range of community-based services, and the closure of other homes to release money. Authority C retained as much as possible of its accommodation, achieving change in the balance of care by diversifying the use of homes, adapting at least one home in each area into a resource centre, and developing specialist EMI resource centres alongside similar developments by local health authorities. Authority B, which abandoned the ESOP plan as a result of the August 1991 benefit changes, made major cuts in services across the board, including reductions in domiciliary services, and the closure of eight residential homes for elderly people in the year up to March 1992 to avoid charge-capping. In a very real sense, the ESOP proposals comprised the residential and community care strategy for elderly people and, in its absence, no clear alternative strategy had emerged. Trade unions strongly opposed the ESOP plans, contending that resource centres would be a better alternative.

Authority D also abandoned plans for large-scale transfers following the benefit changes, and so retained all but the five homes closed to make way for the sheltered housing with care units. In contrast to Authorities C and B, however, it demonstrated a degree of commitment to changing the balance of care by redirecting money originally intended for a new residential home to the development of community-based alternatives. Despite cuts to keep within budget, it closed an additional residential home rather than sacrifice this opportunity.

Decisions regarding what types of residential care and how much of it to retain are important elements in targeting. The results of a study of ten authorities in 1985 showed that targeting of home help services was poor, and that this would limit its ability to substitute for residential care (Davies et al., 1990). In general, the authorities wanted to retain assessment facilities, and there appeared to be broad agreement that this was advisable. There was less agreement over the retention or otherwise of EMI facilities, of short-term forms of provision, and of a proportion of homes for quality control purposes. Authority A had retained its two EMI homes for a variety of reasons. First, it had to retain some homes to meet its statutory obligations under the 1948 National Assistance Act. Second, EMI homes provide crucial backup to the authority's specialist EMI community care scheme, so it wanted to retain close links between the two forms of care. Third, EMI homes are expensive and difficult to run, so the housing association to which it transferred five of its homes and which lacked experience in this type of provision was reluctant to take it on. Authority A also planned to convert one home to EMI usage every two years, indicating a progressive targeting on EMI.

Authority B originally intended to transfer EMI homes into the ESOP, but retain one or perhaps two homes for quality control purposes. The ESOP development team's argument was that *Caring for People* implied a demand-led market, in which companies found specialist niches, so there was no need for the LA to retain such services, and that to do so would be to retain the old mindset of a supply-led market. However, the ESOP development team did have a strong incentive to transfer as many homes as possible since the commercial viability of the enterprise rested partly on its size.

Transferring long-term care makes the most financial sense in terms of maximising income from benefits. Transferring services such as short-term care, emergency admissions and respite care presents problems to any organisation which must maximise its income since the time and therefore cost of administration to apply for benefits is relatively high compared with the income that actually accrues. It also involves income loss through keeping beds vacant, although this is not a problem in homes which have vacancies for any length of time, when short-term care becomes financially attractive. Authority A was negotiating with a local housing association to persuade it to provide short-term forms of care, with a grant or subsidy to cover the additional costs. The authority's concerns were twofold. First, it wanted to have beds available for emergency placements, and the Housing Association Trust agreed to take on emergencies and not charge the client, provided the LA made an assessment and alternative arrangements on the first working day thereafter. Second, the LA wanted the Trust to provide short-term care such as respite care, but it was established early on in negotiations that the housing association would not take these on for financial reasons. The incorporation of short-term forms of provision within residential facilities raises questions about the benefits or otherwise of resource centres, and the complexity of managing them within an increasingly diverse mixed economy of care.

Two authorities foresaw a potential decline in demand for residential care: Authority A because of the planned increase in community alternatives, and Authority C because the unit costs of local authority homes exceeded those of local private and voluntary provision. Authorities A and D both had plans showing how the existence of alternatives to residential care, and the ability for increasingly frail people to be sustained at home, was contributing to a reduction in the amount of residential care likely to be needed. Authority A had piloted and introduced two intensive community-based alternatives to residential care: a home care scheme with health service backing for severely dependent elderly people, and a community care scheme targeted at elderly mentally ill people. The success of these schemes influenced the authority's choice of the way forward. In the short term, the 34 places lost through reaching registration standards were to be replaced with the same number of community care packages. In the longer term, increasingly dependent people will be cared for in the community, and those who do need residential care will go into private or voluntary homes.

Authority D, the county authority, was also taking active measures to develop alternatives to residential care, and had commissioned an outside research unit to undertake a balance of care study to show what services were needed where, including the balance of residential, day and domiciliary care. One area team was already redirecting money originally intended for a new residential home to the development of community-based alternatives. Five homes considered unsuitable for refurbishment were being replaced by sheltered housing units on the basis that this form of accommodation was better able to ensure privacy and independence while giving additional care. This would increase revenue spending and therefore was counter to balance of care arguments, but demonstrated the authority's commitment to providing choice and more homely environments. The revenue saved by closure, before it was required for the replacement, was being put into a bridging fund to replace beds temporarily, through increasing the domiciliary care budget, establishing care management schemes for highly dependent clients to prevent admission to long-term care, and through the purchase of independent sector placements. Together with the health authority and housing agencies, Authority D was also commissioning research into housing needs 'to promote the development of domiciliary, day and respite services to enable people to live in their own homes wherever feasible and sensible' and to carry forward the development of special needs housing.

Clearly, transfers were able to contribute to changing the balance of care towards community services, but benefit changes restricted the use of the transfer mechanism. For local authorities retaining most or all of their provision, the option of closure of homes to change the balance of care was also restricted by government guidance, leaving the extended use of residential facilities as resource centres as the only viable alternative. However, while the concept of a resource centre fits well with the desire to see residential care integrated with community services, and may be a cost-efficient way of using scarce resources, such multiple use of homes has been criticised as creating unhomely environments for residents (see Age Concern Institute of Gerontology, 1991). While transfers could clarify local authority targeting priorities for residential care, only two authorities had a clear strategy incorporating targeting criteria, and linking developments in community and residential care.

Increasing Choice

The term 'choice' may relate to type or amount of service and when and how it is delivered, choice of provider, and choice of whether to have a service or not. In relation to residential care, it can be argued that, while elderly people may initially exercise choice of type of home, location, type of provider and so on, once they have moved into a home they cannot easily signal their dissatisfaction by exiting from the home and finding an alternative (Hirschman, 1970). What is required is a secure and reliable service, therefore, with a choice of options available within the home, and the opportunity and encouragement to state preferences and get complaints heard. Such choice *within* the home will not necessarily be improved by a mixed economy. Indeed evidence has emerged from an ADSS study that the cash crisis in the private residential sector is leading to a two-tier system, with residents reliant on income support facing a loss of choice by being allocated second-class accommodation, such as shared rooms without private bathrooms or toilets, and reduced access to certain essentials such as chiropody and incontinence aids unless they pay for these themselves (Downey, 1992).

Choice also involves a number of trade-offs between interest groups. First, in purchasing services from independent providers, local authorities need to balance client choice against the need for continuity and security of supply, and the benefits of economies of scale that would be achieved by purchasing from one large provider (Lawson, 1991).

Moreover, choice is not always what it seems. The mechanism by which elderly people were automatically entitled to social security benefits for private and voluntary residential care gave people a choice which was taken away when local authorities assumed financial responsibility for publicly-supported placements in April 1993. People are now entitled to an *assessment* but not necessarily to a residential place. The pressure on local authorities to keep people out of residential care is especially strong since budgets are being cash-limited. Local authorities may not have sufficient community alternatives to offer either, so the new financial mechanisms could remove choice, security and protection for elderly people.

To some extent, the transfer of local authority homes could increase availability of choice, security and protection to elderly people by freeing capital and revenue that could then be used to develop alternatives to residential care, such as the sheltered housing units in Authority D, or the intensive community care schemes in Authority A. Transferred homes can also provide an alternative to Part III and private homes.

It is often argued that competition, or at least the threat of competition, is more important than whether homes are publicly or privately owned for encouraging innovation and choice (Millward, 1982; Hartley and Hooper, 1990). Authority B in particular was interested in competition from the point of view of enabling its own residential care to compete with independent providers. And there is a strong possibility that the introduction of a commercial approach, as characterised by the ESOP model of transfer, together with the threat of competition, would have delivered a more flexible and innovative use of resources, and so choice of services to the user. The economic viability of the scheme (to make up the shortfall in benefits payments), and its ongoing ability to compete with the private sector, would depend upon a contract attached to the main scheme, to provide various community services, using the facilities of the homes involved. The impact of change of ownership, and change of rewards and incentives implied by staff share ownership, might also have made a difference to innovation and flexibility of services.

The downside of the competitive equation in Authority B was that the ESOP would have represented the single largest provider of residential care in the authority, and so would have had a tremendous competitive edge, and would eventually be competing with services retained by the LA, such as home care, to the extent that it would not be inconceivable that ESOP would have become a monopoly in due course. Over time, therefore, the ESOP might have yielded less flexible services and less choice overall. In the case of Authority A, which had leased five of its nine homes to one housing association, the transfer represented no increase in competition in the short term, since the leases ran for ten years, which meant that no alternatives would be available until they expired, and competitors might go out of business in the meantime. However, there was a long-term threat to the scheme given that Authority A is on the edge of London where alternative providers are likely to exist. This would force the housing association to demonstrate its competitiveness towards the end of the lease. Interestingly, the change of management from local authority to housing association appeared likely to protect the interests of residents by ensuring the use of facilities was focused on their needs rather than those of the wider community. Having no obligation to serve elderly people living at home, the housing association had little interest in using facilities for day or respite care. Furthermore, the contract stipulated that the provider must maximise income, so the housing association was unwilling to admit residents for short-term stays and emergencies, since the cost of administration needed to apply for benefits rendered it uneconomic.

Authority D specifically sought the variety offered by contracting with two rather than one housing association. It invited a select list of six housing associations to bid for the sheltered housing scheme, with a specification setting out various options that could be bid for, so that smaller associations would be able to apply for part of the scheme if they could not take on the whole. In the event, the authority received four bids, which it evaluated against a range of criteria including cost, value for money, experience of very sheltered housing and adherence to the specification. As a result, it eventually chose two associations on the basis of their extensive experience of sheltered housing with care, and impressive demonstration of quality of life of residents in their existing schemes.

Pfeffer and Coote (1991) point out the limitations of competition, stating that it is wasteful to build two hospitals or residential homes if only one is needed, and that competition does not necessarily generate choice even when it is possible to do so, for a number of reasons. A long contract means that no alternatives will be available until it expires, and competitors go out of business in the meantime as is possible in the case of Authority A. Furthermore, if there is steady demand outside the public sector, competition may be justified, but this is not the case in most health and social care services. Where choice can be maintained, there is no guarantee of quality from the user's point of view, since this depends on the criteria for choosing between competitors. If choice is driven by the desire to contain costs, quality will probably suffer.

Using residential facilities as resource centres is one way of using facilities in a more flexible way and maximising their use, and several LAs were seeking to expand community services in the absence of alternative funds. Authority C had a policy of establishing resource centres for this reason, and an additional incentive was to provide something different from the run-of-the-mill private and voluntary home in order to compete with local independent providers. Authority D was also considering establishing resource centres, and Authorities A and B were planning to diversify the use of their homes. The flexibility achieved in this way benefits both elderly people living in their own homes who come in to use facilities such as respite and day care, as well as the local authority which maximises the use of its facilities. But long-term residents may lose out in terms of loss of privacy and the creation of unhomely environments.

Netten (1993) suggests that such homes can remain attractive to live in by physically separating the locus of day and respite care from permanent residents' living and sleeping quarters, and by limiting the sharing of staff by long- and short-term residents. It is staff continuity and a sense of territory that help to make a homely environment. Netten also argues that specialist facilities provide a positive environment for EMI residents. If LAs develop EMI services within generic homes, the facilities should be physically separate and have their own staff to minimise the disorientation of residents and the disruption of non-EMI residents. Such separation, of course, reduces the economies of scale of providing many services on one site and sharing staff, but here the cost to benefit ratio of quality in relation to price is paramount.

There may be natural limits to the use that can be squeezed out of a home since, if it becomes particularly unhomely, elderly people will not want to live there and demand will fall. This will only be the case, however, if there is an alternative choice of home or of community services, and if elderly people are given sufficient power, through the care management system, to state prefer-ences and get them heard and acted upon.

The Impact of Transfers

Competition has already been discussed in relation to promoting choice, flexibility and innovation, and Authorities A and B transfers did involve the threat of competition. However, whether transfers lead to more efficient services is difficult to assess. Certainly, the purchaser/provider relationship and a contract for clearly specified services may result in improved efficiency, rather than the fact that homes are now owned or managed by independent organisations. In Authority A, contestability (i.e. the ability of new providers to enter the market) was reduced in the medium term since homes were leased for ten years. Also, as Pfeffer and Coote (1991) note, competitors may well go out of business in ten years, and the need to demonstrate efficiency will only become critical for the leaseholder once the lease is drawing to an end. However, at the end of ten years, other organisations could bid to take over the lease, so technically the LA was not locked into a permanent arrange-ment as it would have been after selling or transferring the homes. Authority D's arrangement was somewhat different, since the housing associations would own the sheltered housing units, and the local authority would have to make a commitment to support the schemes at least during the lifetime of any clients for whom it was paying.

Authority A also noted some increase in management costs arising from its transfer, since the housing association running the homes had more managers, and could not operate the economies of scale of the LA. While the LA needed fewer staff for day-to-day management of residential services, there was more work in terms of registration, monitoring and negotiations with the housing association in the short term. Consequently, no central management staff had been shed by the LA, although it may restructure in due course once the transfer is well-established. Undoubtedly the transfer meant another link or two in the communication chain, but since the LA was dealing with just one provider, the gain was probably small. There were also costs involved for the local health authority since admission arrangements for people being dis-charged from hospital into transferred homes took a week longer than before. Whereas heads of homes previously took the advice of the social worker requesting the admission as to whether the person was suitable, the housing association conducted its own assessment in order to demonstrate that the homes were sufficiently independent of the local authority to qualify for in-come support.

It is unclear whether the ESOP proposals in Authority B would have raised management costs had they been implemented. But the fact that it would have involved only one large provider, with a central management core, would probably have limited costs. However, the LA would have needed to create a contract management and monitoring unit at additional cost. Authority D recognised that dealing with one contractor for the provision of five sheltered housing with care units would have allowed economies of scale and ease of negotiation, but it deliberately chose to contract with two housing associations in order to maximise choice and ensure competition. However, unlike Authority A's transfer, both the ESOP and Authority D's scheme do have the potential to yield social gains to justify increased costs.

Residential care has been criticised as inefficient in terms of investment since it benefits a relatively small proportion of elderly people, whereas customised care is considered more efficient and cost-effective in meeting individual need (Willcocks et al., 1987). However, there are counter-arguments that residential settings may be the most efficient means of caring for people in particular circumstances, for instance very physically disabled or mentally confused elderly people (Victor et al., 1992). In fact, the trend in both transferred and retained homes to introduce various forms of short-term provision into hitherto long-term facilities can be seen as one means of countering the argument about efficient investment by maximising the use of resources. In production of welfare terms, the multiple use of facilities where there are long-term residents will improve the degree to which the mix of inputs is adjusted to reflect the costs and constraints in their supply (i.e. input mix efficiency will rise), but will be inefficient at matching services to the valuations placed on them by long-term residents. In other words, output mix efficiency may fall for long-term residents, although it may rise for the people living in their own homes who come in to use the facilities on a short-term basis. Technical efficiency, which is the balance between input and output mix efficiency, will depend upon whether local authorities with a restricted budget place priority on the needs of long-term residents, or on meeting the needs of people living in the community. However, by keeping long-term and short-term facilities separate, the privacy of long-stay residents may be safeguarded (Netten, 1993).

Transferred homes may be more efficient than local authority homes in bridging the social and health care divide, and the joint registration of homes can also help. However, these options will be limited if contracts specify that a provider sells services only to them. There was little evidence of joint purchasing as yet in the four sample authorities, and it was unclear whether transferred homes would be in a better position to bridge the divide than private and voluntary homes, or retained homes that are adapted into resource centres.

CONCLUSION

Efforts to change the balance of care and introduce a mixed economy of social care were characterised by perverse financial incentives and unintended out-comes throughout the 1980s. One reason for this is that the government has been torn between its major goal — of cost-containment — and its policy intentions of encouraging community care. As Evandrou et al. write:

> Throughout the period there has been a steady shift away from a position where the policy focus was on centrally-defined need and equality, with an emphasis on priority groups, targets and planning, to one where the main concern is with public expenditure restraint and a shift in the balance of care provision between the state and the non-statutory sector (1990).

Nowhere is this divide between meeting need and containing costs more clearly represented than in the Department of Health statement that local authorities should provide for those assessed as in need, but 'within available resources' (1992d). As a result, local authorities will increasingly redefine their targeting criteria and raise their charges. This can be seen as moving towards a position in which social care will be selectively provided by the state only to the minority of old people who are officially in poverty. Equality, predictability and security have been replaced by other components of citizenship such as self-determination, independence, choice and flexibility (Baldock and Evers, 1991). Quite apart from the effect of particular political philosophies, however, the recent history of residential care underlines the difficulty of manipulating in unison a range of policy and financial mechanisms to achieve desired goals.

The experience of residential care over the last decade also demonstrates the difficulty of creating change, such as in the balance of care, by taking from one service to give to another. It is more effective and less painful for all concerned to create such change by injections of extra monies, in this case to boost the provision of community care without directly reducing resources to residential care. Having said this, crises can provide opportunities and catalysts for change that may successfully be achieved over a short time-scale, with slower follow-up consolidation.

Given that the option of transferring monies from residential care to community care has gradually been restricted, there appears to be little immediate hope for an expansion of community services except through the use of the special transitional grant after April 1993, which will involve a move away from residential care and towards community care, as well as from local authority to independent sector care. In the meantime, policy and practice guidance and the eight key tasks set a clear joint health and social services agenda, while care management — the linchpin of the whole enterprise — is to evolve slowly, so that the impetus towards change resulting from needs-based assessments and decentralised budgets may be slower in gathering momentum than originally anticipated. Meanwhile residential care, and the concentration of resources it represents, will remain a central feature of the community care agenda.

11 A Case Study of Community Care Implementation

Most local authorities adopted a generally cautious approach to community care implementation, speeding up only when more detailed guidance became available and regular monitoring of progress became established. But a small number of authorities acted quite differently by seizing the initiative and pioneering a way through the implementation minefield. This approach involved considerable risk of making mistakes, but could yield benefits in avoiding crisis management nearer to the date of implementation. This chapter describes the experience of one such authority in the form of a case study. The authority was developing home care services for elderly people in parallel with national policy-forming opinion, and indeed there was regular communication between senior authority staff and central government policymakers. The authority also took part in a number of national studies that led up to the community care reforms, such as *Working Together* (DHSS, 1983) and *From Home Help to Home Care* (SSI, 1987). Consequently, the authority rightly saw itself as pushing forward many of the new ideas for community care development. Perhaps the most interesting and conspicuous local initiative was the promotion of a recognisable form of care management from the early 1980s. This was originally introduced as a small-scale development, parallel to mainstream services, but from the mid-1980s the concept was increasingly being incorporated into mainstream services.

The information for this chapter was obtained through interviews held between 1990 and 1993 with headquarters staff, staff in one area team, and with a number of independent providers. The local authority in question covers a large county council area, and during the period of the research was organised into five areas, each covering dispersed rural communities as well as urban areas, including areas of both wealth and deprivation, as well as coastal retirement areas. The chapter is written in four sections. The first

---

BOX 11. SIGNIFICANT DEVELOPMENTS UP TO 1989

Late 1970s:	Case management scheme established in one small area
Early 1970s:	Case management scheme extended county-wide in parallel to home help service
Mid-1980s:	Policy developed to address structural problems of parallel development
Late 1980s:	Home care management pilots established to integrate care management within home help service; targeting achieved by transferring low dependency clients to independent registers of domestic workers set up by voluntary and not-for-profit organisations
1989:	Home care management went county-wide

---

three represent distinctive periods of development: first, the period before publication of *Caring for People* in 1989 (see Box 11); then 1989 to April 1991, when the authority implemented much of the legislation in spite of the national change in implementation deadlines; and, finally, the period of consolidation and preparation for April 1993. Each of these sections covers the development of policy in relation to national developments, and the process of implementation. The chapter ends with a summary of the authority's overall approach to implementation and the important issues raised, comparing these achievements with the broad national picture described in Part One of this book.

THE PERIOD UP TO PUBLICATION OF 'CARING FOR PEOPLE' IN 1989

The Emergence of Policy on Domiciliary Care for Elderly People
In the late 1970s, the social services department initiated an experimental case management scheme contemporaneously with the pioneering programmes being developed in the United States. This was a success, demonstrating that very dependent people could remain at home; that the need for residential care could be reduced or delayed; and that improvement in morale and quality of life were achieved for lower average costs than residential care. As a result, the scheme was extended across the whole county in the early 1980s. But by the mid-1980s it seemed anomalous to have budget-devolved service-commissioning intensively case-managed care for a minority of users, with social work and home help services operating in the traditional way for other users. The idea that social work for elderly people might be developed with an emphasis on case management began to be suggested. At this time the authority was also a relatively low provider of home help services, with low targeting and extensive cover, and a report to the social

services committee identified the need to co-ordinate services under a single management line, so avoiding earlier problems encountered by a specialist foster care scheme for children also established in parallel to mainstream services. The report also identified that 40 per cent of home help cases received two hours service or less per week, and suggested the possibility of an approach designed to enable such low dependency users to access domiciliary help from private or voluntary providers, particularly those getting appropriate benefits, in order to facilitate targeting of local authority services on those with greatest needs.

As a result, a review of the relationship between the home help service and the case management programme was established. It produced a critical working paper highlighting the essential differences between resource management (i.e. managing provision), and case management. The report recommended the integration of social work and social care, and developed two models for consideration: a preferred model which separated case management from resource management at local team level; and an alternative based on a domiciliary service in which the case management and resource provision roles could be combined in one person. Both models involved the abolition of the separate posts of social worker for the elderly, home help organiser and special scheme organiser, and their replacement by a new post combining all of these skills. Both models required a considerable increase in staffing, reflecting in part the low level of current resources in this area.

As a result, pilot projects were established in the autumn of 1987, in contrasting areas (see Box 12). However, the proposal separating resource and case management was seen as both too radical (involving a very substantial change) and too expensive (in spite of costings having been attempted within existing resources). Consequently, the chosen model took the form of trying to plug a new way of working into existing structures and procedures, and the result was organisational integration without the degree of client-centred integration which had been the key feature of the original intensive case management programmes. Nonetheless, the aim was to develop a more flexible and responsive service, involving users and carers more closely in the decision-making process.

In a medium-term plan produced in 1987, the stated aim was:

> to concentrate more of the social services resources on community care for the most highly dependent and to act as facilitator for the less dependent elderly people by helping them to maximise the social security income to which they are entitled and to employ directly help in the home where appropriate through a social services register of independent home carer systems.

Targeting of the new home care service was achieved by the recruitment of special staff to re-assess all existing users to identify all those receiving up to five hours of home help per week who did not qualify for the new service.

BOX 12. KEY FEATURES OF HOME CARE MANAGEMENT PILOTS

- Home help organisers, specialist social workers with the elderly, and special scheme care managers integrated into teams and each member of staff retitled as a home care manager (i.e. a case manager).
- Each home care manager had a number of home helps and community care assistants (from the special scheme) to deploy within their budgetary limits.
- Each home care manager held a caseload of mainly moderate and high-dependency elderly and handicapped people, together with cases of a high degree of complexity, all of whom would require varying levels of social work or social care. They were also responsible for counselling and social work support for their clients.
- Each home care manager had equal access to day care, residential care and other services as required.
- Each service used had an agreed cost and had to be accounted for from each individual manager's budget, and the cost of each care package had to be regularly reviewed.
- Home care managers would be responsible for the assessment of need and the deployment of home care workers and the recruitment of additional helpers for vulnerable elderly people as appropriate within an overall budget. The home care managers would be responsible to senior workers within the team and thence to a team manager.

In the meantime, rather than running its own independent domestic register as originally suggested, the authority took the opportunity for pump-priming the expansion of an existing non-profit provider of domiciliary care. It later encouraged the development of similar independent domestic registers by other independent providers. These registers operated as agencies, with paid co-ordinators and a list of self-employed domestic workers. After the pilot projects were launched, all lower-dependency clients were gradually transferred to the new registers. All those transferred in this way paid no more for the service they now received than before, since the pilots provided a subsidy, although any new referrals to the registers had to pay the full cost themselves. Some big reductions in caseload were achieved in this way. The authority went on to encourage further expansion of independent domestic registers, particularly to provide competition for the one main provider. When the new home care management service was finally extended across the whole county in 1989, approximately 3,000 home help clients were transferred onto these registers.

As a result of these initiatives, by the time the Griffiths report (1988) and *Caring for People* (Secretaries of State, 1989b) appeared, the authority was well ahead of the game. It was introducing its case management system, and had succeeded in targeting home care services on high-dependency clients by fostering the development of independent sector provision for less dependent clients; it had also started to take on aspects of market management both by encouraging new providers and by starting to develop a regulatory framework through service specifications. Apart from some additional funds raised through encouraging take-up of attendance allowance and by raising its own charges, these changes took place without large injections of money. Overall the new home care service represented a contraction in the role of social services, targeting resources on a relatively small number of high-dependency clients, leaving no capacity for public support for preventive services other than grants to the voluntary sector.

The Process of Implementation
Underlying the whole process of these changes was the tension between those who wanted a fundamental review of the way domiciliary care was delivered, and those who were unwilling or unable to understand the degree of change required. This determined the decision to implement the less radical model, which sought to assimilate case management into existing patterns of provision and models of operation. The two development officers appointed to implement the pilot projects both had backgrounds in the home help service which may also have led to developments oriented towards more traditional practices. Little time was given to absorbing the lessons from the two pilot projects or for staff or clients to be reassured about the changes.

The decision to choose the less radical option may have appeared reasonable at the time, but it left some important areas unresolved. No separation was made between case management and resource management, in spite of the carefully argued case for a split in the original 1986 review. Subsequent development of a purchaser and provider separation in national policy meant that an opportunity had been missed, and a further period of reorganisation and change became necessary later on. The introduction of the new home care management service already represented a huge upheaval for the staff concerned and for those lower-dependency clients who were transferred to independent domestic registers.

LOCAL IMPLEMENTATION IN APRIL 1991

Developments Following 'Caring for People'
The *Caring for People* White Paper, when it eventually appeared in November 1989, endorsed many aspects of the authority's pioneering approach to community care development but went further in a number of respects. Whereas the changes already introduced represented a narrowing of the provider role by targeting an already modest level of provision on those with greatest need, the White Paper envisaged a more radical change, with LAs having only a residual provider function, focused on purchasing and the setting and monitoring of standards. Another aspect of this more radical vision was the

encouragement of LAs to use contracts to specify service provision more explicitly, whereas the authority had just negotiated and signed three-year service agreements with those agencies running domestic registers. The service agreements were not as elaborate as some of the contracts developed in other authorities. The clear separation of purchaser and provider roles and the floating-off of in-house local authority services to form independent units of provision were also outlined by the White Paper. Nonetheless, with its headstart the authority was in a strong position to set about planning and implementing a fairly radical interpretation of the new community care policy. Development continued between 1989 and 1991, and is illustrated in Box 13. Unlike many other authorities, it stood a good chance of having the necessary structures, systems and procedures in place by what was then the required implementation date of 1 April 1991.

BOX 13. DEVELOPMENT FROM NOVEMBER 1989 TO APRIL 1991

June/Sept. 1990   Auditors' reports

April 1991   Implementation of:
- inspection and complaints requirements;
- complete purchaser/provider split at area level;
- home care managers become care managers on purchasing side;
- contracts replace service agreements for independent domestic registers; and
- nine homes floated off into a trust.

In 1990 the authority asked its auditors to conduct a value-for-money study of its plans for implementing the community care proposals, and a number of reports were produced between June and September that year which only loosely followed the continuing SSI development programme (Utting, 1990). These reports broadly reflected senior management thinking, and informed decisions on subsequent developments in the run-up to the eventual phased implementation in April 1993.

The auditors endorsed the department's proposals to separate the purchaser and provider roles at the level of the social services area, and to give providers a semi-autonomous status. They suggested some refinements to the shape of the provider units, recommending that in each social services area in-house services should become 'independent business units' under an area general manager. Accurate unit costs should be calculated taking account of indirect costs, and factors such as future up-take rates and debt charges. Service-level agreements should be developed both for the purchase of care and for support services such as the personnel function. Such services were seen as vital to ensure an even playing field between in-house and independent providers. It was also suggested that purchaser budgets needed to be phased in gradually to allow in-house providers a period to get used to competition. Trading accounts should be established for marketing and similar purposes, and a financial management information system was needed.

The auditors also endorsed the authority's early decision for contracting with private and voluntary residential care providers, which was to promote maximum competition by working on a long approved list, and a similar approach was recommended for domiciliary care. The authority was already beginning the tendering and contracting process through publicity and advertising to prompt potential suppliers to come forward, and using questionnaires to collect better information about suppliers.

Perhaps more significantly, the auditors also suggested that, given the extension of the timetable for full implementation of the community care changes until April 1993, the authority should begin to move towards what it called a 'contract culture'. This involved developing more settled relationships with a limited number of providers in the interests of continuity and security of supply, and higher quality through better relationships between purchaser and provider, allowing early diagnosis and treatment of problems. While client choice would be more limited, case managers would be able to give fuller information about choices to clients. Such an approach could also give rise to economies of scale. A contract culture, they stated, involved the use of explicit criteria to make upfront decisions about which suppliers would be used. They also made recommendations about contract specifications, contract monitoring and the use of information derived from the tendering and contracting process.

The auditors also refined plans for new service development manager (SDM) posts in each social services area, responsible for the planning of services for elderly people and people with disabilities, for arranging and managing larger contracts on behalf of purchasers, negotiating local contracts and prices, monitoring performance and securing compliance, for representing the purchaser interests in dealing with in-house providers, for joint planning and for quality assurance. Care managers would be able to negotiate smaller, one-off contracts themselves with support from the SDM. Essentially, SDMs were meant to act as brokers who helped local purchasers get the best value for money.

The authority had already decided to make care managers budget-holders, but the auditors identified a number of issues still requiring attention.

- The need to think through the scope of the freedom to purchase once buyer budgets were introduced. In the short term, total freedom to purchase either in-house or independent services could pose unacceptable financial uncertainty for in-house providers and the department as a whole.

- The need to consider how to achieve a reasonable level of consistency between care managers in relation to budget deployment given the degree of discretion inherent in assessment and eligibility criteria.
- The importance of recognising the counselling element of care managers' work with clients, which should not be lost.
- The importance of an effective information system to provide care managers and senior managers with information on budgets, service availability and costs.
- The importance of effective training to ensure case managers were equipped with the broad range of skills and competencies required for their role.

The authority broadly followed the auditors' recommendations, and in April 1991 not only implemented the required inspection and complaints aspects of the White Paper, but also introduced a purchaser/provider split at area level. Home care managers became case managers on the purchasing side under divisional managers, so losing their provider role. The independent organisations running domestic registers had their service agreements changed to contracts in July 1991.

Although a considerable amount of work had been done in developing tender and specification documents for residential care, the postponement of income support transfers until 1993 meant that the authority's initial experience of contracts was for domiciliary care only. It had already achieved a degree of sophistication in this field, having developed an array of contracting-out and associated payment mechanisms flexible enough to suit different types and sizes of provider. Nine of the authority's homes (those which would be most difficult and costly to refurbish in line with registration requirements) were transferred to a trust which could raise finance for their refurbishment. The trust was given a five-year block contract to help it through the first difficult years before being exposed to competition. The department had also made some headway in developing a computerised care management information system, although it was not to be fully operational for some time, but the business units were still on the drawing-board at this stage.

The Process of Implementation
In making these recommendations, the auditors stressed the importance of managing the change carefully, particularly of ensuring effective communication between the centre, the areas and field staff. They also commented on the tension in the department between centre-led policy-making and the highly-decentralised approach to operations and service delivery, noting that the views of staff with direct operational responsibilities needed to be properly taken into account. They reported that many field staff felt distant from the changes, and the degree of uncertainty this inevitably created made it difficult for them to commit themselves to the changes, or to take responsibility for emerging problems. These remarks echo the earlier experience of the top-

down introduction of home care management and the degree of disruption caused at field level.

During 1990 a tremendous amount of work was undertaken to prepare for April 1991. Social services staff applied for or were slotted into the new posts either on the purchasing or providing side of the organisation and took on all the changes that implied. In-house and independent providers of domiciliary care attempted to cost their services accurately for the first time. And work was undertaken on systems and procedures to support care management and contracting, such as the design of specifications, service agreements and contracts, payment and information systems. The area restructuring process was such that most divisional managers (area purchasing managers) were still immersed in the day-to-day running of child care, so were unable to get to grips with their purchasing role until early 1991. As a result, the tendering process for domiciliary care was dealt with by the county supplies department until such time as the purchasers had the capacity to take it on, so at this stage the changes were still centrally driven.

Home care managers became case managers on the purchasing side of the organisation in April 1991, leading to another period of upheaval for field staff following swiftly after the introduction of home care management at the end of 1989. This was also a difficult period for the agencies running independent registers. No sooner had they signed three-year service agreements than they were issued with the specified one year's notice of termination, and told that they would have to bid for new contracts to come into force in July 1991. This announcement caused much concern to the voluntary agencies currently running the registers, although it was welcomed by private providers who felt it created a level playing field. Other concerns revolved around potential cashflow problems, such as what would happen if social services area offices ran out of money, the potential loss of preventative services if the authority contracted only for higher-dependency services, the constitutional problems for the voluntary sector, and the fear that contracts would go to those who shouted loudest. These considerations led to some adjustments to the plans for the new system as they evolved at social services headquarters. For instance, originally independent providers were simply to have been accredited by the SSD on the basis of an agreed unit cost and quality control measures, but would not have had a guaranteed volume of work. However, since demand for domiciliary care is relatively unpredictable, providers needed some idea of the volume of work that they would receive in order to be able to calculate unit costs. In the event, in 1990 providers were able to bid for a domiciliary contract let in multiples of 5,000 hours to commence in 1991. Furthermore, contracts which were initially to be for only one year were eventually granted for three years as standard to provide a stable and viable base for providers.

FULL IMPLEMENTATION IN APRIL 1993

Developments to April 1993

Changes in social services senior management in late 1991 heralded a more open and participative style of management, although the commitment to achieving a level playing field to encourage competition, and a policy of gradual externalisation of provision through contracting out or floating off in-house services, remained largely intact. A new project management group was established to prepare the ground for April 1993, which brought together lead managers from key agencies at area level to work on essential issues of implementation, both as determined locally and in line with the requirements of the Foster/Laming letters of March and September 1992. Topics covered included assessment and eligibility criteria, charging and income collection, infrastructure support such as information systems, hospital discharge arrangements, contracting for residential and nursing home care from April 1993, and funding and monitoring arrangements.

During 1992/93 the authority worked to clarify a strategic direction for the next three to five years, especially to identify the essential core services required, either by providing them directly or from external providers. The proportion of direct services was expected to diminish over time. The strategy also sought to clarify the role of care managers, social workers and occupational therapists as a result of the separation of purchaser and provider functions, by recognising that these staff straddled the divide. There was no need for absolute purity of the purchaser/provider split in the organisation of these tasks, although care manager and social worker teams were to remain accountable to the commissioning side of the authority. It was anticipated that social workers would remain the main occupational group for work with children and families, and mental health, while care managers would predominate in elderly and disability teams. Successive drafts of this strategy paper were produced for consultation, which gave rise to some changes, particularly a softening of the policy on externalisation.

The purchaser/provider split. When the purchaser/provider split was originally introduced, it was expected to evolve over time. By 1992 adjustments were needed as it was unclear where commissioning took place, especially at area level, since both purchasing managers (and beneath them care managers) and service development managers were involved in identifying gaps and developing services. There was also an increasing need to reduce overheads and simplify management lines to ensure that spending was directed predominantly to the purchase of services, since establishing the contracting infrastructure had increased unit costs significantly.

The service development function was left intact, but a number of changes were made to the commissioning and providing arms at area level. For example, the number of purchasing managers was reduced to two per area (one for adults, one for children) and renamed 'commissioners', with responsibility to enhance the commissioning function and drive forward the whole process of purchasing and contracting. Existing team managers (managing teams of care managers) were reorganised into a smaller number of locality managers, with a more strategic and managerial role. Those not appointed became senior practitioners working under the new locality managers to provide day-to-day supervision of care managers. Budgets were devolved to care managers for April 1993. The locality manager monitored the budget, ensuring staff operated within agreed parameters. On the provider side, general managers were no longer to be full members of the area commissioning group, although they would still have a say in area strategy.

Strategy for provision. Having identified the essential core services required by the authority, the strategy paper outlined criteria to determine those which might need to be directly provided and those from external suppliers. The authority produced a statement of its criteria.

(a) We have a statutory duty to make sure they are directly provided by the LA;
(b) We provide them because the external market is unable or unwilling to provide them to the standards determined in the department's specifications and at a price the department is willing to pay;
(c) We elect to provide a proportion of a service because it would be ill-advised to be over-reliant on external providers; and
(d) Where we consider that consumer choice and/or public expectation of public provision in the mixed economy is an essential ingredient. Hence, it follows that in some instances, it would be appropriate to retain a market share.

A number of service areas needing to remain directly-provided were also identified:

- assessment services (including care management, social work and occupational therapy);
- child protection services;
- approved social worker services;
- resource centres (former residential homes adapted to include a range of other services);
- day care and social education services for the most highly dependent group of people with a learning disability; and
- services for people with challenging behaviour.

The strategy review noted that, with few exceptions, the law permits rather than prescribes what services must be provided directly, and that the department would take 'a pragmatic and common sense view when considering criterion (a)'. Decisions concerning the proportions of different services to be retained as direct services required more detailed knowledge of the stability and longer-term intentions of external providers, which would be accrued from the purchasing decisions of care managers and from a review of the strategy to be conducted in 1994/5.

Managing directly-provided services. It was proposed that some directly-provided services (whether direct care or support services) should be turned into in-house business units (IBUs) which would operate on a trading account basis without subsidy from the council, and would in due course be subject to competition. IBUs would have the potential to become fully external, providing they established their viability through successful participation in competitive tendering for contracts. The IBU idea dated back to the 1990 audit reports, but had not yet been progressed. The original intention was that IBUs would be progressively exposed to full market competition in preparation for floating-off as fully independent external services, but by 1992 they were no longer seen as a transition phase to independent status. The authority was still pursuing a policy of externalisation by contracting out services to the independent sector, and the ruling that 85 per cent of the special transitional grant for community care should be spent on independent sector services meant the proportion of externally-provided services would gradually increase. However, the strategy paper outlined proposals for piloting a limited number of IBUs. But by early 1994 this strategy had been overtaken by the lack of sufficient capital to bring some resource centres up to registration standard, so the department was looking to find an external provider to take over these establishments. The piloting of resource centres as possible IBUs went on the back-burner pending the result of the local government review of the county later in the year.

The final stages. In February 1993 the community care project management group reported progress to the social services committee. The paper dealt with the specific implementation areas identified in the Foster/Laming letters of March and September 1992, under six headings:

- individual assessment of need and criteria of eligibility;
- charging for services and income collection;
- infrastructure support for community care implementation;
- agreements with DHAs regarding hospital discharge arrangements;
- contracting for residential and nursing home care from April 1993; and
- community care funding and monitoring arrangements.

The report outlined the progress that had been made in each of these areas, but stressed particularly that the oversupply of residential and nursing home beds within the county was likely to lead to some instability, with a risk of at least some home owners leaving the market, leading to serious repercussions for existing residents and for the local economy. The policy would therefore be to play a role in enabling local residential and nursing home providers to diversify to provide a wider range of services — including domiciliary, day and respite care — in line with needs identified in community care plans. This could be achieved by working with other organisations such as economic development agencies, training and enterprise councils and other small business advice agencies, both to assist those who wished to move out of the market altogether, as well as those who wanted to diversify.

The Process of Implementation

The change in management. New leadership brought a number of changes in emphasis. First, there was some loosening of eligibility criteria. The original intention had been that only people assessed as high dependency would receive a publicly-funded service, together with former home help clients who would continue to be subsidised. Under new arrangements each area was required to allocate a budget for this purpose. The May 1993 local elections also created a change in political leadership, when Conservatives lost power to an uneasy alliance of Liberal Democrats and Labour, but the new social services committee allocated new resources for people falling outside the high-dependency eligibility criteria. Those receiving these new services were informally termed 'medium dependency', although this had no formal definition, and were means-tested using the same financial assessment as high-dependency care-managed service.

The position over externalising services had also been substantially modified, with a good deal more caution over the benefits of market forces, and this was reinforced by the change in political leadership. The more open management style was reflected in the project-managed approach to preparation for full implementation in April 1993. In 1992 the department established a programme of work bringing together lead managers from key agencies at area level to work on important aspects of implementation: assessment and eligibility criteria, charging and income collection, infrastructure support such as information systems, hospital discharge arrangements, contracting for residential and nursing home care from April 1993, and funding and monitoring arrangements. This appeared to have been more successful in harnessing area creativity and commitment to change.

Care management. In preparation for April 1993, the most highly qualified and experienced care managers were moved into hospital settings to facilitate discharge arrangements, although they still found themselves operating within a traditional hospital social work role, giving benefit advice and counselling. Two issues were of major importance in 1993/4 and thereafter: ensuring fast and efficient hospital discharge, and avoiding long-term residential and nursing home placements where possible and appropriate. The use of joint assessment beds for high-dependency clients prior to discharge and paid for by the health authority, and the use of respite care beds and short-term placements in residential homes, were being developed or discussed.

Three joint assessment pilots had been established in 1991/2 to test out three separate levels of assessment: level 1 was linked to the screening by GPs of the over-75 population; level 2 drew together care managers and district nurses to conduct joint community assessments; and level 3 concerned assessment for admission to residential or nursing home care. Other initiatives included the drafting of joint eligibility criteria alongside the pilots for access to case-managed services, long-term care and community nursing services; the alignment of care managers for elderly people with GP practices through-out the county; a referral form to be used as the basis for an exchange of information on referrals between GPs and social services; and an information system for the exchange of other information between GPs and care managers.

The process of assessment and care management is outlined in Box 14. A number of issues arose in relation to this system. The purchaser/provider split meant that domiciliary care managers were not able to match a worker to a client, although they could match clients with a provider agency which they felt would offer the most appropriate service. Care managers also tended to receive information on the client third hand once a care package had been established.

For people who did not meet the eligibility criteria for a case-managed service and for whom it was cheaper, or who preferred to arrange their own care, care managers could help with alternative sources of care by giving them a list of local providers. Teams were also able to exercise a degree of discretion within broad eligibility criteria and within the confines of their budgets.

The authority continued to remain at the forefront of good practice in relation to assessment and care management in three ways. First, additional posts were created in 1993/4 to undertake financial assessments, separating financial assessment from needs assessments in line with good practice out-lined in the SSI theme study on assessment (Department of Health, 1994e). Social services and the local health authorities were also exploring ways for NHS staff such as district nurses to take on care management roles with appropriate support, access to purchasing budgets and training. This is again is in line with good practice identified in the SSI care management study (Department of Health, 1994d). The authority was also piloting the con-tracting-out of care management for reviewing the increasing numbers of residential and nursing home placements. Experience in Canada has been that residential care reviews took up an increasing proportion of case man-agers' time, eating into the opportunities for community work (Challis, 1994). By separating out long-term care reviews which do not require the full range of assessment skills, care managers can target their scarce time on new and complex assessments.

Purchasing and contracting. The authority introduced four types of purchasing arrangement according to what was being purchased from whom (see Box 15).

BOX 14. THE PROCESS OF ASSESSMENT AND CARE
MANAGEMENT

All referrals for care are channelled through the duty system at a resource centre where they go to a case allocation meeting. After an initial screening by a care management team, people likely to need a care management service receive a fuller assessment. A person is eligible to receive care management services if they have complex needs requiring intensive and wide-ranging support. The factors taken into account are physical and mental/emotional state, intellectual development, informal support, financial management, and environmental factors. These clients are categorised as high dependency. There is also a medium-dependency category including people requiring more than two but less than five hours help per week, who are on income support and who have a pressing need for help which cannot be provided informally. Such clients receive subsidised services.

If assessment indicates low dependency, the client is informed that they are not eligible for publicly-funded care, and are given a list of local independent providers to approach independently if they so wish.

If high dependency is indicated, the client is entitled to a care-managed package of care. A joint assessment document is completed and placed in the client's home, together with the care plan document. High-dependency clients are given a choice of providers from the range of contractors with hours available. If the service level agreement with in-house providers is undersubscribed, a locality manager interviewed said that a care manager might suggest to a client that they choose this service, although they can choose from alternative services. The private nursing agency and a number of smaller agencies can provide personal care to high-dependency clients under contract.

If an independent agency is chosen, the care manager draws up a service delivery order (SDO) which is sent to the contractor. The SDO includes details of the care required: tasks, numbers of hours together with details of the client's GP, key contact points and so on. There is also space for other information to be added, such as access difficulties. The contractor holds the SDO and invoices the relevant social services area office at four-weekly intervals. These bills are checked for accuracy by a rehabilitation officer.

The decentralisation of budgets. The authority remained committed to devolved budgets for individual managers, but in reality the process was incremental, partly because it had to take place alongside many other organisational changes, and partly because good information and accounting systems needed to be in place beforehand. By early 1994 not all budgets had been devolved, and the speed with which they were being decentralised varied from area to area. Budgets for people with learning difficulties were not yet devolved because of overspend on residential care. But budgets for domiciliary and, in most cases, residential care had been passed down to locality manager level, and the latter would notionally allocate them to individual care managers. The STG resources were also held by locality managers and would only be devolved a year or two after April 1993, once the likely patterns of

---

BOX 15. THE FOUR TYPES OF PURCHASING ARRANGEMENT

- *Service-level agreements (SLAs)* are for in-house services and comprise an agreement between component parts of the same organisation, for instance between the SSD and the legal department, or between a purchaser and an in-house business unit. The SLAs specify volume of services at unit cost and are let on a non-competitive basis.
- *Agency agreements (AAs)* are for voluntary organisations; they are not contracts under law since there is no intention to create legal relations. The authority would not take them to court if there was a problem, but might not use them again. An AA might be negotiated, for example with Age Concern for the provision of day care or transport.
- *Contracts* are issued in competitive circumstances for a specific service over a specified period at an agreed level and cost, to a specification. The intention is to obtain best value for money. Contracts have been issued to voluntary and not-for-profit organisations, for instance for domestic register services, as well as to for-profit organisations and in-house business units.
- *Grants* will continue to exist in order to pump-prime individual projects and to cover one-off expenses in the voluntary and not-for-profit sectors, in recognition of their inability to raise capital and take risks.

---

expenditure became clearer. Most of the domiciliary budget was already committed in block agreements and contracts with in-house and independent providers. Block agreements and contracts also existed for in-house resource centres and the nine homes that had been floated off as a trust. A limited cash element was available for spot contracting, which varied in size from team to team.

Home Care

The specification for home care contracts was developed (and in subsequent years adjusted) in consultation with practitioners and providers. In the first few years, the county supplies department, which had some expertise in contract letting, had responsibility for drawing up the contract. This contract was circulated to all potential providers, who could bid for blocks of a minimum of 5,000 hours of home care. Over time, more flexibility has emerged, with new or small agencies being allocated smaller blocks of work, although the principle of the minimum of 5,000 hours remains. The service development management section of each area also visits interested providers to ensure they can fulfil the terms of the contract, and also monitors subsequent performance. The volume of work specified in contracts was guaranteed, and additional components could be arranged over and above this. Care managers are also able to spot contract with non-contracted agencies if their own budget permits, although there is inevitably pressure to use up the hours already negotiated with particular agencies.

The degree of local control of contracts varied from area to area, including the degree of freedom care managers had to choose between contract-holding agencies, and to negotiate spot contracts. In at least one area, care managers were using spot contracts to test new agencies, prior to recommending them for block contracts.

The 'service provision groups' (SPG) — the name given to the provider side of each area following the purchaser/provider split — agreed a specified volume of services with area purchasers based on what the latter wanted to purchase. This was laid down in a service-level agreement. In general, the existing level of expenditure on in-house home care was ring-fenced from 1991, with all expansion of provision being contracted to independent providers to help ensure the authority achieved the special transitional grant 85 per cent target. Over time, therefore, the proportion of domiciliary care provided by in-house providers will decline in relation to independent sector care. Differences in unit costs and prices among independent suppliers are tolerated in the interests of continuity, quality of care and variety.

Residential Care

A residential care contract for elderly people was introduced in August 1993, a few months after the department assumed responsibility for funding residents eligible for public funding. Unlike the domiciliary care contract, this does not include a guaranteed volume of work, and there are no retained places since there is an oversupply of beds. Instead, private and voluntary homes are placed on an approved list. It is the providers, therefore, who run the risk of demand not matching their supply. It was forecast that there would be fewer new placements after April 1993 than in the past. Given the oversupply of beds, this could lead to major problems for providers, with knock-on effects for existing residents and the local economy. The authority's policy, therefore, is to enable homes that wish to do so to diversify into service areas where there is unmet demand, such as home care services in rural areas. In-house residential facilities were being developed into resource centres which, it was planned, would become in-house business units in due course. These resource centres were already diversifying in 1992/3 into assessment, rehabilitation and post-discharge convalescence so were expected to compete well. No mainstream residential provision was to be retained in-house, and nine homes were hived off in 1991 into a housing trust with charitable status.

Day Care

A contract for day care remained a possibility, although it was unclear in 1992/3 whether this would be a block and volume basis like domiciliary care, or an approved list basis like residential care. The authority's resource centres provide day care, and it was likely that expansion other than in these centres would be developed externally. In-house provision would target high-dependency clients, providing respite for their carers. Agency agreements with local voluntary sector providers were also being negotiated to commence in 1993.

Joint Purchasing and Provision
Links were gradually emerging at a strategic commissioning level between senior social services, district health authority and FHSA staff. At area level, initiatives such as jointly-funded beds in private and voluntary homes are developing. Housing authorities are also getting involved. Joint working with a large health commissioning agency has identified a number of areas for joint commissioning, such as specialist EMI day care, assessment beds, and the provision of social day care and day hospital facilities on the same site. On the provider side, there were signs that in-house providers (and probably independent ones also) were beginning to court GP fundholders. Examples of possible deals included the use of resource centre beds for rehabilitation as they are cheaper and more appropriate than hospital beds.

SUMMARY OF APPROACH AND ISSUES RAISED

The authority remained ahead of other local authorities in a number of ways throughout the period of implementation of the community care legislation, including its policy of care management for elderly people, purchasing and contracting, and the development of information systems. In other fields they have been less good. The model of care management outlined in *Caring for People* (Secretaries of State, 1989b) is similar to that developed by the authority in its experiments and later programmes from the mid-1970s. This local model was developed for elderly people as a way of providing predominantly practical help, but by 1993 the authority still had some way to go in developing the detail of assessment, and in combining elements of assessment, support and delivery.

While many authorities were taken up with the problems of residential care, home care services were high up the authority's agenda by 1990, and care management was already an established operational feature of departmental practice. The authority was also remarkably bold in its development of purchasing and contracting systems for domiciliary care, proceeding with market development and the purchase of care from voluntary and private providers by the late 1980s. Having started early, the authority was able to develop a degree of sophistication in working with independent providers and managing the market before many other authorities had even started.

The authority generally adopted a strategic approach to change, both back in the mid-1980s when considering how domiciliary services should develop, and more recently in implementing the community care legislation. Nevertheless, it still appears to have reacted like many other authorities in emphasising structural issues, and managerial and organisational change. It gave less priority to practice and process issues at lower levels. It was less good at evaluation, and at developing a user orientation, or in involving field staff effectively.

Lack of attention to how staff at middle management and field level would respond to and cope with change was a feature of the authority's approach throughout the period reviewed in this chapter. The problems associated with a 'top-down' style of management were noted both by a Health Advisory Services report on one area in 1990, and by the auditors who assisted the authority with its market development plans in the same year. The more open style of management emerging since 1991 showed signs of starting to address this problem.

Issues

The review of community care policy and implementation in the authority raises a number of issues in relation to structure and organisation, care management training, and market development and management, which are relevant to other social services departments.

Local government review. The large size of the authority enabled it to commission outside professional help in strategic planning, such as the value-for-money study conducted by its auditors. Smaller authorities, such as London boroughs, may not have the financial power to buy in such help. The local government review is likely to divide the authority into a number of unitary authorities, while health commissioning agencies are in the process of amalgamating. While the creation of smaller units would help bring decision-making closer to users and remove certain bureaucratic costs and problems, these smaller authorities may individually lack the capacity for strategic planning of the sophistication and quality demonstrated by the county authority to date. Furthermore, access to services would increasingly be determined by where a person lived.

Care manager training and development. Attention will need to be paid to the training and development of care managers. In the authority's structure they straddle the boundary between purchasing and provision. In assessing clients and constructing care packages, they have a high degree of discretion within broad eligibility criteria. They must also become increasingly computer-literate, and budgetary responsibility is gradually being devolved to them. Care managers consequently need effective training to enable them to operate in a far more complex environment, and to achieve a level of standardisation, so that people of equal need living in different areas have equal access to care. This training must take account of the diverse backgrounds of post-holders from home help, social work and occupational therapy, as well as clerical positions. The relatively weak position of field-level workers has perhaps been a product of the authority's emphasis on management and structure.

Transaction costs. Transaction costs are those associated with organising and regulating services. Such increased costs are inherent in managing a mixed economy, although these costs may be justified by the social objectives of change, such as improved choice, flexibility, and a more local, responsive service. The authority's new contracting arrangements have clearly given rise to increased costs, both from the creation of new service development posts at area level, and from meeting specified standards of services. The latter was causing some concern among purchasers at area level, since budgets did not go as far as they had done previously. For instance, unit costs for residential care for people with learning difficulties and physical disabilities had risen significantly by up to 10-15 per cent. Domiciliary care costs had also risen. It may be possible for the intended outcomes of the community care reforms (choice, flexibility, value for money) to be achieved without a full-blown mixed economy, and that transaction costs can thereby be limited. Comparison over time of the experience of authorities using different approaches will indicate whether this is true.

The development and management of social care markets. The authority's experience of developing and managing community services suggests a number of opportunities and barriers to an emerging mixed economy of care. Independent agencies reported difficulties in recruiting workers in rural areas because of the time (and therefore cost) spent travelling to reach people living in sparsely populated areas. In-house home care services had encountered the same problem over the years. Providing evening and weekend cover was also a difficulty common to all providers. In at least one area, there were reports of private agencies pulling out of contracts because they had underpriced themselves, could not make a profit from providing services in antisocial hours, and because they could not sustain the staffing levels required. The reluctance or inability of 'the market' to fill problem niches is well documented in other sectors. It highlights the limits of market efficiency, and provides one of the key arguments in favour of government intervention.

A service development officer and a number of purchasers commented that the size of provider was significant in relation to quality and reliability. Some organisations that had provided good quality and value for money when small had deteriorated as they grew, losing 'the personal touch' and failing to provide 'quality monitoring'. Some very small providers, on the other hand, lacked an adequate infrastructure and the ability to provide cover. The conclusion drawn was that middle-sized organisations (in domiciliary care terms, those providing 10-20,000 hours per year) were ideal, and that the authority would (and already was doing so in some cases) pay a premium to ensure the availability of good-quality care on this scale. Interestingly, Kamien and Schwartz (1982) also suggest that an industry with many moderate to large firms, and a structure intermediate between monopoly and perfect competition, will have the highest rate of innovation.

Such issues of competitive edge arose time and again in the experience of the authority. In-house home care services were vulnerable because they could not compete on a cost basis since they were tied to nationally agreed terms and conditions of service. In-house home care services in some areas were reported to compete well on the basis of quality, while others did not. Other factors affecting the future of in-house home care were that only 15 per cent of the DSS transfer could be spent purchasing in-house services, and the fact that the cost of large-scale redundancies would be prohibitive. Consequently, the size of in-house services in real terms was likely to remain broadly constant, with any expansion of services targeted on the independent sector.

One local general manager identified a number of niches where he felt in-house services could compete well: providing half-hour slots of care which many independent agencies would not do; covering rural areas and anti-social hours; caring for heavily dependent clients; and testing innovative ideas. He saw partnership with and subcontracting to other providers, including independent ones, as a survival mechanism for the future. Such measures would share skills, facilities and other resources in order to offer a comprehensive service to purchasers.

The authority had begun by developing a market in social care from 1990 onwards, and had by 1993 moved into the field of market management. This involves 'managing down' the residential and nursing home markets while at the same time 'managing up' markets for domiciliary and other services (Wistow et al., 1994). The need for independent homes to diversify because of overprovision, and the authority's policy to assist them in this, has already been noted, but this is by no means a unique issue to the authority. In 1993 the Department of Health in collaboration with KPMG Peat Marwick produced a practical manual for home providers (KPMG, 1993).

A number of innovative schemes began to emerge nationally in the mid-1990s, such as existing well-placed providers setting up community care package franchises which market diversification schemes to home-owners. Similar moves had occurred in the authority, with forward-looking, well-managed homes agreeing contracts with the authority to provide services such as meals and domiciliary provision. Whittingham (1993) suggests that local authorities can facilitate diversification through such means as information on service gaps, developing and sharing design principles, publishing service specifications, providing start-up funding and involving economic development units. The authority's approach was very similar to this. Local alliances and mergers between small home owners are also a way forward, and have already been adopted by some domiciliary agencies in the authority in order to achieve the capacity for a 5,000-hour block contract.

But both Whittingham (1993) and headquarters managers of the authority recognise that diversification was not the answer to acute financial crisis, but was rather a means of building on and reinforcing successful services and adding a competitive edge. The disaster scenario of many homes going out of business has not yet happened either nationally or in the case study authority, with the number of homes in the county actually increasing (over and above the number of small homes having to register for the first time). However, there were homes with high levels of vacancies, and in receivership, and homes were changing hands, although the authority had not yet had to intervene.

CONCLUSION

It is clear that the case study authority was among that relatively small number of authorities pioneering many of the fundamental principles of the new community care reforms. Nonetheless, many of the issues, problems and contradictions now beginning to be experienced by all authorities can be identified within the process of policy implementation. Among the more significant issues to emerge are the crucial importance of developing an effective local care management system based on a sound information technology infrastructure, and comprehensive decentralisation of budgets, but within an overall strategic policy framework and clear practice and eligibility criteria. Despite the lack of emphasis on this in the eight key implementation tasks identified by the first Foster/Laming Letter of March 1992, the authority was able to continue with these developments because of its early experience of integrating care management into mainstream practice. Many other authorities were not so fortunate.

A second important issue relates to the systematic emphasis on organisational, structural and management issues, at the expense of better training, procedures and process activities for the staff required to implement the new systems. The fact that the authority was at the leading edge of such systems development gave it a much greater opportunity to engage front-line and middle management staff in these activities than seems to have been the case in practice.

Despite these reservations, the case study gives a very clear and graphic picture of the struggle of one local authority to translate its own emerging vision of community care into a local reality for users, carers and staff alike which, while inevitably unique in its own way, reflects the multiple difficulties of complex policy change and implementation in any type of public service bureaucracy.

PART THREE
THE CURRENT POSITION

12 Emerging Conclusions

THE POLICY DEVELOPMENT PROCESS

During the past decade the UK has made more progress than almost any other country in developing a radical and coherent community care policy for the new century. There may be better places in which to succumb to disability in old age, but since 1985 few have been so ambitious in transforming their policy framework to the emerging new social policy goals of user and carer empowerment, more efficient and effective use of resources, and clarity over ends and means. Still fewer countries have done so much to ensure operational field agencies adopted local versions of this policy. The change has been rapid and dramatic, and while the outcomes and implications are still far from clear, we believe that a review of the process of adoption and implementation of the policy begins to suggest further policy adaptations that may now be needed in response to this early experience.

By comparison with most other developed countries, the UK has long had one of the most straightforward structures of long-term care — much less complex than the American, Australian, Dutch and French systems, for instance. But despite this apparent simplicity, many important features were in conflict, both with each other and with achieving the ends and means of modern community and long-term care. From the early 1980s radical new argument began to emerge from a variety of perspectives and eventually worked their way through to a new model for community and long-term care of hitherto unparalleled logical coherence. A version of the model was formally adopted in the 1990 NHS and Community Care Act, and has since then been slowly elaborated and worked through at national and local levels.

The history of this process is one of the more interesting attempts to modernise community and long-term care, and ranks as a case study with

Australia and some of the American states, rather than the countries of continental Europe, where policy reforms have either been more modest (as in Austria and Germany) or hesitant (as in the Netherlands). In the early part of this book we have described these developments in broad detail, but in this chapter we place this history into a more specific policy context, before turning to look in more detail at the implications of the implementation process itself. The focus of the paper is on policy for the majority of elderly persons in need, not community and long-term care for those with mental health problems or learning disabilities, where there are important differences in both the distribution of resources and the assumptive relationships between inputs and outcomes (Kavanagh et al., 1995).

We begin by outlining the structures and assumptions of the world into which these new ideas were born, and then consider the conjunction of events and arguments during the first half of the 1980s which converged to make existing policy untenable, and we discusses some of the more important critiques of the old order — not the academic critiques from policy research on community care commissioned by government, because that was intended to impact (and did, in fact, impact) mainly through the thinking in independent state-commissioned reports and policy agencies. We then move on to outline the logic of the model which emerged, showing how it related to its origins, and then how the policy was elaborated at the national level for the benefit of field agencies. After considering each of these stages in turn, we review in more detail the more significant features of the implementation process at both national and local levels, before concluding with a brief outline of some of the potential implications of our analysis of these developments.

The Structures and Assumptions of the 1970s

The features of critical importance were: first, the concentration of policy-making and political accountability, public financing and provision in one organisation with direct political accountability at the national level, and in two organisations at the local level; and second, the contrasting financing principles built into the key legislation for the new local authority social service departments and the National Health Service. Compared with many other countries, what is most striking is the authority, policy scope and functions, and scale of the lead organisations.

The national organisation was the Department of Health and Social Security. The legitimacy of the authority, scale of resources, span of control and political influence of the Department was well established by tradition. Its concentration of authority, responsibility and political accountability contrasts with central agencies in systems built around the separation of powers and distribution of responsibilities between central government agencies each competing at the margin for functions (as in the USA), and with federal systems with responsibilities either at the second level of government or with shared and divided responsibilities between state and federal levels (as in the USA, Germany or Australia).

During the late 1960s, the Wilsonian belief in social modernisation through resource planning was being injected into a cultural tradition which John Griffith's seminal study (1965) of central-local relations described as 'laissez-faire' compared with other central departments. However, the DHSS assumed a more proactive role during the brief periods in which expenditure planning was most in vogue. It was reflected in the attempt at the planning of the health and social services during the early 1960s and early 1970s. In essence, the policy and style of the DHSS in the 1970s was the product of a political fashion for planning across government as a whole more than it was the product of the community care policy network itself.

While the concentration of power within superministries potentially increased rather than reduced the capacity to achieve co-ordination across ministries, a *leitmotif* of policy analysis from the 1960s (CPRS, 1975; Challis et al., 1988), two crucial elements — housing policy for the elderly and the general policy for central-local relations — were (and remain) on the wrong side of a divide between superministries.[1]

At local level, health authorities and local authority social services departments provided most of the collectively-delivered care, had political responsibility for co-ordinating the development of the system, were responsible for most quality assurance activities, and provided the public finance. The local health authorities were appointed bodies, dominated by the medical professionals until the 1980s, accountable to central government for the implementation of national policy. There had been a long-term trend to give priority to the core health services: acute medical care, and primary and community health services. From the 1950s, some patterns of hospital-based geriatric practice made the geriatric consultant an effective interface between the acute care system and the system of long-term care and, for many cases, potentially (and in some cases, actually) a leader of teams which spanned the then health/social care boundary. This was widely envied in Anglo-Saxon writing, and imitated in several countries.[2] The 'general practitioner' — more truly a 'family doctor' than in many European countries — responsible for co-ordinating some primary and community health services and placed at the gate of the acute care system was also a crucial NHS focus for making community care work. However, the British system was internationally notable for the relatively small scale of NHS community care responsibilities compared to the much larger scale of the local authorities'. Following the reforms of the health and social services of the early 1970s, each organisation became more not less self-absorbed in its own structures and responsibilities, at the expense of more effective co-ordination.

In the early 1980s local authorities had a wide range of other responsibilities in addition to social care services for which it was provider, planner and financier. The local authority is directly elected, raising its own tax, but with rapidly diminished power to vary it. To contemporaries, as to those writing about the local government of the 1960s in retrospect, local government was 'more concerned with patronage than policy' (Bulpitt, 1967). Management was based on the hegemony of professional expertise and knowledge, and structured to be a service provider, and as such 'the activities to be carried out are largely prescribed, if not in statute, then in the past working of the authority' (Stewart, 1986, p.10). The dominant features of local authority management were the committee which controlled the department (which considered detail for decision by the local politicians, tended to undermine officer responsibility for broad policy development and lead to the 'fudging' of issues); a bureaucratic style (reflecting principles of top-down hierarchy, uniformity of treatment of persons and cases, and of functional organisation of service at the expense of breadth and flexibility); and of professional influence on perceptions of issues, leading to conservatism and paternalism, the subordination of adaptiveness to changing needs, and 'a concentration on the service rather than on those served' (Simey, 1985, p.5).

Case studies described how local politicians became absorbed by the culture (Dearlove, 1973). Some described how the same councillors would move from the profession-led assumptive worlds of one committee to those of another, and take decisions in each based on inconsistent premises as a result (Minns, 1972). The agenda from the 1960s was to transform local authorities. They had been seen as mere providers of services by loosely co-ordinated departments, almost as loose federations of spending departments, as one of us described them at that time (Davies, 1971). Each department was dominated by one profession. The reformers of the period sought to make them into policy-making bodies, setting priorities between services and to an increasing degree for the territory as a whole. They were to recruit members and officers of higher calibre, and to import some management ideas from the private sector (Mallaby Committee, 1967; Maud Committee, 1967; Royal Commission, 1968; Bains Committee, 1972; Stewart, 1973).

Perhaps to a smaller degree than the Royal Commission and the Maud report, the Seebohm Committee recognised these problems. Parts of the argument reflected the new ideas of the late 1960s. But its actual recommendations and the argument which supported them can now be read for what they were: extrapolations of the Fabian traditions of those who had lobbied for it, and who were well represented by its members (Hall, 1976). The reasons quoted by Seebohm Committee (1968) for the 'growing sense of dissatisfaction' with services included factors other than 'inadequacies in the amount of provision', and 'inadequacies of quality due to lack of staff time and training and old buildings of bad design'. They also included features whose implications for organisation and practice came to be seen differently fifteen years later: 'inadequacies in the range of provision' for needs for which 'no service has a clearly defined responsibility', and for which the services offered 'may not be considered to be the most appropriate'; poor co-ordination in the face of complex needs and the desirability of meeting them 'in a comprehensive fashion'; and 'insufficient adaptability' in the face of changing needs.

The main Seebohm recommendation was for the creation of major new local authority social services departments, with a broad range of service provision and related functions. Other recommendations reflected the general structures of the time rather than anticipated later ideas: for example, the heavy emphasis on social work and the failure to work through the distinction between social work and social care; or the cursory discussion of the co-ordination of acute, community and primary health services with social care; the nature of social planning envisaged; and the creation of a unified family service to solve the problems of co-ordination.

However, what the development by the mid-1970s provided was a local agency of much greater scale than heretofore, recruiting a new and better educated generation of officers, with the authority to take a wide view of social needs and lead the development of the local system of social care, set in an emerging local authority culture in which the agenda was to transform the traditional task of service provision into agencies with a real focus on local policy development and implementation.

Finally, it is important to stress that the post-war legislation provided that core NHS services were financed from the national tax fund, and were free to all users regardless of circumstances and ability to pay, whereas local authorities were to be financed from a central grant supplemented by local taxation and charges to users. The legal obligation was to subsidise the consumption of the poor, not of all users. The subsidy was to diminish fast as the central government squeezed the finances of local authorities from the mid-1970s. From then on these contrasting financing principles became opposing financing principles, and have continued to increase in significance.

The Confluence of Policy-Shaping Ideas and Events: 1974-86

The reforms were the product of the conjunction of events and ideas of the decade starting in the late 1970s. The most powerful forces were those which influenced all public policy, not the critiques of community and long-term care itself, although it was the critique which provided the specific goals and instruments. The critique channelled the broader forces as much as the broader forces adapted the solutions suggested by the critiques. One of the most important events was the oil crisis and the collapse of growth-focused economic policy, resulting in devaluation, strait-jacketed economic policy, the search for cuts in public expenditure, and the break-up of the basis for co-operation between employers, unions and the government. This was one part of the context in which Rose (1975) and others discussed 'government overload': the increasing ambition of policy aims and the increasing gap between performance and expectations. The performance of the traditional agencies of the local welfare state were challenged from different quarters with criticisms first heard during the 1960s. They had much in common, including unresponsiveness to user needs and wishes. By the late 1970s, there were academic critiques of inflexibility and targeting in a wide range of policy areas, including community care (Davies, 1981; Goldberg and Connelly, 1982). In health and social services policy-making, the initial effect of the turmoil of the mid-1970s was to halt progress in implementing old policies without replacing it with a new long-term strategy.

The failure of corporatism was accompanied by a stream of argument from the 'new right' in policy analysis, 'think tanks' echoing for broad public consumption the theoretical arguments of American public choice economists and others. The inflexibility and inefficiencies of government were interpreted as the inevitable tendencies of public bureaucracies. Competitive markets were promoted as an alternative to the inherent weaknesses of public bureaucracies, leading to the 'privatisation' of public utilities and enterprises, the creation of autonomous agencies to perform functions hitherto undertaken by government, the reform of the NHS around the purchaser/provider split, and the 'local management of schools'. Accountability through the ballot box in a public bureaucracy was contrasted by Michael Heseltine with accountability to consumers in a market, and the latter promoted as a better alternative than the former as a principle for reform. Nicholas Ridley, a predecessor to Heseltine as Secretary of State for the Environment (a portfolio which includes responsibility for local government affairs), defined a concept of an 'enabling authority': not primarily a provider, certainly not the near-monopolist provider, but regulator, sponsor and co-ordinator, contracting with independent providers for the supply of services for those for whom it has a financial responsibility. The suppliers would operate in a competitive market (Ridley, 1988).

Though not articulated thus in his Buxton speech to directors of social services, such ideas were certainly being discussed in the policy community at that time (Fowler, 1984). However, not all the arguments that the authorities should play more ambitious enabling roles came from the 'New Right', some seeing authorities flexibly purchasing services in the context of local trade and industry policies as a development from, rather than a reaction against, the reforms of the 1960s, for which it would be necessary to learn from overseas experience (Davies, 1986b, 1990; Davies and Challis, 1986).[3] And from 1979 the Thatcher administration strongly emphasised the contribution that the styles and techniques of private sector management could introduce to the public sector, and pursued it with rigour (Pollitt, 1990).

An immediate response to these emerging developments was the Financial Management Initiative, with the replacement of the Audit Office by the Audit Commission for Local Government, which did much to introduce the new managerialist ideas to a local government system conditioned by the agenda of the early 1970s, and produced powerful critiques of efficiency and effectiveness of community care policy (Audit Commission, 1985, 1986). The term 'new managerialism' was by coincidence used to describe two sets of related phenomena. One sense was the adoption in government generally of some of the values, assumptions and techniques used in private sector management, and in that sense was a powerful influence in all government agencies. The second sense related to the new post-reorganisation local authorities, and was an allusion to local government as a 'political institution constituted for local choice' (Stewart, 1986). Reflecting the second sense, local authorities were defined as 'public sector organisations, not market organisations', making their decisions 'subject to political control, rather than market discipline' (Stewart, 1986, p.4). But this looked a more doubtful generalisation as authorities were forced to fit the market realities of the 'enabling' mould, and a whole host of other local public agencies were created in partial competition with it.

The Model and its Construction: 1986-90

The Audit Commission published a pungent critique of community care, particularly in respect to the excessive reliance on residential modes of care, slow creation of community-based services, and an uneven pattern of local provision. It considered that a community-based service could be provided with current levels of expenditure. This would require rationalisation of funding policy from the centre, a more rational organisational structure with 'local responsibility, authority and accountability for delivering a balanced community-based care services ... more clearly defined', with 'greater managerial authority delegated to the local level'. It concluded that changes were required in the 'organisational framework for community care', and recommended that 'In order to establish how best to achieve this end, a high level review of the current situation should be set in train' (Audit Commission, 1986, p.4). The government response was to invite a report from Sir Roy Griffiths, managing director of Sainsbury, and the model subsequently legislated is in all essential respects the set of arrangements proposed by the Griffiths report (1988).

The Griffiths model. In summary, the Griffiths model may be seen to have six fundamental elements:

1. The central principle was the consolidation of authority, responsibility and accountability for policy and practice decisions and for financing their consequences. In the words of the report: 'a budgetary approach, centrally and locally, which aligns responsibility for achieving objectives with control over the resources needed to achieve them so that there is a built-in incentive and the facility to make the best use of the resources available' (Griffiths, 1988, para. 5.6.). 'The absence of such processes at the national level is inconsistent with any claim that there are serious national objectives to be achieved' (para. 5.7).

This 'fundamental' element of the logic of the report required, it argued, a suitable financial system. The distorting effects of the system as it existed in the early 1980s have been described with eloquence and power in many well-researched analyses (Wistow et al., 1994, for example). In particular, there was the failure of devices to overcome the separation of the funding of long-term social as distinct from nursing and medical care in hospitals (particularly in psychiatric hospitals); and the social security benefit for residence in for-profit rest homes, a subsidy which increased from £10 million in 1980 to £1.5 billion by 1993. But not all the effects have been traced in the literature; for instance, the consequences for the creation and then destruction of promising new modes of care.[4]

What this adoption of this central principle showed was the realisation that mechanisms for financing care (and fiscal mechanisms generally) can helpfully be used to provide incentives to equity and efficiency. But to achieve this, they must be simple, stable and enduring. That is a lesson still to be fully learnt by the British local authorities (Davies, 1989).

2. Griffiths also recommended a clearer focus on community care policy-making and management by the DH, including a Minister of State for Community Care. Central government should have a greater 'direct stake ... in the delivery of its policies at the local level' (para. 5.12.). He therefore recommended specific grants for the financing of community care, not the general grant for all local authority purposes. That was not put into effect, although each annual element of the special transitional grant paid to local authorities since 1993 has been specific.

3. Local authorities were made the lead agencies with responsibility for both 'trade and industry' policy functions and the performance of the 'core tasks of case management'. Griffiths did not use the term 'trade and industry policy'. The point of doing so is to extend the discourse about the range of interventions, to reflect the need to be proactive and not merely reactive, and to provide the unifying purpose for them of the correction of the failures of an unmanaged market (Davies, 1986b, 1990). The study of trade and industry policies in existing mixed economies, for instance in Australia or such states as New York, illustrates that the development of trade and industry policies in current British policy remains narrow, although it is widening year by year.

4. Local authorities were to shift their focus away from direct provision of care and onto needs assessment, social planning and the commissioning and monitoring of care services. The Griffiths report also talked about the enabling authority. 'The primary function of the public services is to design and arrange the provision of care and support in line with people's needs. That care and support can be provided from a variety of sources. There is value in a multiplicity of provision, ... because of the widening of choice, creativity, innovation and competition it should stimulate. It is vital that social services

authorities should see themselves as the arrangers and purchasers of care services — not as monopolistic providers.'

5. Targeting public subsidies on the poor. 'It seems right that those able to pay the full economic cost of community care services should be expected to do so'.

6. Responsibility for performing the core tasks of case management and the management of their performance was to be concentrated. Griffiths calls this 'a keystone' of his proposals. He proposed that a case manager should be assigned wherever 'a significant level of resources' was expected (para. 6.6) or where the case was complex. The concentration of responsibility is associated with the intention to 'align responsibility for achieving objectives with control over the resources needed to achieve them so that there is a built-in incentive and the facility to make the best use of the resources available' (para. 5.6). It is a small minority of case management programmes in the USA and elsewhere which do this in a way which gives the case manager the preconditions for behaving flexibly, resourcefully and responsively to the needs and wishes of clients and informal carers (Davies, 1992). However, Griffiths had seen the British programmes which did this, and took some trouble to learn about the argument and experience.

The White Paper version. In most essential respects the White Paper followed the Griffiths model. It weakened the link between budgeting at the centre and the local authorities by not ensuring that all the long-term care money released in the health services was transferred to local authorities for community care. By contrast, the Bérégovoy proposals for France showed that the greater part of the cost would have been to remove inequalities between major local authorities, 'peréquation' (Chombeau, 1992). Articulation of the budget at central and local levels might have put pressure on the Treasury to face similar tax costs in the UK.

The White Paper fitted the approach to community care into a theme of the administration running through all areas of social policy, that of 'choice and independence', by 'enabling people to live as normal a life as possible in their own homes or in a homely environment in the local community, providing the right amount of care and support to help people achieve maximum possible independence ..., and giving people a greater individual say in how they live their lives and the services they need to help them to do so' (para. 1.8).

The objectives of policy were therefore:

- to develop domiciliary, day and respite services to enable people to live in their own homes wherever feasible and sensible;
- to ensure that service providers made practical support for carers a high priority;

- to make proper assessment of need and good case management the corner-stone of high-quality care;
- to promote the development of a flourishing independent sector alongside good-quality public services, making maximum possible use of private and voluntary providers;
- to clarify the responsibilities of agencies in order to make it easier to hold them to account for their performance; and
- to secure better value for taxpayers' money by introducing a new funding structure for social care, removing the incentive to use residential and nurs-ing home care rather than care in the home.

And these objectives were to be achieved by a variety of changes, which included:

- In collaboration with other professions, local authorities became responsible for assessing individual need, designing care arrangements, and securing their delivery within available resources: that is, to perform case management tasks within a budget.
- A responsibility was placed on the health authorities to make the necessary contributions to multidisciplinary procedures.
- Social services authorities produced and published plans consistent with health authority plans, which were to be inspected by the DH, and the health authorities were expected to help prepare community care plans.
- Local authorities were exhorted and given powerful financial incentives to make the maximum use of the independent sector, securing service under contracting and making other arrangements for financial support of provision, and in other ways 'promoting the mixed economy of care' (para. 3.4.6). To make competition between suppliers from different sectors fairer, an organisational separation of the performance of some of the tasks — care management and its management, the supply of services, the spon-sorship and development of supply and service providers, the quality assurance of services — was suggested.
- Social services took on the responsibility for financing community care.
- Local authorities were required to 'establish inspection and registration units at arm's length from the management of their own services to check standards in both their own homes and independently-owned homes. They were to establish user complaints and inspection procedures and to pub-licise them.
- A new specific grant was introduced to aid the development of social care for seriously mentally ill people.

The White Paper also specifically endorsed the identification of a care manager where an individual's needs were complex or significant levels of resources were involved (para. 3.3.2), and saw advantage in linking care management with delegated responsibility for budgetary management (para. 3.3.5). Local authorities were expected to show in their community care plans how they proposed to apply care management techniques.

The Policy Logic in its Context
This brief review has shown how the policy proposals blended the logics of the elements described earlier. The new policy exploited the structural consolidation of political responsibility, authority and accountability at national and local levels and in important respects enhanced them. It made the vaguer ambitions of the 1960s into concrete goals, and put into effect the lessons of the first type of new managerialist argument. It created a version of the enabling authority concept, and pressed the mixing of the supply economy of care with great determination and powerful new rewards and sanctions. It created the surrogate consumer, the user/carer-responsive care manager, to be the personal broker for cases which would yield the greatest benefits. It was more explicit in its abandonment of some of the vague universalism of the 1960s, and created the first essentials of a 'trade and industry' policy both to develop new market structures, and to avoid any of their potential disbenefits.

THE POLICY IMPLEMENTATION PROCESS

Whatever its content or intention, the impact of policy is inevitably mediated through the process of implementation, and it is to this process that we turn our attention in the next two sections of this chapter. In reviewing these developments our two distinctive title themes consistently emerge: the nature of the central implementation of the community care vision; and the reality of the local response to that vision. We shall deal briefly with each of these themes, and then go on to examine the potential implications of these findings for the next important developments of effective local community care services.

The Central Implementation of the Community Care Policy Vision
The underlying imperatives of the community care reforms have remained remarkably consistent since the _Caring for People_ White Paper was published in November 1989, but the managerial and practice implications of the policy have emerged more gradually, as central government has increasingly extended its control over the implementation process in a variety of ways. The effect of these developments was progressively to increase the ability of central government to influence the local implementation of community care. There is no evidence that this was strategically planned; on the contrary, it appears to have been much more a pragmatic response to emerging circumstances. Reflecting the description of new managerialism as continuity about

ends with opportunism about means, there was great continuity in the vision (by the standards one would expect from implementation theory: cf. the definition 'implementation may be viewed as process of interaction between the setting of goals and actions geared to achieving them'; Pressman and Wildawsky, 1973). Indeed, the vision was for the long run, and was consistently admitted to be so by the policy-makers, even though individual stages in the implementation process inevitably had much shorter time horizons.

We have described the means in some detail in preceding chapters, but particular examples of the process have been:

- the issuing of detailed policy and practice guidance;
- the introduction of regular joint monitoring of progress in both health and local authorities;
- the outlining of key tasks to be achieved within a specific time-frame in the successive series of Chief Inspector letters;
- the creation of the Community Care Support Force; and
- the establishment of specific community care *Regulations* (such as the statutory instrument on choice), and *Conditions* (such as the 31 December Agreements, and the need to spend 85 per cent of special transitional grant on independent sector services).

Each shows a progressive tightening of central control over the local implementation of the community care policy. However, observing the reactions of local authorities suggests that they potentially remain well able to circumvent, or at any rate reinterpret, that central vision if they wish, as shown particularly by our case study authority. In fact, the Department of Health would actually have been able to control the implementation process only to a limited degree had authorities willed it so. That the local reinterpretation of the central vision has been so limited is perhaps the most significant feature of this history. It contrasts remarkably with the experience of some other countries (Davies, 1986a; Challis et al., 1994).

So a study of how these methods were used illustrates more fundamental issues about management authority, political control and democratic accountability. It shows both changes in the balance between different parts of the Department of Health during the stages of the reform (for example, the refocusing of NHS activities onto community care, and the emergence of a distinctive new role in implementation for the new Policy and Business wing of the SSI), as well as changing patterns in the relationship between central and local government. What is interesting is that these are not just local issues. In one form or another they arise in several countries undertaking the reform of community services and long-term care, as illustrated in studies in Europe, Australasia and the United States (Davies, 1992; Challis et al., 1994). That they recur in so many different situations is the essential backdrop against which to view these similar changes in the United Kingdom. In the remainder of this section we shall explore first the issues arising from the perspective of the central implementation of the policy vision and then contrast this with the local response.

The long-term policy vision. The inevitable weakness of the policy from a central perspective is the necessarily long time horizon to get even the minimum foundations in place. While most of the policy fitted well within the central philosophy of the middle period Thatcher administration — user empowerment, expanding the mixed economy and reducing bureaucratic control through new managerialism — it was adopted by an administration predisposed to avoiding the long-term policy planning essential for translating the vision into reality at local level. It is possible that in the early stages even some senior Department of Health officials scarcely recognised the fundamental changes within local authorities required by the Griffiths vision (Utting, 1990, for example). As a result, the initial policy vision was never translated into a phased long-term programme. Despite the title of the White Paper (*Community Care in the Next Decade and Beyond*), no explicit milestones were identified against which progress might be evaluated — the nearest was a table of the implementation programme for the three years to April 1993 outlined in the policy guidance (Department of Health, 1990b), and the short timescales for the various key tasks. More significantly, there was no built-in mid-term review after five years as in Australia, nor even a name for the policy implying a strategic long-run process, despite the emphasis on this in *Agenda for Action* (1988). This inevitably left the implementation process open to interference from the cross-currents of short-term policy management issues as they arose.

Short-term responses. As a result, later developments in implementation often appear to be more a response to emerging problems or short-term preoccupations than to long-term strategic policy requirements. The agenda set out in the 1990 Policy Guidance, for example, was essentially about establishing a 'trade and industry' framework for achieving the key objectives of the *Caring for People* White Paper, particularly around the mechanisms for specifying, purchasing, contracting and monitoring services provided by a growing independent provider sector, rather than being directed towards the essential prerequisite of fundamental change to existing social services organisation and practice, particularly through the introduction and development of comprehensive care management systems to operate successfully within that developing mixed economy of care, as required by the original Griffiths vision. Changes of agenda in the later period of implementation were in many ways even more a response to immediate problems, such as sustaining the independent sector provision of residential and nursing care homes as the burgeoning social security budget was cash-limited by the transfer of responsibility to local authorities — an issue not mentioned directly in either the policy or practice guidance. Other responses which became the focus of specific policy attention, such as the increasing anxiety over hospital bed-blocking and the more general NHS retreat from the provision of long-term continuing care, were not even directly caused by the community care reforms, but by the parallel restructuring of the NHS. These examples usefully illustrate how the absence of an explicit strategic framework linking the implementation stages to a complete argument about changing the system allowed the emergence of short-term issues to override the achievement of the crucial longer-term policy objectives. Perhaps the best example of this is captured by the changing fortunes of the concept of care management.

Care management. Case management, as it was originally termed, was seen by Griffiths (1988) as the *keystone* of his proposals, but this had been reduced to a *cornerstone* by the time of the 1989 White Paper, and then disappeared completely from the early Foster/Laming letters setting out the eight key tasks needed for implementation. Care management as such was only brought back into the implementation process as a cross-cutting theme in later guidance, and in the various implementation monitoring reviews, as those in the inner circle of officials most infected by the early Griffiths vision sought to sustain the longer-term policy agenda. For those at the centre, care management probably never left the agenda; but for local managers and practitioners, effective achievement of the eight key tasks inevitably became the yardstick by which their progress on implementation was evaluated, not least as a result of the active involvement of the SSI Policy and Business inspectors in monitoring progress, largely at the expense of the soundness of their foundations for the longer-term policy vision which care management required.

In retrospect, the various Foster/Laming letters can be seen to be directed more at problems at the interface between NHS *health* and local authority *social* care (with a particular focus on more effective hospital discharge — which is not really surprising given their genesis), rather than at the central requirements for *local authority* social care implementation in the form of care management infrastructures. But the approach went further and ensured that the issue of the distinction between *community* (both health and social) care and *acute* care re-emerged, leading to a steadily decline in the provision of long-term continuing health care by many of the new NHS Trusts (a trend also accelerated by the transfer to local authorities of responsibility for undertaking both the social and financial assessments of those requiring long-term care, as well as payment for that care in appropriate circumstances in *nursing* homes), creating yet more problems for both community health and social care providers as implementation of both the community care and NHS reforms accelerated in the years after 1993. The use of formal agreements between health and local authorities on more effective hospital discharge arrangements as the essential prerequisite for payment of the annual special transitional grant is a particularly interesting example of the use of a short-term pragmatic policy lever to address a longer-term problem, at the same time shifting the burden of responsibility onto local authorities for the consistent failure of the NHS at either national, regional or local levels to implement the specific NHS guidance to district health authorities on hospital discharge procedures (Department of Health, 1989a).

Protecting the independent sector. Another short-term central policy driver was the perceived need to protect the emerging independent sector market (especially in relation to residential and nursing care), which led not only to the skewed distribution formula used to allocate the first year's special transitional grant (1993/94) in favour of localities with well established independent provision, but, initially, the failure to pursue other essential community care changes, such as alternative forms of domiciliary care. Again this was at the expense of ensuring an effective infrastructure was in place for a more wide-ranging development of the mixed economy of care in each local authority area, and was in marked contrast to the views of the majority of local authorities at the time, where most social services directors and chairs did not see the development of the local market as a high initial priority (Wistow et al., 1992b), and led to major difficulties for many authorities in subsequent years when the STG distribution formula reverted to a standard spending assessment basis. The introduction of the 85 per cent rule for the use of the STG as a way of protecting independent sector providers in the early years of community care meant that by 1993 development of a mixed economy was assuming much greater significance for most local authorities (Wistow and Knapp, 1993). In later years, DH statistics clearly show a phenomenal increase in the share of the market catered for by independent home care providers. By 1995, they provided 29 per cent of contact hours brokered by SSDs (Department of Health, 1995).

The involvement of housing. Despite the clear centrality of housing in the widest sense to a policy intended to sustain people in their own homes and communities wherever possible, central government took no specific initiatives to encourage better liaison or to produce more consistent priorities between housing and social care services, and it was not until late 1992 that any guidance on community care was issued to housing authorities (Department of the Environment, 1992). There is evidence that many local authorities were more conscious of the importance of engaging with housing issues than central government (Walden, 1994), and the difficulties of engaging effectively with housing was regularly identified throughout the implementation process (Department of Health, 1994f), particularly the differences in policy emphasis between central government housing policy (co-ordinated through the Department of the Environment) and health and social care policy (co-ordinated by the Department of Health). This is in marked contrast to the position that arose within the similar Australian reforms, for example, where the mid-term review clearly indicated the central importance of housing with a comprehensive health and social care policy, and as a result redistributed central policy portfolios and established a Department of Health, Housing and Community Services (Davies, 1993a). It also contrasted with the development of assisting living in the USA (Mollica et al., 1992; Regnier et al., 1992; Kane and Wilson, 1993). At the very least, some harmonisation and alignment of the planning cycles of the respective key agencies would have been helpful (Department of Health, 1994a).

The central response. All of these examples suggest that, although central policy vision may have remained constant, the perception at local level has been much more fragmented and confused. The metaphor that most graphically springs to mind is of an iceberg responding to the various tidal flows taking it into ever warmer water. While appearing calm and impregnable on the surface, below the waterline the large bulk is being ceaselessly changed and reconfigured. While this process can go on for some time with little appreciable effect, the problem with icebergs is that ultimately they capsize. The difference in this case is that there appears to have been comparatively little happening at a local level to erode the original policy vision other than to respond to the continuing flow of directives from the centre on the one hand and to local issues and problems as they emerged on the other.

As a result, central government officials appear to have concluded that local authorities needed help to absorb the new logics, and to think through the menu of structural developments required, and so began to provide detailed guidance for each. There was very little discernible activity between publication of the 1989 White Paper, the issuing of the Chief Inspectors' letter in January 1990, and the establishment of the various departmental development groups. This whole process was very low-key, and reflected the calm response of the January letter. Only at the end of 1990 was the policy guidance published, followed by a series of practical guidance documents throughout 1991. Not until after the first RHA/SSI monitoring review in September 1991 did the Department begin to move to more focused implementation, through the series of Foster/Laming letters and the outlining of the eight key tasks in March 1992. This strongly suggests that there was no formal implementation blueprint operating within the Department of Health or the NHS Management Executive, but that the various stages of implementation were expected to be achieved within individual local authorities on the basis of the broad policy framework of the *Caring for People* White Paper and developed in the various policy and practice guidance documents. On this analysis, individual authorities did have an opportunity to create a more localised vision within the broad policy framework, rather than awaiting the more detailed directives from the centre that ultimately followed.

Indeed, central government did not initially have the resources or skilled individuals available to produce the explicit guidance needed. There were no blueprints. A process of education into these new logics was necessary within the Department of Health itself in order to begin to produce the materials for local use. Even then there has been a consistent lack of recognition both by central government and by many individual local authorities of the important distinction between first- and second-order change processes (Smale et al., 1994) Much (if not all) of the central guidance has been based on the concept of first-order change; that is to say, of simply doing the same things but in different ways (the proliferation of new assessment forms and proceedures in the early days of community care is a particularly clear example of this, as are the eight key implementation tasks in the Foster/ Laming letters), rather than on the more fundamental requirements of *second-order change*, which is about undertaking completely new activities (such as needs-led assessments), as the total paradigmatic shift of community care really required. Given the very pervasive social work view that they were already undertaking comprehensive needs-led assessments and engaging in case planning and implementation in close partnership with users and their carers *prior* to the community care changes (Marsh et al., 1993), this goes far to explain the disappointing findings on assessment and care management in the more recent monitoring exercises (Department of Health, 1994d).

During this initial period the SSI itself was also undergoing a major restructuring of its own, separating out into an inspection wing on the one hand, and a Policy and Business wing on the other, and it was this latter that eventually appeared to seize the initiative for a more central vision of community care implementation as, particularly at regional level, it saw the potential for a powerful new role within the emerging joint monitoring arrangements to fill the gap left by its move away from inspectorial activities. But at least in the early stages of implementation, local government had more resources available for implementation development than did the centre, and so could have seized the opportunity to create a more heterogeneous response to the emerging policy, as appears to have happened in similar circumstances overseas (Davies, 1992). In the following section we begin to explore the paradox of why this did not appear to happen.

The Local Response to the Central Community Care Vision

The degree of central control exercised by the Department of Health over the implementation of the community care policy raises fundamental questions about the role and authority of local authority elected members. While these are largely beyond the range of this discussion, it is apposite to note how little opposition has been voiced to this exercise of central control from local councillors, trades unions, professional associations or senior managers. This in turn raises important issues about the nature of social services authorities, both at elected member and senior officer level, within the wider political and management framework of local government. This is particularly relevant as a result of the phased transfer of significant new financial resources to social services authorities for community care activities at a time when almost all other areas of local government are in relative decline. The more recent problems of the relationship between the special transitional grant and standard spending assessment for individual local authorities seems to reinforce this point, as does the re-emergence of education as the major policy issue for local electors.

The local vision. Many local authorities had their own visions of community care, although the best were not always quite the same as that of the White Paper. It remains open to discussion whether they would have managed as well in developing the detail of logic and organisational structures by themselves. On balance it seems likely that some could have done so effectively. However, this is not true of all authorities, and it is clear that many could not have managed without central assistance. Indeed, in *Impressions of the First Year* (Department of Health, 1994a), a clear need was identified for 'most agencies to re-visit the purpose of the reforms and provide a clear vision for the next stages of implementation'. Five years after the publication of the *Caring for People* White Paper, this was a disquieting conclusion as to the degree to which the underlying policy requirements had been absorbed by the majority of local authorities.

After 20 years, it is evident that the 1974 reform of local government had produced authorities of immeasurably greater human resources and with a more corporate focus. But the position remains very uneven, with some smaller authorities dependent upon a tiny handful of senior officers, and the proposed move to introduce an increased number of smaller unitary authorities from the mid-1990s onward will inevitably reinforce this position. But history invariably reflects the principle that all policy change remains Faustian: the unexpected almost always countervails the anticipated gain. Among our sample, even the best endowed authorities, acting as the most developed strategic governments of their areas, showed how easy it was to make the range of argument too rich and the key participants too adept at avoiding conformity, so creating turbulence rather than a strategy for clear action.

Resource management. For many local authorities, uncertainties about the budgetary arrangements for community care, compounded by the major changes in general local government funding arising from the introduction of first the community charge and subsequently the council tax, as well as increasing central government controls exerted through the block grant and standard spending assessment systems, have drawn attention away from the consistent long-term policy implementation of community care. Griffiths in particular was very clear about the need for clarity over the level of resources to be available for community care, so that consistent longer-term plans could be developed.

Many social services directors also appear to have devoted substantial energy into ameliorating the traditional restrictions of local authority standing orders, and contracting and financial accounting systems in attempting to implement community care (Department of Health, 1994b) over which there has been little helpful advice or support from central officials. In many cases this has been further exacerbated by the need to depend on central computing capacity and information systems designed for internal audit and financial accounting purposes, and consequently under the control of Directors of Finance, rather than the devolved financial management and commitment accounting systems required for case management and community care (Audit Commission, 1992b). Again there was little recognition of these emerging requirements by central policy-makers, and little in the way of either practical or financial assistance, beyond a marginal increase in the capital expenditure approvals for each local authority. This is in stark contrast to the levels of management and financial resources devoted to information management and technology within the NHS for the implementation of their parallel reforms. Inevitably, these activities and uncertainties drew management attention away from the development of longer-term implementation plans in many authorities.

The organisational response. In many local authorities, the initial response to the emerging central vision of community care was a flurry of structural reorganisation. Perhaps inevitably, in order to assimilate these new logics, all local authorities have had to engage in major restructuring, and discussions about alternative models of purchaser/provider separation (Department of Health, 1991a). The respective merits of specialist or generic services took up a significant amount of management and policy time which in retrospect might have been better focused on the development and introduction of new operational procedures, processes and information systems out of which more appropriate organisational models might have then started to emerge.

More significantly, social services authorities have been required to manage a major cultural change to the prevailing values both within social services organisations as well as within local authorities more generally. These changes are clearly *second-order changes* of the type defined by Smale et al. (1994), requiring a fundamental transformation in the attitudes and responses of individual members of staff, best exemplified by the change from a service-orientated (or *professional*) service to a needs-led (or *consumer*) service. It is increasingly clear that authorities were generally more successful with the structural issues than with the crucial issues of challenging and changing the attitudes and activities of front-line staff. The December 1993 review of training and development (Department of Health, 1994c) concluded that, while in 1992 and early 1993 the emphasis in local authorities had unashamedly been on the managerial agenda for community care, this had now largely been achieved, and it was now time 'to revisit the objectives or vision of the reforms in order to recapture that momentum [of change] and encourage an understanding of the reforms that went beyond proceedures'. As many authorities currently appear to be re-evaluating these present structures with a view to yet more change, it remains to be seen whether this necessary shift in emphasis will now begin to emerge.

Staff development initiatives. In response to a very early recognition of this need to re-orientate staff, in 1989 the Department of Health introduced the specific training support grant (TSG). A major part of the implementation programme within individual authorities has therefore related directly to the training of staff, particularly front-line staff, both on the general background to the community care reforms, as well as to the new procedures and processes needing to be undertaken from 1 April 1993. What is much less clear is how effective these programmes have been at bringing about this necessary organ-isational and cultural change, although the early indications are far from encouraging, largely as a result of the predominantly top-down approach to implementation adopted by senior managers in their understandable attempts to respond to the mandatory eight key tasks in time for April 1993 (Department of Health, 1994d).

This re-visioning process becomes even more important as it is increasingly clear that in many authorities new care manager posts are predominantly being filled by social workers, who inevitably bring their own particular sets of values and vision to the new task, rather than seeing it from the perspective of the original Griffiths concept. As a result, care management in practice is increasingly in danger of being seen as containing the three key elements of social work practice (assessment, care management and counselling) rather than the seven core tasks identified in the practice guidance (Department of Health, 1991c):

- publishing information;
- determining level of assessment;
- assessment of need;
- care planning;
- implementation of care plan;
- monitoring of care plans; and
- review of progress.

The December 1993 review of training and development (Department of Health, 1994c) concluded that 'Training to support care management had for the most part been concerned with systems', and added: 'It was also clear that some staff thought they had been operating a needs-led assessment for some time. Too often the study team heard that staff knew how to assess people who needed residential or domiciliary care. In the view of the study team there was insufficient awareness that residential or domiciliary care are solutions to problems.' It is clear that social workers tend to *believe* that they already have all the necessary care management skills within their traditional roles, and as a result see no reason to change their methods of approach or styles of intervention, although this early review evidence suggests a very high concentration on the *assessment* task rather than the wider *care manage-ment* role (Department of Health, 1994d), with a very heavy emphasis on *describing* rather than *analysing* needs (Department of Health, 1994e). Moreover, 'assessors were not generally agreeing objectives with users and carers at the conclusion of the assessment of need, nor engaging with providers in developing individual care plans'.

User and carer empowerment. Parallel to the Griffiths logic, one sees in some countries a political logic: for example, the accounts of Wisconsin and Australia (Davies et al., 1990), where there were important alliances between executive and pressure groups to increase pressure for confronting the central dilemmas of community care. There is little clear evidence of such activities in the UK, despite some brave attempts by user organisations such as Mind and Age Concern. While the argument of consumer empowerment was clearly a critical element in ensuring wide acceptance of the general community care policy in its initial stages, as yet it appears to have had comparatively little impact in practice, despite the creation of a National Users and Carers Advisory Forum in 1993 by the then Minister of State responsible for community care. Conversely, the recent successful pressure from carers' groups to extend the original community care legislation to cover their needs within the 1995 Carers (Recognition and Services) Act may mark the beginning of a more successful pattern. At a local level the picture appears to be equally patchy, with increasing evidence of users' and carers' representatives being consulted and involved in the development of community care plans, but involvement in the design of individual care plans was still limited (Department of Health, 1994a).

Linking the health and social care agenda. Despite the crucial inter-relationship between health and social care in achieving an effective local pattern of seamless care, the NHS remained predominantly concerned with its own *Working for Patients* (1988) reforms throughout the early period of community care implementation, and it was only as a result of the specific requirement for district health authorities to participate in the new joint SSI/RHA monitoring arrangements initiated in 1991 that the actual lack of engagement began to become apparent centrally, and the series of Foster/Laming letters to both health and local authorities from 1992 onwards began to address this concern. More recently, the growing influence of GP fundholding, reductions in the availability of NHS continuing care, and encouragement from the centre for authorities to engage in joint commissioning and other collaborative activities (Department of Health 1995a) have increasingly concentrated attention on these areas of work, and despite the undoubted difficulties of working across agencies with very different systems of organisation, management, values, responsibilities and accountabilities — particularly at a time of major organisational change — there is increasing evidence of significantly improved inter-agency collaboration as a result of the need to work together over the implementation of both the NHS and community care reforms (Department of Health, 1994a).

IMPLICATIONS FOR FUTURE DEVELOPMENTS

This study was focused on the short period between 1989 and 1993, and only since the completion of the fieldwork in mid-1992 has the long process of implementation in individual field agencies been seriously underway. Despite this potential shortcoming, a number of significant issues arose during this important period of transformation which allow some initial conclusions to begin to emerge, so the main purpose of the remainder of this chapter is to speculate about how the direction of the community care reform process might usefully be adjusted in the light of that experience, and in the face of the contingencies which have pressed in upon every side throughout the process of implementation — and which seem likely to continue to do so in the future. It does so by drawing on insights derived both from our data and from our perspective as interpreters and participants of the history of community care reform both in the UK and elsewhere. Such an interpretation inevitably goes beyond the direct evidence from our early fieldwork, but does so within a broad background of knowledge and experience of social policy issues and developments both here and overseas.

As we have seen, the broad policy objectives of the community care reforms have remained fundamentally consistent since they were set out in the *Caring for People* White Paper in November 1989, although, as we have pointed out earlier in this chapter, some of the short-term policy imperatives have from time to time occluded this vision. But the actual *achievement* of those objectives requires a profound cultural shift, probably a complete paradigmatic switch for social services authorities. As both the Department of Health and the Audit Commission are fond of repeating: 'To implement the new legislation and deliver these [policy] objectives a revolution must take place over the next decade in the way Social Services operate' (Audit Commission, 1992b). We have already indicated that these are second-order rather than the more traditional first-order changes, with implications for both central policy-makers as well as local managers and professionals. Once again, these two aspects reflect our title concerns of the central vision for community care and the local implementation response. We shall consider both of these sets of implications in the remainder of this chapter, but will start with the local perspective before moving on in the final section to consider the wider national policy implications.

Implications at Local Level

Profound change is always challenging for any organisation, but many local authorities appear to be having major difficulties in absorbing the implications of the new policy requirements. This is partly a reflection on the changing roles of elected members and officials within an inflexible organisational framework designed to operate in a very different way than that required for the effective implementation and discharge of much contemporary social policy, and we shall consider this issue in more detail later. But it is also an issue of vision, and of attracting and deploying appropriate staff and resources. The support opportunities for local authority managers in this respect contrast sharply with those for the new managerial executives in the NHS, where thriving networks exist to achieve a rapid interchange of ideas and information between practice, managerial culture and academic institutions, and where innovation and experimentation are more actively encouraged. It is not clear whether this is due to a lack of effective institutions within social services to provide a focus for these activities, or a result of the underlying ethos which moulded the modern social work profession during an era when knowledge, and the definition and development of a small number of core skills, seemed less important than some other qualities. There is some reassuring evidence that this position is now changing, at least among some of the more progressive social services managers, but, without the essential institutional framework to sustain them, both within local government and in a more general professional and managerial relationship, they will still remain isolated from developing ideas. For the present, if social services authorities are to maximise their potential achievements within the existing community care policy framework, a number of specific issues need to be addressed.

Care management. Despite the centrality of care management for the effective implementation of the *Caring for People* reforms, many social services authorities still appear to lack the vision and theoretical background for developing the concept in practical applications to meet local circumstances. In the United Kingdom, care management was developed primarily from an academic base in very few institutions. The lack of training in the application of a corpus of theory supported with empirical evidence and examplars can be seen elsewhere also. It is in marked contrast to the United States and elsewhere, where the driving force of new developments is coming from managers and practitioners in the field as much as from theoreticians. Equally, although a prime objective of the reforms was to ensure the emergence of effective product champions at field level to develop more effective service responses to the needs of individual users and carers (Audit Commission, 1986), there is relatively little sign of this being achieved during the early stages of community care.

The central concern of care management is with the more effective and efficient matching of needs to resources within the framework of user choice. There is now a significant range of evaluation material both from this country and elsewhere to demonstrate the effectiveness of care management, both to improve outcomes and to increase the impact of other home care services, even within existing organisational and legislative structures (Davies, 1993a). While in the past there has been some understandable concern that the very nature of care management experiments themselves, with specially targeted staffing and resources, may be leading to inevitable 'Hawthorn-effect' improvements, there is now evidence that such models work with equally beneficial results when introduced as part of the standard range of services. On this basis, it is clear that local authority managers should be encouraging the development of more effective local care management systems as a matter of urgency, by ensuring greater freedom to assemble more creative care packages and to purchase a wider range of services, by the use of more clearly decentralised budgets and accountability frameworks.

Commissioning. If care managers are to have a wider range of services available to offer to users and carers, significant improvements are also required in the strategic commissioning abilities of many local authorities, both by way of undertaking more comprehensive locality needs assessments against which to balance resource allocation and contracting decisions, and to achieve the break up of the large frequently inflexible blocks of existing service provision. Only by ensuring that better commissioning skills are available to them, and by a willingness to address some of the more difficult issues around direct service provision, will it be possible to ensure that care managers have sufficient choice and freedom to be able to operate at optimum effectiveness. Care management and commissioning are the two crucial complementary activities that need to act in harmony if effective community care progress is to be achieved.

The mixed economy. An important linked issue will be the willingness of senior managers to begin seriously to address the development of a really effective mixed economy of supply. There is no doubt that a number of authorities have had some initial success at harnessing and developing local independent sector markets. What is much less clear is how far local authorities can reduce their own essential core provision and still retain effective control over their activities and fundamental statutory responsibilities in the face of potential market collapse. These issues need a good deal of further exploration and elaboration before either the risks or the potential are satisfactorily established. But the experience from abroad is not always encouraging (Challis et al., 1994).

Similar issues emerge in discussions with senior managers over the nature of the competitive processes they envisage as a result of the development of the mixed economy of care. Competition is being envisaged more in the nature of the competitive *tendering* processes of local government, than in the development of more systematic relationships between commissioners and service providers (Wistow et al., 1994). When Griffiths (1988) referred to competition, variety and choice, he was not thinking just or even necessarily mainly of the influence of competitive processes on the *costs* of services, but of the way in which the enhancement of individual choice could be used to ensure more effective welfare, more closely targeted to the needs and desires of individuals. Competition should be used to produce new forms of services, and different combinations of activities, in order to improve the variety of response to human need, rather than simply to lower the unit costs of services, important as this may be.

Users and carers. If more effective care management and commissioning are to emerge as the levers for more effective community care services, users and carers will need to be engaged fully in both aspects, for it is already clear from the evidence now becoming available that it is only by fully involving users and their carers in individual care decisions affecting their lives that the main objectives of the community care reforms are to be achieved, and equally only by their involvement in the strategic commissioning process can some of the more difficult decisions about future service configurations effectively and confidently be addressed (Morris, 1995).

Collaboration. Effective collaboration is the glue that binds all of these processes together, and this includes collaboration over the identification of need, the commissioning of services, the provision of care, the monitoring of provision, as well as the planning and developing of future activities. Collaboration also needs to involve a whole range of individuals and agencies at different times and for different reasons, and these have been identified in some detail in the recent guidance (Department of Health, 1995). Given the emerging role of GPs within the NHS (and particularly but not exclusively fundholders), it will also become increasingly important to find ways of ensuring that they have access to strategic commissioning activities, as well as being engaged with care managers and other professionals at local level both in planning services and identifying future needs, and in responding to the needs of individual patients and their care plans.

Good collaboration depends on a range of factors, but specifically upon the endowment of local agencies in terms of skilled and available human resources. Some of the current restructuring will inevitably affect the bigger better-endowed authorities which have often in the past shown the lead in policy development and innovation. Scale also offers an opportunity for the spreading of risk which is not always possible in more tightly focused organisations. Scale is also useful in pursuing some key field agency activities: for example, the establishment of more effective internal inspection units and other quality assurance mechanisms. Other functions where economies of scale have potential value relate to the concentration of expertise in human resources, such as in information technology development, and in new skills such as needs-based planning. Local authority training sections similarly require real intensive expertise in the new skills, both to ensure effective staff development, but more importantly to provide an expertise to balance the countervailing power of suppliers of new training opportunities, such as the teaching schools of advanced practice.

Similarly, although many small urban authorities are increasingly linking housing and care services managerially, sometimes also including environment and general community development activities with good effect (Kirklees in West Yorkshire is perhaps the most striking example, but a number of others exist), many of the more significant developments have been in housing association initiatives (putting shelter with care together in new ways, for example). Financial separation of shelter, other general living costs, and care components is crucial for this to work effectively, as shown in an increasing number of long-stay resettlement developments (Knapp, 1993, for example).

Implications for Further Policy Development

Agenda for Action provided a concise and elegant vision on which to predicate the development of more effective social care services into the next millennium. The *Caring for People* White Paper elaborated that vision into a new policy framework, but largely on the basis of existing organisational structures and agency responsibilities. For example, although implemented through the 1990 NHS and Community Care Act, the new policy requirements are based firmly on the pre-existing legislative framework for adult care services which has accumulated since the 1948 National Assistance Act, supplemented by new guidance and directives. As a result, as the new community care reforms begin to gather pace, a number of the tensions both within and between these traditional organisational relationships are being brought into much sharper focus, particularly the nature of the relationship between health and social care services. It is too early to argue that these tensions could lead to the failure of the policy, but it is increasingly clear that the community care vision as outlined by Sir Roy Griffiths will not achieve its full potential unless these fundamental structural relationships begin to be addressed and resolved. This is the emerging challenge for central government over the final years of the decade, and in this final section we review some of the more critical of these tensions.

The role of local authorities. The new entrepreneurial enabling local authorities will need new structures, new systems and new roles, possibly even new electoral arrangements, if they are to undertake their new responsibilities positively and effectively. At present they are based around an outdated council and committee system adequate enough for the traditional role of local service provision, but insufficiently flexible and responsive for the commissioning challenges required by their new role in the reforms. It is disappointing that the creative energy in so many local authorities is currently being dissipated by the Local Government Review, rather than directed towards a serious reappraisal of the long-term role of elected local government. If the emergence of a range of smaller unitary authorities during the latter half of the 1990s begins to identify the need for such a radical change in approach, then this may have been worthwhile — despite the inevitable turbulence of their establishment.

But whatever the structures, public accountability through elected representatives inevitably lends itself to short-termism, rather than the sustained

longer-term vision that is required to commission for major policy implementation, instead of the more mechanistic provision of direct services. During
the 1980s these problems became more serious with a further decline in the
numbers of those participating in local elections (often only around 40 per
cent of the register), the emergence of increasing numbers of hung councils,
and greater instability of control both within and between parties. Political
instability of this nature may be a simple correlate of local (as well as national)
political values and cultures, and the distance individuals and communities
now feel from the democratic process. If so, the problems are too difficult to
be tackled simply by redrawing boundaries, introducing some form of propor-
tional representation, or having annual elections for a proportion of the seats.
Perhaps the only way would be to shift the balance of local authority functions
away from the technocratic and back towards the political. The emphasis in
the 1974 restructuring was towards the technocratic, based on the provision
and purchase of services within a framework of more sophisticated local
service policy, which led to the creation of a number of large local authorities
(some of the largest multipurpose authorities in the world). The more recent
argument behind the Heseltine review has been a re-emphasis on the political,
through a reduction in size and hegemony as a way of allowing the emergence
of more local citizen values, but this is unlikely to have any significant effect
unless local authorities are freed up to respond to such local initiatives through
greater decentralisation of policy definition, and through their own local
income-generating powers. Reforms of this sort would remove the new forms
of the old paradox long noted by John Stewart (1986): local government is
no longer organised around the mediation of local conflicting interests but
around the commissioning and provision of services, which is inevitably a
much narrower and more technocratic role.

This tension between the political and the technocratic remains a key
dilemma for policy areas such as community care, and is a fundamental
reason why technocratic health commissioning will never fit well with the
essentially political role of local authorities, an issue to which we will return
in the next section. For the present, local government review is in the process
of establishing an increasing number of smaller multi-purpose authorities in
many areas, of which social care services will inevitably be a large component.
Effective bulk purchasing and market power require significantly sized authorities, while investment in new service ventures and other more risky market
development require an adequate risk pool to share it across. Redcliffe-Maud
(1969) argued that economies of scale in the valued functions of the day set
the minimum size of authorities. Today's policy wisdom emphasises the
power of the market and the need to reduce local authority direct provision
and encourage a more comprehensive mix of suppliers through the implementation of effective trade and industry policies designed to stimulate an
expanding mixed economy of care. These new unitary authorities are likely
to be well placed to press for the creation of a new range of commissioning-

cum-trade-and-industry-policy (CTIP) agencies extending across a number of local authority areas. These would be at arm's length from individual local authorities who would exercise influence through the use of local taxation to provide more powerful incentives for more effective commissioning and service delivery. Many such CTIP agencies would have wide geographic territories and, not being directly governed by local politicians, could be financed with similar grant arrangements to those now in existence. Such agencies might create the hybrid culture more appropriate to the provision of long-term care, and could employ a wide range of professional staff, including health care staff where appropriate (Davies, 1993a).

An alternative might be the eventual organisational separation of the political from the CTIP functions — perhaps health/social care agencies such as those suggested by the Audit Commission (1986) or by some academics (Ferlie et al., 1985). A further possibility might be to shift the responsibility for the more costly forms of community care to the health services.

Health and social care purchasing authorities. One of the most fundamental difficulties facing the further implementation of community care is the largely artificial boundary between community health and social care services which has been growing since the transfer of community health away from local authorities to the NHS in 1974. Moreover, health and social care services are essentially inter-dependent, and the success of some crucial developments, such as the Tomlinson proposals for improving London health services, depend on the community care authorities adjusting flexibly and creatively to these changes (Tomlinson, 1992). This boundary is exacerbated by the fundamental differences in the organisation, roles, responsibilities, financing and culture within the NHS and local government. These differences have been well rehearsed elsewhere (Association of Metropolitan Authorities, 1994), but perhaps the greatest distinction is between the concept of universal free health care regardless of ability to pay, and increasingly targeted and means-tested local authority care services. This distinction leads to endless difficulties for professional staff from both sides of this divide jointly trying to provide seamless care to increasingly vulnerable people, and leads to further perverse incentives to cost-shunt from one authority to another.

The policy has created new boundaries of responsibility at which the opposing financial principles distort incentives. The policy drew the boundary of social services to include much — but not all — long-term care. So long-term community nursing was excluded. So were the hospital and long-stay beds used predominantly for nursing and social care, although conversely local authorities were provided with a proportion of the special transitional grant to purchase nursing care in independent sector homes. Yet there is great potential for substitution across these activities, with potential improvements in quality of life for patients as well as improvements in the utilisation of resources, as is clear from the experience overseas (Davies, 1993b).

Not only are there great practical difficulties in drawing the boundaries between such essentially different agencies, there are also clear limits to the degree of service substitution that can be achieved with agencies operating on opposite sides of the boundary. For example, a wide variety of models for geriatric practice already exist (Brocklehurst et al., 1989), and these are matched by equal diversity of NHS continuing care provision. Local patterns should and do change, not least to ensure maximum utilisation of historic patterns of services and resources, and it would be damaging to discourage such local adaptations.

At the same time, advances in health technology will make demands for new mixes on the boundary of health and social care. The United States demonstrates how intensive high technology nursing at home can save costs. So can the tooling up of nursing homes to cope with sudden decline cases (Zimmer et al., 1988). And hospital stays are already being reduced through the use of non-invasive investigations and trauma-reducing surgical procedures. But such reductions require significantly better health and social care home support services if they are to be truly effective. The largest potential saving in costs will come from the substitution of *acute* hospital beds, not from the substitution of residential or nursing care beds by community alternatives, the predominant emphasis in the academic argument so far (Davies, 1986a).

The best-known recent example of these difficulties is the significant retreat from continuing health care services by many NHS Trusts in the early days of community care and the emphasis on speedy rather than necessarily effective hospital discharge, which created major problems both for local authorities and for NHS Community Trusts, and this difficulty is only now beginning to be addressed by guidance (Department of Health, 1995b). As a result, the increasing attention being given by local authorities to taking over the (non-elected) role of commissioning local health services — currently the responsibility of District Health Authorities (Association of Metropolitan Authorities, 1994) — is hardly surprising, even though it is happening at a time when Local Government Review is leading to the creation of a new generation of small unitary authorities, whereas the NHS is seeking major improvements in scale by the integration of DHAs and FHSAs into new commissioning agencies, and encouraging the merger of many smaller health authorities and Trusts. While this approach clearly has a number of attractions for local authorities, it is unlikely in itself to lead to any greater clarity of responsibilities, and while a better integration of community health and social care services might result, the problem of charging for local authority as opposed to free NHS services will remain. The boundary between NHS acute care and community health and social care provides a more difficult and clearly defined boundary to negotiate than is currently the case between the potentially more flexible local interpretations of health and social care.

Existing commissioning patterns appear to be adding to the tensions, and better and more effective resource utilisation will only be achieved with some new form of comprehensive and integrated commissioning mechanisms. The existing Department of Health exhortation (1995a) to improve collaboration through joint commissioning is a way of making the best use of the existing financial and legislative frameworks, but it is not a mechanism for addressing the more substantial issues of input resource substitution through more comprehensive commissioning that will be required to make the major impact required by the original policy vision.

The role of general practice and the primary health care team. The emergence of new larger health commissioning authorities brings into sharper focus yet another essential paradox of the current reforms in the form of the increasingly powerful emergence of GP fundholders, and the recent policy moves towards a primary care-led NHS (NHS Executive, 1994) — with three new levels of fundholding (including a number of pilot experiments in total fundholding) — will increase yet further the current role of general practice. As a result of these developments, GPs have recovered some power of initiative. But even in the long run and in the absence of dramatic change in policy, their response in the care of elderly people will differ greatly and with it the degree to which they will become the focus of new care management. Some local authorities are already moving fast to base care managers in general practices to a degree unthinkable only a few years ago.

Given the justifiable emphasis on effective collaboration within the policy vision as set out in much of the guidance, these developments seem likely to hinder rather than assist the process. While the principles for collaboration set out in the *Accountability Framework for General Practitioners* (NHS Executive, 1995) suggest that the problem of engaging GPs within the local district health commissioning process is now more clearly recognised, it is unlikely to provide a really effective mechanism for the comprehensive engagement that will be necessary to ensure that a flexible and responsive supply of high-quality local health and social care services is available. Indeed, it is difficult within the present arrangements to identify any clear incentives for GPs to participate in these activities at all. Unless these fundamental difficulties are addressed with some clear policy initiatives as a matter of urgency, they will have serious implications for the longer-term development of community care goals, let alone for the most effective care services for individual patients, their families and other carers.

Housing. The enormous improvements in health care achieved in the early parts of this century came about largely as a result of an increase in emphasis on public health rather than from improvements in individual patient treatment. The same continues to be true today, and it is becoming increasingly clear that significant long-term health care benefits (and hence potential reductions in resource expenditure) can be achieved only through more effective health education programmes, and through improvements to housing and the environment. This is equally true for community care. A policy which is predicated on keeping people in their own homes rather than in more expensive institutional alternatives requires a significant contribution from improvements in both the type, mix and availability of suitable and adaptable good-quality housing. Moreover, housing is not only where people live and receive services; in an increasing number of cases it also represents the accumulated equity from which they are likely to have to contribute financially towards their future care needs.

So far, apart from the brief circular on housing and community care services issued in November 1992 (Department of the Environment, 1992), housing has not figured high on either the local or national agendas, and although as we have noted a number of local authorities have linked their housing and social services functions together within one directorate, there is little evidence of more tangible integration at a more local level. Nor is this particularly surprising given the policy differences between the two major responsible departments. If better local integration is to be achieved, central government will need to set a better example of more effective joint working between the Departments of Health and Environment, initially by creating some clear new machinery for co-ordinating and reviewing policy in this area, and for developing a series of joint initiatives, possibly on the basis of some forms of targeting joint funding, for exploring and encouraging new developments and initiatives in this crucial area of activity.

Financing and benefits issues. The most significant way in which the White Paper differed from the Griffiths proposals was in its failure to ring-fence long-term care funds. Similarly, the White Paper had almost nothing to say about some of the longer-run comments and recommendations about funding mechanisms in *Agenda for Action*. Once the special transitional grant finishes after 1996/97, local authorities will be expected to manage long-term care needs on the basis of their annual standard spending assessment grant, and it is increasingly clear that eligibility criteria for community care services are having to be set very high as a result of financial constraints in many local authorities.

As we have already argued, the community care reforms have created a sharp boundary between the domains of two contrasting financing principles: those of the NHS and those of local government. This has two immediate consequences. The first, relating to the issue of substitutability of service inputs across the acute and community (health and social) care boundary and their differing marginal costs, has already been identified. The second is the related issue arising from potential distortions in decisions over individual cases, as a result of perverse incentives for users to remain in 'free' NHS services which their condition no longer requires, so using resources that could better be utilised in supporting more seriously disabled patients, rather than to be discharged to more appropriate nursing or residential care services where they will normally be expected to make a significant financial contribution. A similar perverse incentive exists for local authorities, as the net cost to the authority for a place in a residential or nursing care home is likely to be less than the costs of a comprehensive home-based community care package, once the financial contribution from the user is taken into account. Consequently, the financial interests of the *community* as a whole are completely at odds with the financial interests of the *user*, and are causing major ethical dilemmas for all the professional staff involved.

These developments have brought into sharper relief an underlying problem with the UK system of long-term care that has been largely hidden in the past: the lack of a suitable financing mechanism which allows those with modest or middling income or capital who fall outside the criteria for complete coverage by the state for their care costs to meet their contributions for potentially long periods of care at the end of their life. These problems are not dissimilar to those currently being actively discussed in the United States and France (Davies, 1994). Experience overseas provide a rich source of ideas for future financing mechanisms. The precise form of any new benefit will need careful discussion, but for the present it is increasingly clear that a more urgent review is required of the whole range of both existing and potential future taxation and benefit arrangements, taking account of the already substantial flows of resources between health, housing, social care and income support agencies. For instance, it has been shown that the French equivalent of the dependance allowance has been much more effective in reducing the probability of admissions to homes (Davies et al., 1997). The result, and the difference in scheme policies and practice, beg questions about a large British benefit, the attendance allowance. If it is intended to help to make it unnecessary for persons to enter institutions for long-term care, its targeting should be tuned for the purpose, the levels should be better tailored to the needs of those at risk, and brokerage care management help should be on offer to recipients to help those requiring such assistance to use it to best effect. Also, experiments in various American states, and the technical discussions prepared for the Pepper Commission (1990), have shown significant possibilities. So also is the evidence that a social security benefit like the attendance allowance has had more impact on making admissions to homes unnecessary in France than in England (Davies et al., 1997). What is needed is some overarching political initiative that will begin to bring these crucial and yet disparate strands together into a more integrated and comprehensive policy framework.   ·

Inter-dependencies. Finally, it would be difficult to overstate the crucial interdependencies of all of these separate strands of activity. Each has a crucial contribution to make to the policy in its own right, but if some more effective mechanisms can be devised to harness each element to some more overarching policy structure, then the final outcome is likely to be significantly greater than the sum of the individual parts. Just as the essential challenge to local authorities and other front-line agencies for the immediate future is to ensure the effectiveness of services and responses within the existing legislative and financial frameworks, the challenge for central government is to begin to forge new linkages between currently disparate major departments of state, to identify new alliances and initiatives, and to achieve a more co-ordinated response. Only in this way will the Griffiths vision be given an effective operational framework which in turn will enable front-line agencies to achieve the optimum benefits from the policy for the ultimate benefit of the nation as a whole.

CONCLUDING REMARKS

For the present, the essential changes in individual authorities still appear turbulent and disruptive, abounding with contradictions, side-tracking and occasionally even back-tracking, with failures of communication between agencies, as well as between management and front-line staff, although this is probably inevitable at a time of such rapid change. We have already indicated that one possible reason for this degree of turbulence could be the lack of recognition by both central government and many individual local authorities of the important distinction between first- and second-order change processes (Smale et al., 1994).

It is also clear that progress varies significantly between individual authorities, and while it is far too easy for social policy case studies to overstate the importance of personalities (for to a significant extent the environment attracts or selects the senior officers it wants and deserves), the effectiveness of senior executives clearly depends on the symbiosis with that environment. Accidental absence of symbiosis is easily confused with personal ineffectiveness. The real breakthrough in policy analysis of the 1970s showed that there were patterns across authorities, and that individual authorities were not *sui generis* as was believed by many policy analysts of an earlier time. However, we did see that styles were personal and of enormous importance. Above all, that was true of the directors. But it was true also of other important participants in the process. Authorities had different and unique human resources at their disposal. Changes in dispositions did indeed result in important changes in direction, and changes in the effectiveness of policy development within each chosen direction, as shown in our case study authority, for example.

Given the great diversity of the 109 English local authorities and their respective committees and senior officials, it seems remarkable that the general level of community care implementation has been so effectively channelled by the central policy vision into the relative homogeneity of the reality of the local response. However, as increasing diversion from more traditional patterns of care begins to emerge, and new independent sector providers become established (often as a specific result of the 85 per cent STG requirement), it may be that increased diversity and variation will begin to emerge. But this will require the application of a greater vision of local community potential between local authority elected members, senior officials and local communities than is currently apparent from the evidence in the great majority of authorities (Department of Health, 1994a).

If there is one over-riding impression which sums up the state of local authorities as the lead agency policy formulators at this stage of community care implementation, it is that few of them are pushing the development of new activities and systems beyond those outlined in the continuing flow of Department of Health guidance. As a result, the provision of this very detailed guidance from the centre, which was originally intended to act as a stimulus for further development within individual local authorities, may in fact have stultified the very developments and innovations it was intended to nurture and sustain. One of the lasting legacies of the new community care reforms, and the increasing centralisation of activities, may therefore be a *decrease* in the responsiveness and diversification of local authorities, and the provision of more standardised services. This is arguably a complete antitheses of the very flexibility and diversity that the community care policy changes were intended to achieve. Yet, for the present at least, it is the Department of Health guidance which provides most local authorities with their only entrée into the new intellectual world of community care.

This study has focused on a short period between 1989 and 1992, and only since the completion of the main fieldwork has the long process of implementation been seriously underway in most authorities, but we have tried in our own way to capture and evaluate some of the most important elements of that experience, and even at this early stage some significant indicators of current issues and future directions are beginning to emerge, and will require attention by both central government and local field agencies if implementation momentum is to be sustained. For the present, the jury is still out on the issue of community care, but the verdict from both users and carers is already becoming increasingly clear. Those responsible for guiding and implementing these crucial policy reforms would do well to heed that verdict while the opportunity for change is still available.

NOTES

1   The co-ordination of housing and care policies, particularly for elderly people, has become more important in several countries as the modernisation of community and long-term care has proceeded. The Australians recognised this at the mid-term review of their Aged Care Reform Strategy, and subsequently redistributed central portfolios to create a Department of Health, Housing and Community Services. The implementation documents about community care planning in the UK have paid increasing attention to housing, and local authorities

are increasingly changing their departmental organisation in the same way. However, the responsibilities remain unaltered at the central government level. Similarly, the Department of the Environment retains responsibility for the overall operation and financing of local authorities.

2   However, models of geriatric practice differed (Evans, 1983), some geriatric consultants preferring to spend their time less in managerial and more in clinical roles. The same variations existed for the psychiatry of old age. The community nurses were important NHS providers in community care.

3   Taking one of the oldest symbols of the welfare state — the school meals service — a case study showed how social change had created variation in need between individuals and so the populations of small areas and, similarly, variations in the factors causing uptake; how the relative costs of mitigating the nutritional consequences of child poverty differed between small geographical areas; and how the needs were being met with an inappropriately uniform response by authorities. In consequence, the benefits of the large subsidy were not received by proportions for whom they would be of most benefit, and the public money was not spent in the most cost-effective way. A solution would be for local managers to be set the task of mitigating the nutritional consequences of child poverty, to be allocated budgets to do so, being held accountable by the examination of outcomes (Davies, 1978). That was an almost identical model to the Kent Community Care Project whose initial design was stated in Davies (1974), save that the allusion to contracting supply was more explicit, and the budget was to be held by field workers.

4   An example was adult fostering/boarding out. Its value has been shown in the Oregon evaluation (Kane, 1989). It is a case which illustrates two important features of the problem: first, how the old DHSS (and in other examples, such as the system of grants and other government departments) was rapidly making the knot ever more complex; and second, how the responses of suppliers were (and are) accelerating, this in turn inviting a faster response from the DHSS. This is the road to Kafka's castle.

References

Age Concern England (1991) *Some Financial Issues for Older People Related to the Community Care Reforms*, Astral House, London.

Age Concern Institute of Gerontology (1991) *Multi-purpose Homes for Elderly People*, King's College, London.

Alaszewski, A. and Manthorpe, J. (1991) Literature review: measuring and managing risk in social welfare, *British Journal of Social Work*, 21, 277-90.

Allen, I., Hogg, D. and Peace, S. (1992) *Elderly People: Choice, Participation and Satisfaction*, Policy Studies Institute, London.

Allen-Meares, P. and Lane, B.A. (1990) Social work practice: integrating qualitative and quantitative data collection techniques, *Social Work*, 35, 5, 452-8.

Askham, J. and Thompson, C. (1990) *Dementia and Home Care*, Age Concern England, London.

Association of Directors of Social Services (1989) *Community Care: Agenda for Action — Response to Sir Roy Griffiths Report*, ADSS, Manchester.

Association of Directors of Social Services (1992) *Private Residential Care in England and Wales: The Report of a Survey by the ADSS*, ADSS, Manchester.

Association of Metropolitan Authorities (1994) *The Future Role of Local Authorities in the Provision of Health Services*, AMA, London.

Audit Commission (1985) *Managing Services for Elderly People More Effectively*, HMSO, London.

Audit Commission (1986) *Making a Reality of Community Care*, HMSO, London.

Audit Commission (1992a) *Community Care: Managing the Cascade of Change*, HMSO, London.

Audit Commission (1992b) *The Community Revolution: Personal Social Services*, HMSO, London.

Auditor General (1988) *First Triennial Review of the Home and Community Care Program: Final Report of the HACC Working Group*, Home and Community Care Program Working Group, Department of Community Services and Health, Australian Government Publishing Service, Canberra.

Austen, C. (1983) Case management in long-term care: options and opportunities, *Health and Social Work*, 8, 1, 16-30.

Austen, C. (1981) Client assessment in context, *Social Work Research and Abstracts*, 4-12.

Bains Committee (1972) *The New Local Authorities: Management and Structure: Report of the Study Group on Local Authority Management Structures*, HMSO, London.

Baldock, J. (1993) Patterns of change in the delivery of welfare in Europe, in P. Taylor-Gooby and R. Lawson (eds) *Markets and Managers: New Issues in the Delivery of Welfare*, Open University Press, Buckingham.

Baldock, J. and Evers, A. (1991) Citizenship and frail old people: changing patterns of provision in Europe, in N. Manning (ed.) *Social Policy Review 1990-91*, Longman, Harlow.

Barclay, P. (ed.) (1982) *Social Workers: Their Role and Tasks*, NISW/NCVO, London.

Barr, N. (1987) *The Economics of the Welfare State*, Weidenfeld and Nicolson, London

Barrett, S. and Fudge, C. (eds) (1981) *Policy and Action — Essays on the Implementation of Public Policy*, Methuen, London.

Barry, N. (1987) Understanding the market, in M. Loney, R. Bocock, J. Clarke, A. Cochrane, P. Graham and M. Wilson (eds) *The State of the Market*, Sage, London.

Bartlett, W. (1991) *Quasi-Markets and Contracts: A Market and Hierarchies Perspective on NHS Reform*, School of Advanced Urban Studies, Bristol University, Bristol.

Bayley, M. (1982) Community care and the elderly, in F. Glendenning (ed.) *Care in the Community — Recent Research and Current Projects*, Beth Johnson Foundation, University of Keele.

Bebbington, A. and Charnley, H. (1985) *Domiciliary Care Project: Entry into Care*, Personal Social Services Research Unit, University of Kent at Canterbury.

Black, J., Bowl, R., Burns, D., Critcher, C., Grant G. and Stockford, D. (1983) *Social Work in Context: A Comparative Study of Three Social Services Teams*, Tavistock Press, London.

Booth, T. (1990) Taking the plunge: Contracting out?, *Community Care*, 6 July.

Brewer, C. and Lait, J. (1980) *Can Social Work Survive?*, Temple Smith, London.

British Standards Institution (1987) *British Standard Quality Systems*, BSI, London

Brocklehurst, J.C., Davidson, C. and Moore-Smith, B. (1989) Interface between geriatric and general medicine, *Health Trends*, 21, 48-50.

Brown, P., Hadley, R. and White, K. (1982) A case for neighbourhood-based social work and social services, in P. Barclay (ed.) *Social Workers: Their Role and Tasks*, NISW/NCVO, London.

Brunsson, N. (1982) The irrationality of action and action rationality: decisions, ideologies and organisational action, *Journal of Management Studies*, 19, 1, 29-44.

Bulpitt, J.G. (1967) *Party Politics in English Local Government*, Longman, London.

Burke, T. and Moss, F. (1990) Right place, right time, right stuff..., *The Times Higher Education Supplement*.

Cabinet Office (1991a) The Citizen's Charter: Raising the Standard, Cmnd 1599, HMSO, London.

Cabinet Office (1991b) *Competing for Quality*, HMSO, London.

Central Policy Review Staff [CPRS] (1975) *A Joint Framework for Social Policy*, HMSO, London.

Centre for Policy on Ageing (1984) *Home Life: A Code of Practice for Residential Care*, CPA, London.

Cervi, B. (1991) Income support restrictions thwart SSD trust plans, *Community Care*, 4 July, 3.

Challis, D.J. and Davies, B.P. (1986) *Case Management in Community Care*, Gower, Aldershot.

Challis, D.J., Davies, B.P. and Traske, K. (eds) (1994) *Community Care: New Agendas and Challenges from the UK and Overseas*, Personal Social Services Research Unit/British Society for Gerontology, University of Kent at Canterbury.

Challis, D.J. and Ferlie, E. (1986) Changing patterns of fieldwork organisation. I: The headquarter's view, *British Journal of Social Work*, 16, 181-202.

Challis, D.J. and Ferlie, E. (1987) Changing patterns of fieldwork organisation. II: The team leaders' view, *British Journal of Social Work*, 17, 147-67.

Challis, D.J. and Ferlie, E. (1988) The myth of general practice — specialisation in social work, *Journal of Social Policy*, 17, 1-22.

Challis, L., Fuller, S., Henwood, M., Klein, R., Plowden, W., Webb, A., Whittingham, P. and Wistow, G. (1988) *Joint Approaches to Social Policy: Rationality and Practice*, Cambridge University Press, Cambridge.

Chombeau, C. (1992) Le projet du gouvernement sur les personnes agées dépendantes, *Le Monde*, 22 December, 10.

Davies, B.P. (1971) *Variations in Services for the Aged: A Causal Analysis*, Bell, London.

Davies, B.P. (1974) Proposal for a Kent Community Care Project, Kent Community Care Project Paper 1, Personal Social Service Research Unit, University of Kent, Canterbury.

Davies, B.P. (1978) *Universality, Selectivity and Effectiveness in Social Policy*, Heinemann, London.

Davies, B.P. (1981) Strategic goals and piecemeal innovations: adjusting to the new balance of needs and resources, in E. Goldberg and S. Hatch (eds) *A New Look at the Personal Social Services*, Policy Studies Institute, London.

Davies, B.P. (1986a) American experiments to substitute community for institutional long term care: lessons for evaluation and policy, in C. Phillipson (ed.) *Dependency and Interdependency in Old Age: Theoretical Perspectives and Policy Alternatives*, Croom Helm, Beckenham.

Davies, B.P. (1986b) American lessons for British policy and research on long term care of the elderly, *The Quarterly Journal of Social Affairs*, 2, 3, 321-4.

Davies, B.P. (1989) Why we must fight the eighth deadly sin: parochialism, *Journal of Aging and Social Policy*, 1, 217-36.

Davies, B.P. (1990) The 'trade and industry policy' metaphor and the Griffiths report, in W. Bytheway and J. Johnson (eds) *Change in Later Life*, Gower, Aldershot.

Davies, B.P. (1992) *Care Management, Equity and Efficiency: The International Experience*, Personal Social Services Research Unit, University of Kent at Canterbury.

Davies, B.P. (1993a) Thinking long in community care, in R. Page and N. Deakin (eds) *The Costs of Welfare*, Avebury, Aldershot.

Davies, B.P. (1993b) La réforme des soins communautaires - création et mise en oeuvre d'une politique nationale: du désordre au modéle et du modéle au ...?, *Gérontologie et Société*, 67, 112-26.

Davies, B.P. (1994) Maintaining the pressure in community care reform, *Social Policy and Administration*, 28, 3, 197-206.

Davies, B.P. and Challis, D.J. (1986) *Matching Resources to Needs in Community Care*, Gower, Aldershot.

Davies, B.P. and Ferlie, E. (1982) Efficiency-improving innovations in social care: Social services departments and the elderly, *Policy and Politics*, 10, 181-205.

Davies, B.P., Bebbington, A. and Charnley, H. (1990) *Resources, Needs and Outcomes*, Gower, Aldershot.

Davies, B.P., Warburton, R.W. and Fernández, J. (1995) Do different case management approaches affect who gets what? Preliminary results from a comparative British study, *Care Plan*, 2, 3, 26-30.

Davies, B.P., Fernández, J. and Saunders, R. (1997), Effects of benefits in cash and kind and entry of elderly persons to institutions for long-term care in England and Wales, *Ageing and Society*, forthcoming.

Davies, M. (1981) *The Essential Social Worker*, Heinemann Education Books, London.

Davies, M. (1985) *The Essential Social Worker*, 2nd edition, Gower, Aldershot.

Dearlove, J. (1973) *The Politics of Policy in Local Government*, Cambridge University Press, London.

Dekker, W. (1987) *Bereid tot Verandering: rapport van der Commissie Structuur en Financiering*, Ministry of Health, Welfare and Cultural Affairs, The Hague.

Deming, W. (1982) *Quality, Productivity, and Competitive Position*, MIT Centre for Advanced Engineering Study, Cambridge, Massachusetts.

Department of the Environment (1991) *Local Government Review: The Structure of Local Government in England*, Department of the Environment, London.

Department of the Environment (1992) *Housing and Community Care*, LAC (92)13, DoE/DoH, London.

Department of Health (1989a) *Discharge of Patients from Hospital*, HC(89)5, Department of Health, London.

Department of Health (1989b) *Discharge of Patients from Hospital*, LAC(89)7, Department of Health, London.

Department of Health (1990a) *Caring for People: Community Care in the Next Decade and Beyond. Implementation Documents, Draft Guidance, Assessment and Case Management*, HMSO, London.

Department of Health (1990b) *Community Care in the Next Decade and Beyond, Policy Guidance*, LAC(90)12, HMSO, London.

Department of Health (1990c) *Caring for Quality: Guidance on Standards for Residential Homes for Elderly People*, HMSO, London.

Department of Health (1991a) *Implementing Community Care: Purchaser, Commissioner and Provider Roles*, Guidance Document prepared by Price Waterhouse, Department of Health, London.

Department of Health (1991b) *Community Care: Review of Residential Homes Provision*, HMSO, London.

Department of Health (1991c) *Care Management and Assessment: Practitioners Guide*, HMSO, London.

Department of Health (1991d) *Care Management and Assessment: Managers Guide*, HMSO, London

Department of Health (1991e) *The Right to Complain: Practice Guidance on Complaints Procedures in SSDs*, HMSO, London.

Department of Health (1991f) *Purchase of Service: Practice Guidance and Practice Material for Social Services Departments and Other Agencies*, HMSO, London

Department of Health (1991g) *Inspecting for Quality: Guidance on Practice for Inspection Units in Social Services Departments and Other Agencies; Principles, Issues and Recommendations*, HMSO, London

Department of Health (1992a) *Implementing Caring for People*, EL(92)13)/Cl(92) 10, Department of Health, London.

Department of Health (1992b) *Implementing Caring for People*, EL(92)65/ Cl(92) 30, Department of Health, London.

Department of Health (1992c) *Community Care*, EL(92)67, Department of Health, London.

Department of Health (1992d) *Implementing Caring for People: Assessment*, Cl (92)34, Department of Health, London.

Department of Health (1992e) *National Assistance Act 1948 (Choice of Accommodation) Directions*, LAC(92)27, Department of Health, London.

Department of Health (1993) *Implementing Caring for People*, EL(93)18, Department of Health, London.

Department of Health (1994a) *Implementing Caring for People — Impressions of the First Year*, Department of Health, London.

Department of Health (1994b) *Implementing Caring for People — A Special Study of Purchaing and Contracting*, Department of Health, London.

Department of Health (1994c) *Implementing Caring for People — Training and Development*, Department of Health, London.

Department of Health (1994d) *Implementing Caring for People — Care Management*, Department of Health, London.

Department of Health (1994e) *Implementing Caring for People — Assessment Special Study*, Department of Health, London.

Department of Health (1994f) *Implementing Caring for People — Housing and Homelessness*, Department of Health, London.

Department of Health (1995a) *Practical Guidance on Joint Commissioning for Project Leaders*, Joint Commissioning Project Group, Department of Health, London.

Department of Health (1995b) *Developing Continuing Health Care Policies: A Checklist for Purchasers*, Department of Health, London.

DHSS (1976) *Priorities in Health and Personal Social Services*, LAC(92)12, HMSO, London.

DHSS (1977) *The Way Forward: Priorities in Health and Social Services*, HMSO, London.

DHSS (1981a) *Care in the Community*, HMSO, London.

DHSS (1981b) *Report of Study Group on Community Care*, DHSS, London.

DHSS (1981c) *Growing Older*, HMSO, London.

DHSS (1983) *Working Together*, HMSO, London.

DHSS (1985) *Progress in Partnership*, DHSS, London.

Donabedian, A. (1982) *Explorations in Quality Assessment and Monitoring*, Health Administration Press, Michigan.

Downey, R. (1992) Home truths, *Social Work Today*, 5 March, 11.

Evandrou, M., Falkingham, J. and Glennerster, H. (1990) The personal social services: 'everyone's poor relation but nobody's baby', in D. Hills (ed.) *The State of Welfare: The Welfare State in Britain since 1974*, Clarendon Press, Oxford.

Evans, J.G. (1983). Care of the elderly in a defined community, in J.M. Graham and H.M. Hodgkinson (eds) *Effective Geriatric Medicine: The Special Work of Physicians in Geriatric Medicine*, Harrogate Seminar Reports 7, Department of Health and Social Security, London.

Ferlie, E. (1980) *Sourcebook of Innovations*, Discussion Paper 261, Personal Social Services Research Unit, University of Kent at Canterbury.

Ferlie, E., Challis, D.J. and Davies, B.P. (1985) Innovation in the care of the elderly: the role of joint finance, in A. Butler (ed.) *Ageing: Recent Advances and Creative Responses*, Croom Helm, London.

Ferlie, E., Challis, D.J. and Davies, B.P. (1989) *Efficiency Improving Innovations in the Community Care of Frail Elderly People*, Gower, Aldershot.

Firth, J. (1987) *Public Support for Residential Care*, DHSS, London.

Fisher, M. (1991) Defining the practice content of case management, *Social Work and Social Sciences Review*, 2, 3, 204-30.

Fisher, M. and Marsh, P. (1993) *Social Work in Practice*, Report to Westminster City Council Social Services Department, London.

Fitchett, M. (1991) M25 syndrome, *Health Service Journal*, 5 December, 24-5.

Flynn, N. and Common, R. (1990) *Contracts for Community Care*, Caring for People implementation document CCI 4, Department of Health, London.

Fowler, N. (1984) Speech to Joint Social Services Conferences, Buxton, 27 September.

Friedman, L. (1985) *Microeconomic Policy Analysis*, International Student Edition, McGraw-Hill, Singapore.

Gaster, L. (1991) Quality and decentralisation: are they connected?, *Policy and Politics*, 19, 4, 257-67

Gibbs, I. and Corden, A. (1991) The concept of 'reasonableness' in relation to residential care and nursing home charges, *Policy and Politics*, 19, 2, 119-29.

Glastonbury, B., Cooper, D. and Hawkins, P. (1980) *Social Work in Conflict*, Croom Helm, London.

Goldberg, M. and Connelly, N. (1982) *The Effectiveness of Social Care for the Elderly*, Heinemann Educational Books, London.

Goldberg, M. and Warburton, W. (1979) *Ends and Means in Social Work*, Allen and Unwin, London.

Gostick, C. and Scott, T. (1982) Local authority intake teams, *British Journal of Social Work*, 12, 395-421.

Griffith, J.A.G. (1965) *Central Departments and Local Authorities*, Allen and Unwin, London.

Griffiths, R. (1983) *Report of the NHS Management Enquiry*, DHSS, London.

Griffiths, R. (1988) *Community Care: Agenda for Action*, HMSO, London.

Hadley, R. and McGrath, M. (1981) *Going Local: Neighbourhood Social Services*, Bedford Square Press, London.

Hall, P. (1976) *Reforming the Welfare: The Politics of Change in the Personal Social Services*, Heinemann Educational Books, London.

Hambleton, R. and Hoggett, P. (1990) Beyond excellence: quality local government in the 1990s, Working Paper 85, School for Advanced Urban Studies, University of Bristol, Bristol.

Handy, C. (1985) *Understanding Organisations*, Penguin, London.

Hartley, K. and Hooper, N. (1990) Industry and policy, in P. Curwen (ed.) *Understanding the UK Economy*, Macmillan, London.

Henwood, M., Jowell, T. and Wistow, G. (1991) *All Things Come*, Briefing Paper 12, King's Fund Institute, London.

Hirschman, A. (1970) *Exit, Voice, and Loyalty: Response to Decline in Firms, Organizations and States*, Harvard University Press, Cambridge, Massachusetts.

Hoggett, P. (1990) Modernisation, political strategy and the welfare state: an organisational perspective, Studies in Decentralisation and Quasi-Markets Paper No 2, School for Advanced Urban Studies, University of Bristol, Bristol.

House of Commons Social Services Committee (1985) *Community Care, Second Report*, HC13, HMSO, London.

House of Commons Social Services Committee (1990) *Community Care: Third Report. Funding for Local Authorities*, Session 1989/90, HC277, HMSO, London.

Hudson, H. (1991) *Assessment of Need and Research Methods*, University of Stirling, Stirling.

Hudson, J. (1983) The changing character of quality assurance: activities in acute care hospitals, *Effective Health Care*, 1, 2, 75-84.

Hunter, D., McKeganey, N. and MacPherson, A. and colleagues (1988) *Care of the Elderly: Policy and Practice*, Aberdeen University Press, Aberdeen.

Hunter, D. and Judge, K. (1988) *Griffiths and Community Care: Meeting the Challenge*, King's Fund Institute, London.

Isaacs, B. and Neville, Y. (1976) The needs of old people: the 'interval' as a method of measurement, *British Journal of Preventive and Social Medicine*, 30, 79-85.

Isaacs, B., Livingstone, M. and Neville, Y. (1972) *Survival of the Unfittest — A Study of Geriatric Patients in Glasgow*, Routlege and Kegal Paul, London.

Ivory, M. (1991) Department of Health sets limits on private care trusts, *Community Care*, 15 August, 3.

Johnson, N. (1990) *Reconstructing the Welfare State: A Decade of Change 1980-1990*, Harvester Wheatsheaf, Hemel Hempstead.

Jones, G. (1969) *Borough Politics*, Macmillan, London.

Juran, J. and Gryna, F. (1980) *Quality Planning and Analysis*, 2nd edition, McGraw-Hill, New York.

Kamien, M. and Schwartz, N. (1982) *Market Structure and Innovation*, Cambridge University Press, Cambridge.

Kane, R.A. (1990) Case management: what is it anyway?, in R.A. Kane, K. Urv-Wong and C. King (eds) *Case Management: What is it anyway?*, University of Minnesota, Long-Term Care Decisions Resource Center, Minneapolis, Minnesota.

Kane, R.A. and Kane, R.L. (1981) *Assessing the Elderly*, Lexington Books, Lexington, Massachusetts.

Kane, R.A. and Wilson, K.B. (1993) *Assisted Living in the United States: A New Paradigm for Residential Care of the Frail Elderly*, American Association for Retired People, Washington DC.

Kavanagh, S., Schneider, J., Knapp, M.R.J., Beecham, J.K. and Netten, A. (1995) Elderly people with dementia: cost-effectiveness and the balance of care, in M.R.J. Knapp (ed.) *The Economic Evaluation of Mental Health Care*, Arena, Aldershot.

Kelly, A. (1991) The new managerialism in the social services, in P. Carter (ed.) *Social Work and Social Welfare Yearbook, Vol. 3*, Open University Press, Buckingham.

Klein, R. and O'Higgins, M. (eds) (1985) *The Future of Welfare*, Basil Blackwell, Oxford.

Knapp, M.R.J. (1984) *The Economics of Social Care*, Macmillan, London.

Knapp, M.R.J. (1993) The roles of costs research, in J. Beecham and A. Netten (eds) *Community Care in Action — The Role of Costs*, Personal Social Services Research Unit, University of Kent at Canterbury.

KPMG Peat Marwick (1993) *Diversification and the Independent Residential Care Sector: A Manual for Providers of Residential Care Homes*, HMSO, London.

Kramer, R. and Grossman, B. (1987) Contracting for social services: process management and resource dependencies, *Social Services Review*, 61, 32-55.

Lawson, R. (1991) From public monopoly to maximum competition: one authority's approach, *PSSRU Bulletin*, No. 8, Personal Social Services Research Unit, University of Kent at Canterbury.

Lawson, R. (1993) The new technology of management in the personal social services, in P. Taylor-Gooby and R. Lawson (eds) *Markets and Managers: New Issues in the Delivery of Welfare*, Open University Press, Buckingham.

Letwin, O. (1988) *Privatising the World: A Study of International Privatisation in Theory and Practice*, Cassell, London.

Lipsky, M. (1980) *Street Level Bureaucracy*, Russell Sage, New York.

Lutz, B., Bland, R. Cheetham, J. and Yelloly, M. (1991) *Report of the Development and Testing of Screening and Assessment Instruments*, Social Work Research Centre Paper 12, University of Stirling.

Mallaby Committee (1967) *Report of the Committee on the Staffing of Local Government*, HMSO, London.

Mattison, J. and Sinclair, I. (1979) *Mate and Stalemate — Working with Marital Problems in a Social Service Department*, Blackwell, London.

Maud Committee (1967) *Report of the Committee on the Management of Local Government*, HMSO, London.

Millward, R. (1982) The comparative performance of public and private ownership, in Lord Roll of Ipsden (ed.) *The Mixed Economy*, Macmillan, London.

Minns, R. (1972) Homeless families and the organisational determinants of deviancy, *Policy and Politics*, 1, 1-21.

Mollica, R.L., Ladd, S., Dietsche, R.C., Wilson, K.B. and Ryther, B.S. (1992) *Building Assisted Living for the Elderly into Public Long-Term Care Policy: A Guide for the States*, Center for Vulnerable Populations, National Academy for State Policy, Portland, Maine.

Morris, J. (1995) *The Power to Change*, Kings Fund Centre, London.

National Association of Health Authorities and Trusts (NAHAT) (1992) *Care in the Community: Definitions of Health and Social Care — Developing an Approach. A West Midlands Study*, Research Paper 5, NAHAT/West Midlands RHA, Birmingham.

Neill, J. (1989) *Assessing Elderly People for Residential Care: A Practical Guide*, National Institute for Social Work Research Unit, London.

Netten, A. (1993) *A Positive Environment? Physical and Social Influences on People with Senile Dementia in Residential Care*, Ashgate, Aldershot.

NHS Executive (1994) *Developing NHS Purchasing and GP Fundholding: Towards a Primary Care-led NHS*, (EL(94)79), Department of Health, London.

NHS Executive (1995) *Accountability Framework for General Practitioners*, (EL(95) 54) Department of Health, London.

Norman, A. (1981) *Rights and Risks*, Centre for Policy on Ageing, London.

Oakland, J. (1990) *Total Quality Management*, Heinemann Professional Publishing, New York.

Opit, L. (1991) The measurement of health service outcomes, in W. Holland, R. Detels and G. Knox (eds) *Oxford Textbook of Public Health*, 2nd edition, *Volume 3: Applications in Public Health*, Oxford Medical Publications, Oxford.

Ovretveit, J. (1993) *Co-ordinating Community Care*, Open University Press, Buckingham.

Patel, C. (1991) How can the (long-term care) industry mature in the 1990s, Paper at the Laing and Buisson Conference, March, London.

Payne, M. (1977) Integrating domiciliary care into an area team, *Social Work Service*, 14, 54-8.

Pear, R.A. (1966) Introduction, in D. Peschek and J. Brand (eds) *Policies and Politics in Secondary Education: Case Studies in West Ham and Reading*, Greater London Papers No. 11, London School of Economics, London.

Pepper Commission (1990) *A Call for Action: The Pepper Commission. Final Report*, US Government Printing Office, Washington, DC.

Peters, T. and Waterman, R. (1982) *In Search of Excellence*, Harper and Row, New York.

Pfeffer, N. and Coote, A. (1991) *Is Quality Good For You? A Critical Review of Quality Assurance in Welfare Services*, Institute for Public Policy Research, Social Policy Paper 5, London.

Phillips, M. (1991) The home stretch, *Community Care*, 29 August, 17.

Pinker, R. (1982) An alternative view, in P. Barclay (ed.) *Social Workers: Their Role and Tasks*, NISW/NCVO, London.

Pollitt, C. (1987) Capturing quality? The quality issue in British and American health policies, *Journal of Public Policy*, 7, 1, 71-92.

Pollitt, C. (1990) Doing business in the temple? Managers and quality assurance in the public services, *Public Administration*, 68, 4, 435-50.

Powell, E. (1961) Address to NAMH 1991 Conference, *Report of the Annual Conference of the National Association of Mental Health*, NAMH, London.

Pressman, J. and Wildawsky, A. (1973) *Implementation*, University of California Press, Berkeley, California.

Redcliffe-Maud Committee (1969) *Report of the Royal Commission on Local Government in England (1966-1969)*, Cmnd 4040, HMSO, London.

Regnier, V., Hamilton, J. and Yatabe, S. (1992) *Best Practices in Assisted Living: Innovations in Design, Management and Financing*, National Eldercare Institute on Housing and Supportive Services, University of Southern California, Los Angeles.

Ridley, N. (1988) *The Local Right: Enabling Not Providing*, Policy Study No. 92, Centre for Policy Studies, London.

Ritchie, J.H., Dick, D. and Lingham, R. (1994) *The Report of the Inquiry into the Care and Treatment of Christopher Clunis*, HMSO, London.

Robinson, R. (1991) *Managed Competition in the NHS*, Kings Fund Institute, London.

Rose, R. (1975) Overloaded government: the problem outlined, *European Studies Newsletter*, 5, 13-18.

Rowlings, C. (1981) *Social Work with Elderly People*, Allen and Unwin, London.

Royal Commission on Local Government in England (1968) Report, Cmnd 4040, HMSO, London.

Salter, C. (1992) The day centre: a way of avoiding society's risk, *Critical Public Health*, 3, 2, 17-22.

Scott-Whyte Commission (1985) *Supplementary Benefits and Residential Care*, DHSS, London.

Secretary of State (1968) *Report of the Committee on Local Authority and Allied Personal Social Services*, (*The Seebohm Report*), HMSO, London.

Secretaries of State (1989a) *Working for Patients*, Cmd 555, HMSO, London.

Secretaries of State (1989b) *Caring for People: Community Care in the Next Decade and Beyond*, Cmd 849, HMSO, London.

Seebohm Committee (1968) *Report of the Committee on Local Authority and Allied Personal Social Services*, Cmnd 3703, HMSO, London.

Shenfield, B. (1957) *Social Policies of Old Age*, Routledge and Kegan Paul, London.

Silverstein, N.M. (1984) Informing the elderly about public services: the relationship between sources of knowledge and service utilization, *The Gerontologist*, 24, 1, 37-40.

Simey, M.B. (1985) *Government Consent: The Priniple and Practice of Accountability in Local Government*, NCVO/Bedford Square Press, London.

Sinclair, I., Crosbie, D., O'Connor, P., Stanforth, L. and Vickery, A. (1988) *Bridging Two Worlds: Social Work and the Elderly Living Alone*, Avebury, Aldershot.

Smale, G. (1995) *Managing Change through Innovation*, National Institute for Social Work, London.

Smith, G. (1980) *Social Need*, Routlege and Kegan Paul, London.

Social Services Inspectorate (1987) *From Home Help to Home Care: An Analysis of Policy, Resourcing and Service Management*, Department of Health, London.

Social Services Inspectorate (1989) *Homes Are For Living In*, HMSO, London.

Social Services Inspectorate (1991) *Assessment Systems and Community Care*, Department of Health, London.

Social Services Inspectorate (1993) *Inspection of Assessment and Care Management Arrangements in Social Services Departments: Interim Overview Report*, December, Department of Health, London.

Steele, J. (1991) Information for citizens, *Policy Studies*, 12, 3, 47-55.

Steinberg, R. and Carter, G. (1983) *Case Management and the Elderly*, DC Heath, Lexington, Massachusetts.

Stelzer, I. (1989) Privatisation and regulation: oft-necessary complements, in C.G. Veljanovski (ed.) *Privatisation and Competition: A Market Prospectus*, Institute of Economic Affairs, London.

Stevenson, O. and Parsloe, P. (1978) *Social Service Teams: The Practitioner's View*, HMSO, London.

Stewart, J.D. (1973) *Management-Local-Environment-Government: A Few Words Considered*, Institute of Local Government Studies, Birmingham University, Birmingham.

Stewart, J.D. (1986) *The New Management of Local Government*, Allen and Unwin, London.

Straus, A. and colleagues (1973) The hospital and its negotiated order, in G. Salaman and K. Thompson (eds) *People and Organisations*, Open University Press, Buckingham.

Streatfield, D. (1992) Inside information technology: The computer minefield, *Community Care*, 30 January.

Taylor-Gooby, P. and Lawson, R. (eds) (1993) *Markets and Managers: New Issues in the Delivery of Welfare*, Open University Press, Buckingham.

Tester, S. and Meredith, B. (1987) *Ill-informed? A Study of Information and Support for Elderly People in the Inner City*, Policy Studies Institute, London.

Thatcher, M. (1993) *The Downing Street Years*, Harper-Collins, London.

Thompson, C. (1987) The assessment of depression in elderly people by non-clinicians, in C. Phillipson, M. Bernard and P. Strang (eds) *Dependency and Interdependency in Old Age: Theoretical Perspectives and Policy Alternatives*, Croom Helm, in association with the British Society of Gerontology, London.

Tomlinson, Sir B. (1992) *Report of the Inquiry on London's Health Services, Medical Education and Research*, HMSO, London.

Ungerson, C. (1987) *Policy is Personal: Sex, Gender and Informal Care*, Tavistock, London.

Ungerson, C. (1995) Gender, cash and informal care: European perspectives and dilemmas, *Journal of Social Policy*, 24, 1, 31-52.

Utting, W. (1990) *Care in the Community*, [Cl(90)3], Department of Health, London.

Victor, C. and colleagues (1992) An option to keep open, *Health Service Journal*, 13 February, 22-23.

Wagner, G. (1988) *Residential Care: A Positive Choice*, HMSO, London.

Walden, D. (1994) Speech to launch *Practical Guidance on Joint Commissioning for Project Leaders*, May, Department of Health, London.

Webb, A. and Wistow, G. (1982) *Whither State Welfare? Policy Implementation in the Personal Social Services 1979-80*, Royal Institute of Public Administration, London.

Webb, A. and Wistow, G. (1986) *Planning, Need and Scarcity: Essays on the Personal Social Services*, Allen and Unwin, London.

Webb, A. and Wistow, G. (1987) *Social Work, Social Care and Social Planning*, Longman, London.

White Paper (1983) *Financial Management in Government Departments*, Cmnd 9058, HMSO, London.

Whittingham, P. (1992) Inside information technology: integrating care, *Community Care*, 30 January.

Whittingham, P. (1993) Diversity in adversity, *Community Care*, 18 November, 14-15.

Willcocks, D., Peace, S. and Kellaher, L. (1987) *Private Lives in Public Places: A Research-based Critique of Residential Life in Local Authority Old People's Homes*, Tavistock, London.

Williams, E.I. (1986) A model to describe social performance levels in elderly people, *Journal of the Royal College of General Practioners*, 36, 422-3.

Williamson, O. (1975) *Markets and Hierarchies: Analysis and Antitrust Implications*, Free Press, New York

Wilson, G. (1991) Models of ageing and their relation to policy formation and service provision, *Policy and Politics*, 19, 1, 37-47.

Wintersgill, C. (1991) Separate identities, *Social Work Today*, 17 October, 22.

Wistow, G. (1989) Open forum, *Insight*, 11 October, 7.

Wistow, G. and Brooks, T. (eds) (1988) *Joint Planning and Joint Management*, Royal Institute of Public Administration, London.

Wistow, G. and Henwood, M. (1991) Caring for people: Elegant model of flawed design?, in N. Manning (ed.) *Social Policy Review 1990-91*, Longman, Harlow.

Wistow, G. and Knapp, M.R.J. (1993) Developing the mixed economy of care, Paper presented to ADSS Research Conference in Bristol, November.

Wistow, G., Leedham, I. and Hardy, B. (1992a) *Preliminary Analysis of a Sample of English Community Care Plans*, Nuffield Institute, University of Leeds.

Wistow, G., Knapp, M.R.J., Hardy, B. and Allen, C. (1992b) From providing to enabling: local authorities and the mixed economy of care, *Public Administration*, 70, 1, 25-45.

Wistow, G., Knapp, M.R.J., Hardy, B. and Allen, C. (1994) *Social Care in a Mixed Economy*, Open University Press, Buckingham.

Wolfensberger, W. (1972) *The Principle of Normalisation in Human Services*, National Institute on Mental Retardation, Toronto.

Wynne-Harley, D. (1991) *Living Dangerously: Risk-taking, Safety and Older People*, Centre for Policy on Ageing, London.

Zimmer, J.G., Eggert, G.M., Treat, A. and Brodows, B. (1988) Nursing homes as acute care providers: a pilot study of incentives to reduce hospitalizations, *Journal of American Geriatric Society*, 36, 124-9.

Name Index

Subject Index